I0558307

One Last Confession

S. JOHN DIAMOND

.

AOS Publishing, 2024

Copyright © 2024

S. John Diamond

All rights reserved under International
and Pan-American copyright conventions

ISBN: 978-1-990496-45-5

Cover Design: Chanelle Poupart

Visit AOS Publishing's website:
www.aospublishing.com

To Judie, Alexis, Samantha, Michelle, and Milo

CHAPTER ONE

We met over a lawn chair—a broken-down, rusted piece of junk. I wanted to throw it out.

He did not. We shared a garden in the Plateau.

I lived in the upstairs apartment.

He and his brood lived downstairs.

Mother had willed the property to me after she passed. I was going to sell it. But life intervened. I had walked out of the priesthood and needed a place to live. Pastoral parishes gave way to an urban setting complete with noise and the Orensteins.

The children, and there were several, eyed me with suspicion. After all, I was an interloper, a fox in the henhouse. Maybe that's going a bit too far.

With the boys, I could discuss hockey. With the girls I had nothing in common.

English is my mother tongue, I acquired Quebecois and Inuktitut, and they seemed to work pretty well. I read Hebrew and Latin, courtesy of a classical seminary education, but spoke neither.

There was a small kitchen where I cooked elaborate meals for one. The leftovers I threw away; sharing with the neighbours was not an option.

Orenstein's beat-up van was forever breaking down. I knew how to keep the thing going. Working in the north, one became, of necessity, handy at such things.

So I took the opportunity to ask him if I could throw the lawn chair out.

"Why, it offends you?"

"Yes, it is a rusted piece of junk."

"I like it. I use it to sit outside—a little quiet spot."

"I would not want to interfere with your peace of mind, but really?"

"I have something more important to talk to you about," Orenstein said with his voice in a lower register. Almost conspiratorially. Speaking to me, but not really looking at me. "I want you to come with me to the Children's Hospital to meet with a social worker there," he said with an air of weariness. The task was not likely to be pleasant.

"There has been a report, a suspicion, that one of the local children has been abused. He was at the hospital being treated for something or other and someone noticed bruises which could not be explained. The child would not talk. The parents likewise were not helpful. The Rabbi has asked me to meet with the social worker to see what can be done."

"You could confront the parents."

"Not an option at the moment," was the curt answer.

"How is it that you are involved?'

"I am the fixer; I solve problems. Sometimes life presents issues which fall outside boundaries. They call me."

He was not tall, exactly, but not small. He had a grey beard and wore a black skullcap.

He had a deep voice that commanded respect. Sometimes he wore a black fedora.

"Why do you want me along?"

"You have experience in these matters, no?"

"In the Native communities in the north. But not here. Here I am out of my depth, and I am retired."

"You'll drive me, then?"

CHAPTER TWO

We drove in silence. Shmully was busy on his cell phone, mostly receiving calls. To whoever called, he gave curt answers in Yiddish and Hebrew and occasionally English. He took some notes on a dog-eared scratch pad.

I turned right onto Sherbrooke Street, heading west. He turned off the phone. Out of the side pocket of the passenger door, he took a small prayer book, also dog-eared. He began to mumble quietly to himself, his eyes half-closed.

We passed the university on the right. The nicest walk in the country is walking west on Sherbrooke by the old greystones that have been transformed into art galleries and boutiques. Tall, majestic apartment buildings were interspersed with more modern condominiums.

At Atwater, I turned left. I found parking on the street about two blocks from the hospital. I started fumbling for change to put in the meter. "A toonie will be enough," was the reply to the question I did not ask.

"Are you sure?"

He had put on his black hat over his skullcap. He had on a white shirt, black vest, and black slacks. His shoes were black walkers.

At the entrance, we saw parents and children. Many of the youngsters were in wheelchairs. The information desk was on the right. The social work department was in an annex on the other side of the building. We went out and around. The receptionist told us that Ms. Lang would be with us shortly.

I was beginning to worry about the meter.

The reception area was decorated in what might be called utilitarian chic. A few plants were scattered around. The chairs were basic, which after a while I found uncomfortable. Between the chairs and the reception desk was a coffee table piled haphazardly with magazines. On the walls were posters with warnings about abuse in all forms—family, neighbourhood, workplace.

From the rear, behind the reception area, a woman appeared. She was short, about fifty, and all business. We both stood.

"I am Martha Lang," she said. "And you are here, why?"

3

"To discuss the matter concerning Yoel–Joel Goldberger," Shmully said in his deepest, sagest voice. "Rabbi Shinder has asked me to . . . to intervene."

"I had hoped that the Rabbi would be here with the family. They have been very difficult people to deal with. And you are?" she said, looking directly at me.

"Mr. Glasheen is my assistant." I guess I had received a promotion.

She stared at both of us. "Follow me," she said curtly.

We were led into an office behind the reception area. Her desk was a pile of files. We could barely close the door to sit in the two chairs in front of it. She stood, we sat. A plaque on the wall read, "Martha Lang, Master of Social Work."

"I want you to tell the Goldbergers and the Rabbi that I am going to submit this file to the Social Welfare Court, unless—"

"Unless, Ms. Lang?" Orenstein said quietly. There was no air in the room.

"I have a case here of child abuse, pure and simple. The child will not talk, and the parents keep referring this whole thing to this 'Rabbi Shinder'."

Silence. Slowly, Orenstein lifted up his head to stare right at her. "Are you sure?"

"Sure, I have a report here which details the evidence. I cannot give you the report to read in its entirety, but there were marks found on the boy's body which could only have come from a severe beating. And any attempt to find out what's going on has been met with total denial and lack of cooperation."

"That's why I am here, Ms. Lang," Orenstein said almost in a whisper.

"You can get to the bottom of this, really?"

"I perhaps have an *entrée* into this situation which you do not have. I would ask you to hold back from proceeding to the court for a couple of weeks. Now, may we see the report?"

She gave a file to Shmully, which he handed to me.

Scanning down the report, I noticed that the signature had been erased. These folks were careful.

The body of the document contained the usual stuff. "Marks consistent with . . . blows to the buttocks and thighs." There were a lot of "consistent withs." Too many for the whole thing to be an accident.

4

I looked up and put down the report. "If we find out how, we will find out who and when. Did this happen here?"

Ms. Lang sat down in her chair for the first time. "I would like to say no. But he did not come in that condition. Of that we are certain. There was a family member around the child from the minute he got here."

"Why was he here, exactly?"

"Pneumonia."

"How long was he here?"

"Not long enough, in our opinion; the family wanted him home. Twenty-four hours. We filled him full of antibiotics and he left."

"And he was not left alone for an instant."

"Ms. Lang, I will report back to you in a week with a complete explanation in this affair," Orenstein said quietly.

"An explanation? I don't want an explanation. I want to know who did this. Am I very clear?"

"One week?"

"One week, then. Please leave your phone numbers with the receptionist."

"Of course."

We left our numbers and returned to the van. There was one minute left on the meter.

Before starting up, I looked at him. He was staring straight ahead.

"Ah, I assume you have a plan? She meant what she said. We both know that transferring this to the court and the police is what she should do, what she is obligated to do."

I think I saw a nod. I hoped I saw a nod.

"Second question. What's the relationship between Rabbi Shinder and this family?"

"Daughter and son-in-law."

I feared as much.

"So I am beginning to understand their reluctance to be present."

"Yes, and why they asked me to intervene."

He turned to face me. "You have been a big help this morning. Let's get going. The meter has expired."

CHAPTER THREE

I really wanted to see a movie. It was Saturday night. The hockey season was weeks away, and besides, I did not want to spend the evening indoors alone. Checking the listings, I saw that everything was aliens and violence. The rep cinema had some really obscure-looking stuff, too outré-looking even for me. Looking elsewhere in the paper, I saw *La Bohème* was playing at the concert hall. Surely I could buy a single ticket.

Dressed in slacks, button-down blue shirt, and a blazer that still fit, I walked down the Main toward Place des Arts. I passed bars that were beginning to fill up, a movie theatre that still showed X-rated movies with a sign that said, "couples free on Monday and Tuesday," and the Deli, where you can have an intimate smoked meat sandwich while packed together with a hundred perfect strangers. The line to get into the place snaked up the street. Portuguese restaurants with white tablecloth-covered tables sat waiting for the evening crowd. Standing outside a renowned steak house was a doorman dressed in livery to usher people into this monument to 1950s dining. Still popular, the restaurant offered a reduced priced menu after nine p.m.

Most of the people I passed were young college kids out shopping for the week. There were a few grey-hairs like me but not a lot. I was in the minority also when it came to body art; I had none. Many had very elaborate and colourful designs. I stopped at a coffee shop to carry out a cup of strong brew, which I sipped. At Sherbrooke Street, I went downhill past buildings that would soon be gentrified but now appeared in need of tenants.

Farther down were shops selling the latest electronic devices at discount prices, or so the signs proclaimed. I turned right on de Maisonneuve into a jungle of construction cranes and road-working machines. They were building a new concert hall, remaking the area.

Managing to find an entrance to Salle Wilfrid Pelletier, I was a half-hour early for the curtain. The uniformed attendant informed me she had a single aisle seat.

"*Premier* first *balcon*," she said through the glass cage.

"Fine." I downed the last of the coffee and went up to my seat.

The theatre was quickly filling up. There were obviously a lot of disgruntled hockey fans.

Over to my left a few rows down, I noticed our social worker, Ms. Lang, who came in just before the curtain. She was with two other women.

The performance began. The stage had the look of a very modern garret with the outline of Paris drawn in the background. The singers were all young and enthusiastic. Above the stage, two screens displayed the lyrics, one in English, one in French. The role of Mimi was played by an elfin singer whose voice belied her small frame. She was impressive; her acting was real. She was alternatively flirty and vibrant, this along with the knowledge that she was deathly ill.

At intermission, I went to find the bar to get some cold water. Standing in front of me was Ms. Lang. She was served first and turned to leave the queue. She spotted me, paused, and went on to join her friends. I paid for the drink and went to stand against the wall.

I was sipping the overpriced drink when a voice to my left said, "I did not know Sam Spade liked opera." It was Ms. Lang, who had managed to sneak into the spot next to me.

"Sometimes one needs a change of pace, and besides, my colleague is off duty today."

"You have to admit, the two of you do make an odd couple: a religious Jew and an Irishman—you are Irish, aren't you?"

"*Pure laine.*"

"You're his chauffeur?"

"Yes, and mechanic."

"You applied for the job?"

"No, I was volunteered."

"Otherwise you're . . .?"

"Retired."

"From what?"

"The priesthood."

"Oh my, you are *pure laine.*"

The house lights dimmed for the start of the second act. Neither of us moved toward our seats.

"We could continue this conversation after the performance."

"Yes, we could, as long as we do not talk shop."

Meanwhile, we both seemed glued to our spots against the wall.

"Your friends will miss you."

"How do you know I'm here with anyone?"

"I saw you come in just before the curtain."

"Yes, I am notoriously, chronically late. My friends keep me on time. I'm more interested in your former calling. Why did you retire? And besides, poor Mimi dies in the last scene."

"There is no easy answer to that question. And you have just ruined the suspense for me."

"You were not one of those priests who attacked children."

"No. I was one of those priests who went where they had been molested."

She looked at me full in the face.

"So working with Orenstein is pretty much old hat."

"Sort of. Except I do not have the authority and weight of the Church on my shoulders and the smouldering pain of my parishioners to deal with. It was time to get out while I still had my soul intact. And you? Did you always want to be a social worker?"

"Psychologist, actually, but I hate rats. So I chose social work."

"You seem to have a lot of files on your desk. Are you a one-woman show?"

"More or less. I am the only full-time person."

"So coming to the opera on a Saturday night is a rare outing?"

"Yes."

"I really do not want to keep you from your friends."

"No. I want to know more about you and Rabbi Orenstein."

"It is Mr. Orenstein; he is not ordained."

"What exactly does he do?"

"He is a fixer of sorts. He solves problems. Like our young friend in the hospital."

"And your job is to drive him around town, listen to the goings-on. And fix his car. You enjoy this?"

"'Enjoy' is not the right word. I am retired from the priesthood; I am not retired from life. And I get to spend time with someone who is not much different from me."

"How did you meet Orenstein?"

"We are neighbours. I live upstairs in my late mother's flat. She taught at the old Catholic School Commission in Outremont and could not afford to live where she taught, so she rented then bought this apartment in the Plateau."

"Father?"

"Long gone. He felt it his duty to uphold the Irish male stereotype—wine, women, and song. They found him in a hotel room in Detroit. His attacker was never found. You have parents?"

"Mother is still around. Father passed some years ago. My parents were mostly not together. They never divorced, just apart. Mother and I abide one another; I go weeks without seeing her or calling. I call, she complains; she calls, I complain. Not exactly warm and close."

"I have one work-related question to ask you."

There was a slight narrowing of the eyes. Whoops, I may have blown it.

"Do you have to?"

"No. At least not here, not now"

"Monday, then. I have your coordinates. You will respond?"

"Scout's honour, yes."

The performance was getting out; Martha's friends joined her, eyeing me. I was introduced by name and not by title, current or former.

No doubt as they went home, I was going to be discussed.

Leaving the theatre, I turned on my phone. There was a message from Shmully. The Sabbath was over—back to work.

Later as I was walking up the Main, he called. I was to meet him opposite the X-rated cinema!

CHAPTER FOUR

Directly across the street from the theatre, I spotted the van. The driver's side door opened as I walked up. Orenstein moved around to the passenger side. It had started to rain, and the temperature had dropped.

"Are we here for some specific reason?"

"I believe we are waiting for someone to come out of the picture show."

"What?" I started the motor to put the defroster on so we could see out and to warm up. "We are waiting for someone you know?"

"The son of someone."

"Wonderful. Whatever happened to a flashlight under the bed covers?"

There was a double feature, according to the billboard outside.

"How long are we going to wait?"

He turned to look at me. "Until we are satisfied."

He gave me his camera. I got out of the van and took some pictures of the building.

Customers, mostly single men, went in and out.

I turned the motor back on. We could see out again.

Out of the theatre came the figure of someone much slighter and younger than the rest. He was wearing a pulled-up hoodie with a baseball cap. Standard garb for the area.

He did not run up the street, exactly. We started to follow. Our young friend was moving at a speed-walking rate with his head down.

Several blocks before entering our *quartier*, he disappeared down an alley. I stopped driving to see what would happen next. He reappeared wearing the more conventional hat and suit. Under his arm was a garbage bag. He resumed his determined pace, now not looking out of place. He put the bag, which presumably contained the hoodie and baseball cap, next to a house on our street. He went into a building that was used as a synagogue to join up with a group of young fellows who were involved in some after-Sabbath activity that we could see going on from the street.

"Now what?"

Orenstein was writing notes. Without looking up: "Any experience with this sort of thing?"

"Occasionally I would be called upon to give my version of sex education courses. I have interviewed couples who were about to get married. Sometimes in confession, I would hear some admission of some sexual indiscretion. Never have I confronted an adolescent who has slipped out of an X-rated movie theatre."

"Neither have I. Our next move in this affair will become obvious in the next day or two."

He was sounding more solemn than usual. Where is a woodshed when we need it most?

CHAPTER FIVE

On Sunday morning I awoke early, as was my custom. Some habits die hard. I perused the Internet for news both local and international. There had been a fire overnight on the Main. Our X-rated movie theatre had sustained unspecified damage. I decided to go down to investigate.

The rain from the previous night had stopped, and the streets were still wet. Leaves from the trees were littering the ground in celebration of autumn. I had a jacket on, and my head was covered with my Montreal Canadiens baseball cap.

Dog walkers and joggers were out early this morning. Police cars had blocked the intersection where the cinema was located. Fire trucks and hoses were everywhere. The fire had been put out. Damage was confined to the roof of the building. The adjoining businesses had sustained water damage. Some firemen were milling about rolling up hoses, and others were drinking coffee. I approached one of the men, who wore a yellow fireman's hat. "Much damage?"

"Not too bad. There won't be any movies for a while."

A fellow emerged from the store next door, cell phone to his ear, yelling, "What do I pay you premiums for?" His windows had been knocked out and his door had been yanked open and was hanging askew.

I looked up and there was Orenstein. He nodded in my direction. He was standing on the northwest corner diagonally opposite the theatre. I wandered over. We stood beside one another, eyeing the scene. I hesitated to ask what I believed to be the obvious question. I cleared my throat.

"Glasheen, don't even suggest I had anything to do with this," he muttered.

"Just wondering."

"I am not unhappy this happened, however. It's what we might say *besheart.*"

"What?"

"Ordained, in the stars."

"Or arson."

"I will leave that to others to determine."

S. John Diamond

Declining a lift, I decided to walk back to the apartment. Though it was early, there was a fruit and vegetable store open, and I went in to replenish my supply.

Leaving with my purchases, I ran into a tall, frock-coated man. We exchanged excuse-mes. He looked down through his glasses at me, "You're Glasheen."

"And you are?"

"Shinder, Rabbi Shinder."

I must stick out around here like a sore thumb.

"I want you to come to my office later today. You do work on Sundays?"

"Yes, and your office is where?"

We agreed on a time and he told me the place.

Going home, I opened my old PC to discover a message from Martha Lang: "What is your question?"

"Was there any semen around Joel's bed?" I typed.

Immediately there was a response. "You suspect there was?"

"Yes."

"Nothing mentioned. The bed would have been stripped and the room wiped clean."

"You may have a new volunteer."

"You think it may happen again?"

"I do."

"An inside job?"

"That would be my theory."

"Couldn't be a family member?"

"Could be, but I do not think so. Could be an opportunistic hospital employee. This is an awful business. The person who did this is lurking out there, somewhere, and will do it again whether in the hospital or in a park or in a parking garage."

"Meanwhile, we do not know how Joel is, how he is dealing with this. Interesting how the victim gets shunted aside."

"I am meeting with Rabbi Shinder later today."

"You will give me a report."

It was not a question. "Perhaps he wants to talk about the weather or the latest about Christians and Jews."

"Bullshit."

13

"Listen, I have no agenda. I will see where the conversation goes. Though I agree the subject should come up, he may have something else on his mind. If it does, and I hope it does, I will give you some details."

"Not some."

"Let us end this for now and I will contact you later. Coffee, maybe?"

"Sure. Just let me know where and when."

"Over and out."

I had not eaten. I turned on the radio; the Sunday morning radio show was on the CBC. There was a conversation about breast cancer. I turned the sound lower.

With brewed coffee and some toast, I looked up the sports site. There was a report about the Canadiens training camp and the latest crop of rookies who were trying to make the team. The news came on the radio and there was no mention of the fire at the theatre. Not a big item.

There was a rap at the back door. Shmully was standing there.

"Busy day and it's just ten a.m. You are going to meet with Rabbi Shinder. We are going together.

"I suspect he wants to talk about his grandson and also some other issues. We will walk over."

"Sure."

He left. My toast was cold and my coffee lukewarm. I started over.

By now the radio show was talking about the Middle East—Israel and its neighbours and the Arab Spring. Though I rarely paid attention to that conflict, given my current situation, I was becoming more attuned to what was going on there.

CHAPTER SIX

I was standing on the walk outside, waiting for Orenstein, who emerged from his house with a torrent of Yiddish trailing behind him.

His wife, Bella, was standing there, broom in hand. When she saw me, she smiled slightly, looked up and down the street, and went back in, slamming the door behind her.

We walked in silence down the block. As we turned the corner, several men of varying ages passed, nodding in Orenstein's general direction. They averted their eyes from me; I was invisible.

Rounding the next corner, we came to a house with a front door up some stairs. At street level was another door through which a woman emerged. She looked away, not making eye contact as she walked by. She was not dressed in the same conservative manner as most of the women in the area.

In we went, down some stairs into the basement. There was a big room lined with bookshelves on either side. At the rear was a big desk, behind which Rabbi Shinder sat. He ushered us into two seats in front. His desk was neat. He had removed his frock coat and was wearing a vest over a white shirt.

"Terence Joseph Glasheen. I knew your mother. We were neighbours for a time when you were attending to your duties. She was a fine lady. When we made a request to enlarge our Shul, the borough held numerous hearings. Your mother came to the meetings to support our cause. Others were not so supportive. In the end, it was agreed that we would simply refurbish the building, but these things are not forgotten.

"In the matter of young Joel, his wounds have healed. We have arranged for visits with a psychologist, a member of the community, to deal with the emotional side of this outrage. And of course, his family has been the source of much support. We shall see if there are any lingering effects. He remembers nothing."

"Could I interview him? I suspect this was not an isolated incident and I think it will happen again."

"No. At least not yet. I understand that the social worker is very anxious to involve the authorities."

"She is obligated to do so. She has given us a week to come up with some answers. And even if Joel is unresponsive, we have no choice but to allow the police to interview him."

Shinder took off his glasses and rubbed his eyes. "It would be in our best interest to find the culprit."

"I have a number of questions about all this."

Eyes turned my way.

"The attack occurred in the hospital. According to the social worker, the child was never left alone. Do we know who was there? At any time was he taken for a test like an x-ray, when he would have been alone waiting? He would have been transported by a porter to the area of the hospital where these things take place. We have no timeline. It would be useful to interview Joel even if we get nothing. We might unearth some memory which might prove useful. The police are going to have to interview him. We all need to acknowledge that.

"Putting that off is a double-edged sword. The longer we wait, the more their suspicions will be aroused. And the longer we wait, it may be more likely that Joel will remember something that can help in the investigation. Someone needs to speak to Joel's parents to outline the realities of the situation."

Shinder was leaning back in his chair. "My daughter and son-in-law are not willing to subject their son to a grilling by the police. They are aware that the authorities need to be involved."

"Is there any other child from the community in hospital?"

"Not to my knowledge."

"Should that occur, we should know."

"You have a plan?"

"Just that the hospital needs a new volunteer to check on things."

"You would be comfortable with that?"

I nodded.

Orenstein, who had been silent, finally spoke. "I know someone in the Youth Protection Squad. Someone who might be counted on to handle this matter with . . . sensitivity. I will arrange a meeting tomorrow. Rabbi, I was waiting for your permission to involve the authorities. I also would like to know if there are any other kids from the community in hospital. I think that we should know that, anyway. And I want permission to speak with Joel. I agree with Glasheen on that one. I think we can stage-manage the interview so as to not offend anyone."

16

Shinder did not immediately respond. Finally, to Orenstein he said, "Shmully, you do not need my permission for anything; you have *carte-blanche*. I respect that, because of my relationship with Yoel, you have chosen to wait until things settled down a bit. News of this outrage has spread through the community. The hospital has been cast in a negative light.

"Our children—all children—should be safe in a situation like that. I have had a phone call from the chairman of the board expressing his concern and his commitment to get to the bottom of this."

Rabbi Shinder was beginning to display a political astuteness that intrigued me. His bookish demeanour was deceptive.

"You gentlemen are here for two other issues. A young woman's parents wish to know if a certain gentleman is appropriate for marriage. They have reason to believe that he is not. And secondly, there is the matter of convincing a man to give his wife a *get*."

"A *get*?"

"A religious divorce, without which she cannot remarry within the faith."

"Our young suitor owns real estate around here." He placed a typed list of some addresses on his desk in front of us. "Levi Epstein is his name and the buildings are owned under different names, different company names. There may be some ties to interests in Israel and in New York City.

"The family wants to know if this gentleman is worthy of their daughter.

"As for the fellow who is denying his wife a divorce, his name is Moishe Greengarten. He also calls himself Mike Green. He owns a company in Ville Saint-Laurent." On a separate piece of paper were details about Green.

Just then a voice from upstairs yelled down, "It's time to go—you promised."

"Ah. I need to go out with my wife, some shopping." In a low voice he added, "*Shalom Bayit*—Peace in the House."

We left by the same door we came in.

Once on the street, we walked in silence. Again, many passed acknowledging Orenstein and averting their eyes from me. I had never been so invisible in my entire life. Being a village priest usually carried with it a certain prestige. Here, nothing.

"Peace in the House?"

"Yes, away from the tumult, and a little calm within. Good for the soul. An exercise in getting along. Everybody is right. Domestic peace."

"So what is our next move?"

"Tomorrow is soon enough. I also am going to run some errands."

"Why did you wait this long to mention that you had a contact in the Juvenile Squad?"

"Timing. I did not want to tip my hand. The parents could have shipped the child to relatives in New York. Or they could have sent him to Israel to be with his aunt, the mother's sister who lives there. I wanted to make sure that he was still here."

"Tactful."

"In this matter, yes. We are juggling a number of plates. Any one of them falls and it is all over. We really need to find out who did this before he strikes again."

"He?"

"Statistically speaking."

"I am going to meet with the social worker later today for coffee. I want to pitch the idea of my spending a few nights there as a volunteer. Keep an eye on things. Would be helpful if she bought the idea."

"I want to arrange the meeting with the police for tomorrow; perhaps we can use your apartment?"

"I will dust first."

"Whatever."

"The first building belonging to our Lothario is within walking distance. I think I will wander down to take a look."

"We will check in later."

CHAPTER SEVEN

Time for a nap. I had no errands to run. I put on the Broadway recording of *South Pacific*. Lying on the couch, I picked up the current *New Yorker* and started reading from the back.

The next thing I knew my cell phone was vibrating.

"You were going to call me." It was Martha. "Let's meet."

"I was taking a well-deserved nap."

"Meet me at the Coffee Bar on the Main in half an hour."

I took a quick shower and shaved. I made a note to get a haircut. Maybe Martha would know someone.

Walking out into the afternoon sunshine, I passed Shmully's kids, who were playing ball hockey in the street. I stopped to watch. I was offered a stick to have a go at the goalie. No words were spoken. They all stopped to watch. They had homemade nets. I lined up the tennis ball and lifted it into the net minder's pads. He sent it back my way. This time I faked a slap shot and went into deke. He made the first move and I tucked the ball into the corner of the net.

I handed the stick back: a feeling of triumph. Stares all around.

"Good day, gentlemen, and thanks for the offer."

I arrived at the coffee place first. Several tables were occupied by students with laptops. I went to the counter to buy a coffee and something sweet. Martha appeared at my side.

"I'll take the same. It's on me." The young man behind the counter obliged, and we went to find a place to sit in the back where it might be quieter.

"Do you know a hair stylist?"

"Uhm, around here? Just a second. I'll call Elyse, she would know."

"Elyse?"

"Fundraiser extraordinaire and knows everything about that sort of stuff. She has an encyclopedic knowledge about local goings-on."

A cell phone appeared and the call was made. Elyse came through. I was provided with a name and a phone number.

One problem solved.

"Your meeting with the Rabbi produced what?"

"Some agreement that the culprit needs to be found and that I would spend an evening or two at the hospital to keep an eye on things. Can you arrange that?"

"It would be easier if you were still a priest. The chaplain and I are buds. To go through the volunteer process requires an orientation and a vetting process that could take weeks. You could pretend to be visiting someone—or a number of someones—without raising too much suspicion."

"And the chaplain is?"

"Ferguson—Reg Ferguson."

The name meant nothing to me. "Could you arrange a meeting with this fellow?" She nodded. "And how is your internal investigation going?"

"Nobody knows anything. Nobody saw anything. The board chairman has spent some time doing damage control and yelling at the head of security. None of this has produced any results."

"You mean that no one has come forward to confess?"

"Are you planning to interview the child?"

"Yes."

"And what do you expect from that?"

"Nothing."

"Nothing?"

"I have no expectations. So maybe we will receive some nugget that can shed some light."

"You have had experience interviewing before?"

"One of my duties was juvenile court liaison. I got used to talking to monosyllabic Inuit teenagers."

"How did you manage that?"

"Guile, deceit, bravado, humour, and pure bullshit."

"And I am sure you are not giving away all your trade secrets."

"We live in a highly verbal culture and we deal with folks who are inarticulate, who have no language to explain their pain."

"Is that why you left the Church?"

"Partly. I no longer had enough language. I, too, became inarticulate. The Church had provided me with a blueprint, with a map. But the map no longer matched the terrain. I ran out of language."

"You know, working in the hospital is not much different. There are some days when I feel I am making absolutely no difference. Let's lighten this up. More coffee?"

"No, I think I will pass."

"Me, too."

"So you will arrange for me to meet with the Reverend Ferguson?"

"Yes. He is in the building certain days of the week. But he manages to come by to have a chat with me on a regular basis. I will let you know when he is available."

"Plans for the evening?"

"Dinner with Mother. And you?"

"Need to go home and dust the apartment."

"Want to come to my place and do the same?"

"Some other time, maybe."

"You better watch out. I may take you up on that."

We left the coffee shop and shook hands at the curb. She headed south and I went north.

I thought, *That was a nice talk, a lot deeper than I would have thought possible a few days ago.*

And, one of Levi Epstein's buildings is nearby. Time to visit the suitor.

CHAPTER EIGHT

Turning right onto Pine, I walked east a couple of blocks. There on the north side of the street was a five-storey building with apartments upstairs and small shops at street level.

There was a tattoo parlour, a barber shop, an antique store, a cell phone outlet, and a used clothing place. There was an alley on one side, and up the alley in the rear of the building was a sign that read *Studio de Massage*. It was *Ouvert*—or so the flashing sign said in the window.

The door was locked, so I rang the bell. A youngish blonde woman dressed in slacks and a t-shirt opened the door. "You want massage?" She had an East European accent—Russian, maybe.

"Do you have a card or a brochure?"

"Card. Very nice massage. Very young, pretty girl. Good price."

"Thank you. The card will do nicely."

She closed the door behind me. It was not a slam, exactly.

I wandered back down the alley toward the street and into the main entrance to the apartment building. I looked briefly at the names on the roster; none were remarkable.

Beside each one was a code for getting in. The vestibule had been refurbished and was spotless.

Back outside, a big, black SUV rolled to a stop. Out came a large, bearded fellow with a black hat and frock coat. He came around to the sidewalk.

"You are looking for an apartment?"

"No. I was looking for someone who might live here. Guess not."

"I have nothing for rent, all filled up. Come back and see me when school is over, next spring. I have too many students here."

"I will keep it in mind."

I wandered down the street toward the Main; crossing to the other side, I noticed the big fellow walking up the alley.

I turned to come back, looking up the alley; no one was there.

I tried the massage parlour door; it was locked and the electric sign was turned off.

I went back to the street, crossed, and sat on a bench next to a bus stop.

I waited. How long does it take to collect the rent? About a half hour later, Levi Epstein, for I was sure that was him, came back down the alley, got into his car, and drove off.

Back up the alley, the sign had been turned back on. I rang the bell.

The same blonde woman came to the door. This time she had on a robe and flip-flop sandals.

"Change your mind?"

"How much for half an hour?"

"Fifty dollars."

I went in. She showed me to a room down a dimly lit hallway. She opened the door. "Get undressed. I be back."

The room was clean and had a massage table near the wall. There was also a shower stall. The aroma of incense was more pungent than I would have hoped.

I disrobed down to my underwear and sat on the table.

A few minutes later, the same woman came in.

"My name is Magda. Fifty bucks, please."

I paid her. Orenstein and I would work out the finances later.

"What kind massage?"

"What are the choices?"

"Soft, hard, medium; and where you want?"

"Medium and in my lower back."

"Please take off pants. More comfortable."

"Do you mind if I leave them on?"

"You choose."

She had taken off her robe to reveal a not-bad figure dressed in a bra and panties. I probably should have bolted then. In the name of sleuthing, I stayed.

There was the sound of waves coming through a sound system which added to the relaxing environment. She kneaded away. I was lying on my stomach. Conversation was not practical.

After about fifteen minutes, she asked me to turn over and she turned down the lights. This was more ambience than I wanted.

"You want extras?"

"Extras?"

"For forty bucks I take off my bra. For a hundred I nude. For two hundred complete."

"No, no, just a massage, thank you."

"You afraid? I clean."

"Maybe next time."

"You cheap."

I wanted to change the subject if I could. I also wanted to get out of there as quickly as possible.

My research had produced the results I had predicted. Orenstein would no doubt be proud. And how do I tell the Rabbi how I came to the conclusion that Mr. Epstein may not be the marriage material that the family is looking for?

The lights came back on and she put on her robe.

"Where are you from? "

"From Ukraine. You know where Ukraine is?"

"Part of Russia."

"No! No! Separate country. Why you want to know?"

"Just asking."

"My English is not good for you? I come here, make me take French classes. Funny place."

"Well, thank you. I will get dressed now."

She left and closed the door with a small bang.

I dressed in record time and left the room.

Sitting in the waiting area near the door was the big frock-coated man.

Magda was nowhere to be seen.

"You checking up on me?" His accent was Bronx tinged with something else I could not recognize. There was an air of menace.

"Excuse me."

"I do not believe that you are a lonely middle-aged man who simply wanted a massage on a Sunday night. You were the one hanging around outside before, right?"

"You can believe whatever you want. I paid for the service, which was quite acceptable. Now I would like to leave."

"Get out of here and don't come back. I do not want to see you around here again." He got out of the chair and came right up to me. "Do you understand?"

He turned to unlock the door. He opened it for me.

I turned slightly as I went out. "Thank you for your hospitality."

I walked down the alley to the street. The door slammed again.

I had witnessed more doors slamming in the past few hours than I had in years.

In hindsight, I should have got when the gettin' was good.

Now, how would I tell Shmully that I had been excommunicated from a massage parlour? I walked with a certain hop to my step all the way home, laughing to myself.

I spent the rest of the evening preparing for the interview tomorrow with the police. I dusted and vacuumed the entire flat.

CHAPTER NINE

Shmully came up at nine in the morning. "How was your night?"

"Fine; I actually slept well for a change."

"They will be here at ten."

"Ah, I did some research last night. That fellow Levi is not a good catch."

"How did you find out?"

"He has a building on Pine Avenue, which I visited. Very disagreeable fellow; chased me away."

"Could have told you that. I made some calls to Israel and New York. Real estate is just one of his enterprises. He is the visible associate for several others who wish to remain anonymous. You discovered the spa?"

Just then the bell sounded.

Two people came up the stairs. The first introduced herself as Constable Elbaz and the second was a tall, trim gent who was Beaulieu, Marc Beaulieu. Neither one was in uniform, and except for the name tags on their lapels, one would not know they were police.

Ms. Elbaz sat in the overstuffed chair that required refurbishing. A relic from a bygone era; the damn thing should have been thrown out. She opened a binder to take notes.

So Beaulieu was going to do the talking: he looked over at Shmully. "You did not call me to discuss our fifteen minutes of fame. So why are we here? And who is this gentleman?" He spoke with no trace of an accent.

I was simply introduced as Orenstein's assistant. Neither one of us was going to take notes. To the best of our ability, we'd try to keep this off the record.

Orenstein was in a difficult spot, or so I thought.

"We have reason to believe that a young member of our community, a young boy, was abused." Beaulieu nodded and said nothing.

Orenstein continued, "To the best of our knowledge, the attack took place in the Children's Hospital while the child was there for medical treatment."

Elbaz was taking notes. I was curious to know what she was writing.

26

"The social worker . . . what's her name . . . Lang . . . she has not contacted us. You have anything to do with that?"

Orenstein sat not taking his eyes off Beaulieu. "We wanted to do our own investigation into this horrible affair."

Beaulieu started to pace. "You know we have to interview the boy. Do you want me to read you the riot act?"

Orenstein sat calmly in the other overstuffed chair.

"That won't be necessary."

"I gather you are getting nowhere. Have you interviewed the boy?"

"Not yet."

"There is more to this story than you are telling."

"Perhaps."

"Orenstein, you are still a pain in the ass."

Orenstein made no response.

The policeman stopped pacing. "What sort of deal can I offer you? You have given me nothing to work with."

"My colleague and I wanted to speak to him first. Then he is all yours."

"He is still here? He hasn't been shipped out of town?"

"He is still here, to our knowledge."

"We will be back here Thursday. Make sure the interview has taken place."

Orenstein nodded.

Beaulieu looked at Ms. Elbaz, who had folded her binder. Time to leave.

Without shaking hands, they went down the stairs and out the door.

"Now what?"

"We go interview the boy."

"How do you know Beaulieu?"

"Series of jewellery robberies which involved teenagers. He was a hero for a few minutes."

Orenstein then left by the back staircase. As was becoming his habit, he told me just what he thought I should know, leaving me to infer the rest.

I made a mental note to take the two old chairs and throw them out.

A little while later, Ms. Lang called. "You can meet with Reverend Ferguson any time you want." She gave me his number, and I repeated it to make sure I had it right.

Orenstein called a few minutes later. "We have a meeting with Yoel's parents at four this afternoon at their house. We can walk over. I will call you later."

Ferguson, the chaplain, took my call immediately. We arranged to meet in the chapel in the Children's Hospital at noon.

CHAPTER TEN

The chapel was on the main floor down at the end of the corridor. I went in and sat on one of the benches. The room had subdued lighting. It was set up as more of a meditation space than anything else. A quiet room.

In walked a chubby, white-haired gentleman with a full white beard. Santa Claus; how perfect for a children's hospital. "You're Glasheen?"

"And you are Ferguson."

"So you want to volunteer here?" I nodded. "Martha told me a little about you. You are a priest. You worked in the north and now you are retired. You used to being around children, sick children?"

"Part of my duties was ministering to the sick."

"You really have not answered my question. How do you see yourself operating around here?"

"I thought I would come in the evening, put on a white or blue coat, and mingle with the patients. Maybe read them a bedtime story . . . that sort of thing. Then, as the night goes on, I would wander from floor to floor checking on things."

"You have a cross you can put in your lapel?"

"Somewhere."

Ferguson had blue eyes behind wire-rimmed glasses; he took them off to wipe them on his tie. "You left the priesthood why, exactly?"

"Exactly? I do not know why exactly. I cannot give you a long, detailed explanation. Was I involved in the abuses which took place? Not directly. Was I aware of others who were abusers? Only after the fact. Was I aware that these things were being covered up? Yes. Did I or do I have a crisis of faith? Probably. Was I good at what I did? Yes, and then I ran out of gas. I was empty. I went on retreats; I took time off. Nothing seemed to rekindle the magic. I have been a priest all my adult life. I am now sixty years old. It was simply time to retire."

Ferguson looked at me when I finished. "You had no issues with your bosses?"

"They had issues with me."

"How is that?"

"The word that comes to mind is messy."

"Messy?"

"I do not like disorder. I know the world is not like that. But they could not make things tidy."

"You are referring to the abuses."

"Yes, and their inability to recapture the joy of the Church."

"Or your inability to transcend all that stuff."

"I guess after a while it got to me. I could no longer get excited."

"Was there one event which triggered your leaving?"

I paused and took a breath. "I am still not sure I can talk about it yet."

"Painful."

I nodded. "Listen, my mother was dying here, and it was a convenient out. I came down to tend to her and her affairs. She went quickly and of course she had her papers perfectly in order. I wrote a letter to the bishop and that was it."

"So you chauffeur a religious Jew around town and do good deeds."

"Some would say we meddle."

"Some would also say that we religious are by definition meddlesome."

"And you, here, in the hospital?"

"I no longer have a pulpit. Many churches have closed, and the congregations have joined together. I fill in as needed. I mostly operate here and at an old age home nearby. I prefer here."

"There is something more hopeful about children."

"Married?"

"Was. I am a widower. She died five years ago, no kids." He spread his arms. "These are my kids."

"Your family?"

He nodded. "I guess you could say that." He paused, then said, "Talk."

"Her name was Molly. She was around ten and she was interested in the world. She would hang around and talk. She asked questions. She was curious about Chicago. Do not know why, really. Perhaps the name. Anyway, we studied up on Chicago. The Internet is a wonderful teaching tool, especially in isolated communities in the north. And if it could be arranged, we talked about visiting the city. Well, Christmas came around, and I got busy with my duties.

S. John Diamond

"We lost contact over the holidays. In January, I looked forward to resuming our after-school meetings. No Molly. She was not around. She had stopped going to school. I went looking for her. I could not find her. It was as if she no longer existed. No one knew where she was.

"It was a small community; everybody generally knew everyone's business, or so I thought. One day I was called to the school to meet in the principal's office. Molly, along with several adults, was present. That bright little girl was present in body only. Someone mentioned selective mutism. Something had obviously gone terribly wrong in her world. Had she been beaten? Had she been raped? All possibilities, no answer. There was going to be a council. In the meantime, my best efforts produced no response. I wanted to be alone with her. But right then that was impossible. The elders were holding sway and closing ranks. Her parents claimed complete bewilderment. Her brother, a young burly fellow, chose to blame all this on me and everyone else. This through a translator. He speaks perfectly good English. We were excluded from the healing process. The meeting ended, and we all went our separate ways."

"And now you live in Montreal among religious Jews. You are nothing if not eclectic." There was a twinkle in his eye and a warmth in his voice, which was reassuring.

"When do I start?"

"It's up to you."

"Perhaps tonight?"

"I will meet you here at six with a blue volunteer coat. Bring your cross."

I checked the clock. I needed to get back home to meet up with Shmully for the appointment with Joel and family.

31

CHAPTER ELEVEN

It was a warm late September afternoon, so I decided to walk back to the 'hood: east on Sainte-Catherine Street then up Saint-Laurent Boulevard. I arrived home slightly out of breath and was greeted on the front steps by one of Orenstein's children, who told me that Shmully would be a bit late. The van had broken down again. A few seconds later, a taxi came to a screeching halt by the curb. Out jumped Orenstein, who congratulated the cab driver in several different languages.

He handed me a small black device. "Keep this in the pocket of your suit coat and turn it on when we start to interview the boy." It was a small—very small—tape recorder. As we were walking, I tested the mechanism to see that it worked.

We reached the house, which of course was right next door to the Rabbi's. I should have known. Up a few stairs to the landing, exactly four o'clock. The door opened without our knocking. A tiny, slim woman with a kerchief around her head ushered us in.

Shmully introduced himself and then nodded at me. "And this is my associate, Mr. Glasheen."

She looked my way and nodded. She did not offer to shake hands.

I turned on the recorder.

We were ushered into the front parlour. Everything was spotless. I did not want to sit down on the sofa for fear of offending the order. There was a glass case that housed an array of candelabra. Each one was more ornate than the last. And, of course, books. One wall was lined with shelves full of serious-looking tomes with spines imprinted in Hebrew, which I did not have a chance to look at. In walked a very thin gentleman, who nodded at Orenstein.

"And you are?"

Orenstein answered for me. "He is my assistant, Mr. Glasheen. This is Avrum Goldberger, father of Yoel."

The father nodded but did not offer his hand.

We were still standing. This was getting awkward with gusts of uncomfortable.

We still had not met the boy.

Orenstein in his deepest, most measured voice proceeded to explain why we were there. His tone spoke to the seriousness of the situation. He very slowly reviewed the facts as we knew them. We were offered seats.

Avrum, dressed in black, had kept his fedora on. In a high-pitched voice, he started to explain his position. "I have sought the advice of a lawyer. Though I have some legal training, I felt that I required someone who would be more objective."

Orenstein interjected, "In fact, you completed your legal studies but chose not to continue on."

"Yes, well, that is in the past. And now we have to deal with the horror of the attack on my son."

I decided to interject myself into the proceedings by going on a slightly different track.

"According to the social worker, your son was never left alone from the minute he arrived."

Goldberger looked down and, speaking more slowly, he acknowledged that was not quite true.

We were silent.

"I received a phone call during my watch. It was the middle of the night here but seven hours ahead in Israel. I went into the corridor and started down the hall. I was so involved in the conversation I lost track of time and place. When I came back, Yoel had been attacked. He was immediately seen to by the medical staff. They were magnificent.

"However, my son has been bruised. He could not have seen anything and, even if he had, he was sufficiently medicated so as to render anything he said suspect."

"The boy is going to need to be interviewed. It might be easier if we did it first. The police had to write a report so they will be along in a few days." Shmully stated this in as matter of fact a manner as possible.

The father took this information in. "I would like to have my lawyer present when the police question Yoel."

"As you wish. However, that may not be wise at this point. They are simply going to complete a report."

"You have met with the police?"

We both nodded.

"So this meeting is something you negotiated with them?"

Again, nods.

"We have until Thursday to get back to them," Orenstein said.

"We thought that maybe we would send the boy to Israel to live with relatives. We chose not to do that. You know he is small and frail for his age. Why would anyone attack him like that?"

A sombre Orenstein waited a second. "We know that this has been a very devastating experience for all of you."

"I know my father-in-law has been in touch with the president of the board of directors at the hospital. That still does not negate the fact that we are being encouraged to sue. I would prefer not to. I would prefer that this, this . . . culprit be identified and prosecuted."

"So would we. Maybe by speaking gently with Yoel in as unthreatening a way as possible. Mr. Glasheen has experience in this." Orenstein looked directly at the father and asked, "Do you suspect anyone?"

"No. I know of no one who could do this. No one I know is capable of this kind of outrage."

"Will you let us speak with the boy?"

"I want to be present."

Orenstein nodded. I wanted to talk to the boy alone.

At the door of the parlour, the thin woman appeared as if she had been paged, which she had not. "Avrum, are you sure?"

Again, she did not look at us or acknowledge we were even there.

"Go get Yoel."

A minute or so later, in walked a junior version of the father.

Thin, small, with a dark suit, white shirt, black fedora, and glasses. He looked about twelve years old.

"These two gentlemen want to speak to you about your time in the hospital."

Avrum looked directly at Shmully. He ignored me. I reached into my pocket to check the recorder. The thing was vibrating slightly in my hand, so I guessed it was working.

Orenstein began, "As your father said, we want to ask you some questions about your time in the hospital. Is that okay?"

A shrug.

"Why were you there?"

"I had pneumonia."

"You were attacked when you were there? Yes?"

No response, then a nod.

"You were pretty banged up. It must have hurt."

Silence. Avrum interjected, "Yoel, you can talk to these men—they are on our side."

Mostly Joel was looking at the floor.

"Did you have an oxygen mask on?" I asked.

A slight nod.

"Could you see around it and look at your attacker?"

"I was asleep. I woke up. Someone was standing there. I was groggy."

"Did you recognize your attacker?"

"No."

"If you saw this person again, would you recognize him?"

"I don't know."

"Was the person big or small?

"It was dark. I really could not see."

"You felt pain."

A slight nod of the head.

"Is there anything you would like to tell us about that night that you have not thought of before? Do you think about that night when you are asleep? Do you dream about it?"

No response.

"Those are really tough questions for him to answer, don't you think?" said the father.

"I guess I was wondering if there is something that you remember, that you may have forgotten about until now."

The father interjected, "Didn't you have some special visitors?"

"Some hockey players came to visit me. They gave me a small Canadiens crest."

"That is exciting. How do you think they will do this year? Will they make the playoffs?"

A look up, a slight smile, a nod.

"So you are a fan?"

"Yes."

"And how are they going to do this year?"

"They are my favourite team and they are going to do great."

Well, well, some life.

"Have you been to a game?"

"Maybe this year if Abba can get some tickets."

"I am sure your father can arrange that.

"Now what are we going to do about your injuries in the hospital?"

He shrugged.

There was no place else to go.

Orenstein looked at the father. "Well, that appears to be all for now. If there is anything else, please let us know."

Goldberger nodded. "And what about the police?"

"We will give them a report and see where that goes."

With that, we left the house. On the way out, the boy's mother was standing in the hallway at the door to the kitchen, her thin frame silhouetted in the rear windows. She was wiping her hands on her apron. She gave a slight nod as we went out the front door.

CHAPTER TWELVE

"Well, that went pretty much as I had thought it would."

We were walking side-by-side toward our street.

Orenstein did not respond. He was looking more dour than usual.

"I think they are lying."

"Mr. Glasheen!"

"I think they know who did it and are too numb to believe it. They are in denial."

"Interesting theory. So it was an inside job. A family member."

"Yes."

Just then the young man from the X-rated theatre came walking down the street. He was alone with a big, blue velvet bag under his arm.

Orenstein stepped right in front of him to impede his progress.

In a very low voice he admonished the kid, "Stay away from places you do not belong."

The young man turned white and attempted to walk around Orenstein. Shmully deftly cut off his move. "Do you hear me?"

A slight nod.

I was impressed. No lecture. Just right to the point.

We continued walking in silence. I was wondering how we were going to handle the police.

Orenstein was unusually silent, distant.

"When do you want to hear the tape?"

"Later."

"I am going to spend tonight at the hospital. I met with the chaplain."

Shmully did not respond. We continued walking in silence.

My cell phone vibrated. It was Martha Lang. I did not take the call.

"I will call Beaulieu to arrange to see him tomorrow morning. And you need to go home and prepare for tonight. I don't like any of this all the way around." He was walking with his head down.

"We could quit this case."

"No. Not an option."

"It is always an option."

"I am not in the habit of walking away; and I will not, especially in this matter."

"Are you not just being stubborn? It is possible that this one is beyond us. It is also quite likely that this is an inside job, that the abuser is a family member."

He stopped and looked up at me. "And if it is, so be it. We will follow this wherever it leads."

"You do not care what this will do to the community?"

"That's exactly the point. I do care. The community will be better for it."

"You know that we will find the culprit?"

"The guilty party will make himself known to us. Whether it's when you are in the hospital or somewhere else. This person will reveal who he is. We just need to be vigilant."

"I am not sure I share your certainty."

"We need to prepare for the meeting with the police. I want to listen to the tape recording."

I reached in my pocket to give him the tape recorder.

"My volunteer job beckons."

"Later."

"Later."

CHAPTER THIRTEEN

As I lay in the bathwater, I was thinking about Shmully's determination. That determination to forge on was admirable, but at what cost?

He is who he is by sheer will. A religious and moral man in a world not really tolerant of that. His sights are set above us all.

What to wear to capture a pedophile? White runners, white athletic socks, pressed jeans, no jeans, lightweight blue corduroy, and button-down checkered shirt.

Something to eat and a snack for later. My pectoral cross was neatly wrapped in a sock in the back of a drawer.

I found a knapsack from my camping days and left the apartment.

With no helmet, I rented one of the bikes from the street corner, figuring there would be a similar docking place near the Children's Hospital. There was, and I managed to arrive in one piece.

Two phone calls, two voicemails. Both Martha and Ferguson were busy.

The information desk inside the front door was closed for the day. From behind me, Martha appeared. "Where have you been all afternoon?"

"Here I am. What is on your mind?"

"I wanted to know how the interview went."

"As predicted."

"He said nothing."

"Joel spoke, all right. He just did not or could not tell us anything of value. He did get a crest from the hockey team; some players were doing rounds."

"Did he seem okay? Were there any signs of distress?"

"That is the thing, he seemed healthy as hell. His father is considering a lawsuit."

"I am not surprised."

"Well maybe if we find the guilty party that will be avoided. The father has a law degree, by the way."

"Let's find the bad guy and we will deal with the rest of it in due course. Okay?

"I was to tell you that Reg was going to be held up. So you are on your own. Let's get you a blue volunteer jacket. Do you have a plan of action?"

"Should I?"

"It would help."

"I thought I would wander around, make chit-chat, and offer to read to the kids who are alone."

"Do you know how to play computer games?"

"No. But I am a quick study. Are there any kids here from the community?"

"Not that I am aware of. I think I will stay with you for a while, introduce you around."

We took an elevator up a couple of flights. We exited onto a floor in front of a nurse's station. I had neglected to put my cross onto the lapel of my blue coat—I left it in my pocket.

Martha introduced me to a couple of nurses who were sitting behind the counter. I was simply a new volunteer. The corridor ran off to the left and right. It made no difference to me which way I went since the venue was all new to me.

The first room had a young fellow in street clothes lying on a crisp white bed with a tube going into the back of his hand. He smiled as I walked in. Martha stayed out in the hall.

"My name is Terry."

"So's mine!" he said cheerily.

"What is new?"

"Not much. I am getting out of here soon. "

"Great. How are you feeling?"

"Pretty good. Much better than before."

His chart was attached to the end of the bed. I was tempted to look at it. I chose not to. A nurse came in to look at the medication. Everything was in order, and she quietly left.

"Well, then, what would you like to talk about?"

"Nothing, really. Do you play chess?"

"As a matter of fact, I do. Is there a chessboard?"

"Don't need one."

From the bedcovers, he produced a tablet with a chess app.

In less than five minutes, he had beaten me in game one.

Game two was about to begin when Martha came into the room.

"I have got a meeting upstairs which was just sprung on me. I see you two are having fun. I will call you later."

Game two produced the same result. At least I was learning how to use the gizmo. Young Terry manipulated the thing with ease.

By game three, it took him about ten minutes longer to beat me. My young friend was tiring; the medication was continuing to be administered.

"Do you need to nap?" I took the tablet from his hands and put it in the night table next to the bed and then quietly left the room.

Next door was a whole family who was there to visit Sheryl, they told me.

"Anything you need? I am the new volunteer."

Several people had gowns on. I retreated into the hallway to find one as well. When I went back in, I was greeted with, "I want my hair back and a pizza—all dressed."

"Pizza, maybe; hair, afraid not."

She was tiny and dressed in hospital patient garb.

One of the adults said, "We need to fatten her up."

"What a great idea. Surely one of the local pizza joints delivers here."

"She has trouble keeping food down with all this medication she is taking."

Just then a figure dressed in a clown outfit appeared, making all kinds of strange sounds—talking gibberish, really, but almost making sense. The child laughed uproariously. It was infectious; everyone got the giggles.

Ribbons appeared out of the patient's nose, balloons were magically blown up. Good fun all around.

I walked back out into the hall with a promise to myself that I would return to visit her soon.

Martha came down the corridor. She was wearing a white coat.

"It was an all-hands case conference. So I had to act the part."

"Anything interesting?"

"Maybe to you. A young Inuit girl with selective mutism. We are bringing her in for an evaluation."

"And her name would be—"

"Molly," we said in unison.

I did not know whether to laugh or cry.

"I have told you more than I should have."

"Do you want me to fill you in on the rest of the story?"

"You know her?"

"What village is she from?" I knew the answer even before I asked. "When is she coming in?"

"In the next few days. We have to wait for a bed to be available."

"How long will she be here?"

"Three months . . . which we can stretch a little if necessary."

"Then what?"

"I don't want to talk about that now. There are several alternatives."

We were still standing in the corridor. The lights had dimmed. Visitors were starting to leave. Suddenly a rush of emotion swept through me. I took a step and stumbled.

"Do you want to go to have coffee? You don't look like you are in shape to do any more visiting."

With difficulty I moved down the corridor. We were walking side by side in silence. Martha put her arm around me. We took the elevator to the main floor where there were food dispensing machines.

Once in front of these robots, I could not bring myself to choose anything.

We sat on a bench in silence.

"It hurts, still."

"How's that?"

"She was special. And then numbing silence. No rhyme or reason. And then the hostility from the family and the community. Well, I guess there will be a second act. She is here and maybe she will get the help she needs. And then what—she goes back to where she comes from?"

"So maybe there will be an act three."

"What do you mean?"

"Didn't you always want to become a foster parent?"

"Oh, come on, now. You are not serious. An old priest looking after a twelve-year-old Inuit girl in the Plateau?"

"The two of you will fit right in."

"This conversation is really premature. She is not even here yet. By the way, in actual fact, she is still only eleven."

"You want to go back upstairs?"

"Not really. But my knapsack is at the nurse's station."

Back upstairs to fetch the bag, I wandered down to Terry's room. He was still asleep. Sheryl's room was empty! There were flowers and stuffed animals and a very eerie feeling.

Outside, it was dark, and there was a light rain falling. Leaves were plastered to the sidewalk and curb. Just then, Orenstein appeared in his van. I got in on the passenger side.

"Your timing was excellent."

"Martha called me to tell me you had had a jolt. I thought it wise to come to your aid. No child abusers tonight?"

We drove in silence. "I listened to the tape recording and the cops should be pleased that they can finally interview the child."

"Did you hear anything useful?"

"No. Only how much father and son sound alike."

We reached our house. "What time tomorrow?"

"Eight."

CHAPTER FOURTEEN

Sleep was hard to come by. I woke often during the night. The Internet provided some respite. I checked out various sites for news and sports. I showered around five. A jolt of very good espresso was a useful antidote. I took a broom outside to sweep the front steps. Leaves had gathered unattended.

Just before seven, first light appeared. Shmully and his older boys came out to go to the local Shul for early morning prayers. I went back inside and decided to prepare a bed in the back to plant garlic.

I dug on my side of the garden and felt eyes from the first floor watching me. The work was not hard and strangely relaxing. Working in the earth took my mind off the issues of the day. After the first frost, I would plant the garlic cloves. For mulch I would use leaves I had gathered in the backyard and put in a makeshift bin.

Back inside, I made more coffee and some toast. The radio had the usual morning fare of weather and traffic and local news. There had been a frost in the Laurentians, so my garlic planting was not too far off. I debated whether to take another shower and chose not to. I started rereading an old *New Yorker* that had been lying around. Still good reading months later. I dozed off in the chair. A rap at the back door woke me.

Shmully arrived ten minutes early for our meeting. At exactly eight o'clock, the doorbell rang, and up came the two constables. This time, Marc sat and the woman Elbaz stood. She was about to say something when Orenstein mentioned the recording of our meeting. Out came the tape recorder and we started to listen.

When it was over, she looked at Orenstein. "You are wasting our time. We have to interview the boy. We know where Joel lives and we intend to leave here and immediately go to his house. You have interfered enough in this affair and produced nothing."

Beaulieu, who was taking notes, looked up to ask, "Have you any leads?" We both shook our heads.

"I am beginning to agree with Constable Elbaz. Is the boy still here?"

"To our knowledge, yes. Though this morning he probably will be in school and his father will be out and about. That leaves the mother, who may be difficult to interview."

"They are expecting us?"

"Yes."

"We are in charge. You are not to communicate with them to alert them that we are coming. Is that clear?"

We both nodded.

Orenstein, looking at Elbaz directly, started to talk to her in a language that was barely recognizable. "*Arrêt*," she said, holding up a hand. He switched to French to finish his thought.

"Finally some agreement from you."

Shmully nodded. With that, Marc stood, and they both left. No handshakes. No other courtesies.

At least they felt in control.

CHAPTER FIFTEEN

Orenstein showed no emotion at being lectured by the police. He seemed to accept it as a matter of course. I wanted to know how he felt about what had happened.

He looked me in the eye and, ignoring my question, announced, "I am going to pick up my van. I brought it to a garage I know. Late tomorrow morning, I have an appointment with this Green fellow. He is the guy who has to give his wife a *get*. I would like you to drive me. After that, I want to get the van washed and park it in the alley until next Wednesday. Rosh Hashanah is Monday and Tuesday."

"One question. What language was that?"

"Ladino."

"Ladino?"

"Judeo-Spanish, Hebrew, and Arabic. Like Yiddish in Europe."

Another thing to look up. My learning curve was rising on a daily basis.

"Tell me more of the story about how you met Beaulieu."

"He was after some kids who were involved in jewelry robberies. I was helping the store owners whose employee was behind the thefts. Justice was served." He went into his flat without any other word.

Martha called.

"What is on your mind?"

"Do you own a suit?"

"I think so. Why?"

"I have an invitation from Elyse, the fundraiser, to dinner on Sunday night. It's Jewish New Year, and I am always invited and I never go. I make up some excuse."

"You are asking me out on a date?"

"Yes."

"Then I had better get my one suit cleaned."

"You mean you will go with me?"

"Yes, I will. And what should I bring?"

"You let me deal with that."

"We will go fifty-fifty on whatever it is."

"If you insist, but it is not necessary."

"I do and it is."

She rang off. The suit hung at the back of the cupboard. The jacket still fit. And better still, pressing was not required. After the meeting with Orenstein tomorrow, I would go around and find a decent shirt and tie. I was beginning to feel like I had been invited to the prom.

I started reading up on Rosh Hashanah. This induced a nap while sitting at my desk. I went to lie on my bed and slept until four. Studying up on the Days of Awe had taken a lot out of me, but I got the gist of it.

Orenstein was going to be largely tied up with religious things for the next month. I decided to go out to buy a chicken. Walking around the corner, I came to Fogel's.

The place was a madhouse. Luckily, they had self-service. Maybe I got caught up in the atmosphere; I bought two chickens, cut up, and some stewing beef. This came to more money than I was expecting. Standing in line at the cash, I was stared at. I paid; the fellow did not look at me and threw the change on the counter. I wished him Happy New Year. He looked up and managed a slight smile.

The idea of having stew appealed to me. Looking up recipes on the 'net, I found several, but none really struck home.

Mother had a recipe box, which I had not thrown out. Looking through the various entries produced some interesting results, including a newspaper clipping of me on a snowmobile with the caption about the "Trailblazing Priest." I had forgotten the article; I know I had not kept it. I spent a lot of time travelling around from community to community in the north. Back then, it was fun, adventurous. But the truth was the Inuit had marked trails so professionally that it was impossible to screw up. After all, their livelihood depended on being able to get around in winter. They never paid attention to the markers, so I suspect they had trail-blazed for us white folks. I needed to go out and tend to the sick and the well. In the box was also a snippet from a college newspaper about a student production of a play in which I had a starring role. On a dare I had tried out for this part, which I got. I was physically right, I was told. It was great fun. And I worked really hard at getting my role down pat. It was a humorous piece which the whole cast took seriously. Getting laughs is hard work.

And I got into it with much encouragement from my far better and more polished fellow cast members. Mother came to all the performances. She sat in the same spot and laughed uproariously in all the right places. It was a piece that had been written by one of the students who wanted to enter it in a summer festival. I left for the seminary before the production reached its ultimate destination. I do not know how it all turned out. I lost contact with those guys. Some of them were really creative and talented.

In general, I felt lost at the university, and this play was a way of feeling connected.

Joining the priesthood was a way of providing structure and meaning to my life. So spending the first few months on my hands and knees cleaning floors was a rude introduction to my higher calling. Now I was living on a pension in Montreal. The arc of my life had led me to this point. So now I needed to put my own stamp on my existence, to put my own sense of order on things. Define what was important and what was not. Finally work out my own structure.

Should I sell this place? Surely the market would be in my favour. Shmully would be a candidate to purchase; he and his clan could use the space. And Molly? What to do about that?

Living the next few years through the eyes of an adolescent Inuit girl, was that really what I wanted? Was there enough room here for that, both physically and emotionally? And what would she want?

Maybe the idea would be as foreign to her as it was to me? As always, there would be two sides to the equation. Whether to foster on my part and her willingness to be fostered? Two unknowns at the moment.

The stew was unmade. I put the meat in the freezer for another time. I had lost interest in the whole endeavour. Maybe a pizza and beer would do the trick.

Outside on the landing, Mrs. Orenstein was sweeping leaves off the porch.

She looked up to nod in my general direction. In the time I had lived upstairs, we had never engaged in conversation. If she needed to speak with me, she sent one of her sons. The nod and the smile were a step up in communication. She held to the custom of not speaking to men who were not family and, in my case, not Jewish. I headed off to find some food.

Eating alone in a restaurant prompted me to stop at a store on the Main to buy some reading material. One copy of today's *New York Times* remained—too much reading. The local newspaper would do.

48

There was a restaurant that advertised *"Pizza au four"* and in smaller letters, "wood-fired pizza." Perfect.

I was ushered to a table for two near the back. I placed my order and the waiter brought me a beer. It was a local brew that tasted rather good.

The newspaper headlines contained an account of a woman who wanted her sentencing delayed because she had just had breast enhancement surgery! I believe the word that describes this best is *chutzpah.*

My cell phone rang. I had meant to turn the damn thing off. It was Martha Lang. "What is up?"

"Molly is coming in next week. I thought you should know."

"Thanks for telling me. Now what?"

"She will be integrated into the unit. She will be interviewed and tested to determine her level of functioning. Usual hospital stuff. You might want to think about your next move."

After a long pause, I folded the newspaper and sat sipping the beer while staring out into the street from the back of the eatery.

The pizza was placed down on the table before me. I stared at it, not having the energy to begin eating. I finished the beer and called the waiter over to ask him to put the pie in a box, paid, and left. Walking back to the flat I passed many of the same young men I had seen in the area before. This time there were almost signs of recognition.

Back home, I turned on the TV to catch part of a Thursday night NFL game, or at least the pre-game show, which seemed to go on forever. Switching channels to the all-news station, I was treated to a discussion about the Middle East. There was general agreement that the area was a mess and there was no practical way to intervene. Then there was a human-interest piece about a Palestinian boy whose parents made it to a medical facility in Israel so that he could be treated.

The family was interviewed as well as the child. Everybody was thankful for the help that was made available. Such a tiny country; so full of impact despite its size, so totally disproportionate to the enmity that surrounded it. How can so many people hate a country?

I dozed. Molly's face appeared. Behind her was an image of the Sacred Heart. And behind that, my mother. They were all talking to me at once. A chorus of admonitions. I awoke with a start, sweating.

Maybe it was the beer. Old body memories die hard.

CHAPTER SIXTEEN

I went back to bed only to wake with a start at five. I looked outside into the darkness. Hearing meows, I went to the back door to see a young marmalade cat on the porch. The cat was not running off. I made some coffee and went to the computer. The news sites were all devoted to the American election. The Canadian sites had several pieces about the end of Parliament as a useful tool of government. The cat was still meowing outside the door.

I filled an aluminum pie tin with some milk I had in the fridge. The date stamp showed it had almost expired. Waste not, want not. The animal drank enthusiastically. I refilled the plate. Just then someone went out on the lower balcony to tend to the garbage. With that, the cat took off into the lingering darkness. I left the milk on the landing and went back indoors. The weather was going to be iffy. Rain mixed with high winds, courtesy of a storm coming up the East Coast. Our van did not work well in damp weather. Taking Orenstein by the hand to see a new vehicle should be on the agenda. This one had outlived its usefulness.

I went to the corner store to get the local newspaper. Even though I could have read it online, there was something about holding a paper in hand. Folding and unfolding the pages was a unique pleasure. I dozed off. Shmully called to tell me he wanted to go at ten. I went to make more coffee and some toast. I stood eating the toast at the counter beside the sink.

I went back to one of the overstuffed chairs with the coffee to read the rest of the paper. I looked up the note about the hair salon place. It was too early to call. But I would call to get my hair cut for my big date. I dozed again. I had tuned the computer to the sports radio station. They were blathering on about this and that. Nothing of great import.

In my drowsiness, I fixated on Joel's attacker. I was convinced that we knew roughly who this person was. It was just a matter of time before he emerged from the shadows. I could see this was more a matter of faith than a rational conclusion from evidence. In fact, it was quite a stretch since nobody appeared obvious as the culprit. The list of possibilities included mother, father, grandfather, grandmother. None seemed likely. Perhaps it was a hospital employee. I hoped for the latter, though I had my doubts. In fact, I had doubts about the whole mess. Nothing was making any sense.

At exactly ten a.m., Shmully called. It was time to go.

I joined him in the van. We drove to the expressway. Today he had on his black suit, white shirt, and a vest. On his head was the big, black fedora. Very formal.

He took out his shrivelled prayer book. Exiting the expressway, we came upon construction cranes and bulldozers. Men in hard hats were standing around. One or two of them were doing some sort of work. Shmully interrupted his meditation to tell me the address and give me general directions as to where to go.

At the far end of Ville Saint-Laurent, we came upon a row of modern factories all looking more or less the same. The signs outside indicated different entities. Some were for sale. And some had "For Rent" signs outside.

We drove into the parking lot of one that said, "KnitRite." There was parking in front of the door in a spot marked "Visitors." We went in.

Directly in front of us to the right of a circular staircase was a receptionist. On the wall behind her was a very large portrait of a well-turned-out gentleman. Perhaps the founder of the company. The receptionist was stylishly dressed in a scooped-neck sweater that showed a bit of cleavage. She was not young, perhaps in her forties. If Orenstein noticed her, he was not letting on. He simply asked to see Mr. Green. She phoned somewhere to announce our presence.

We were told to take a seat and that Mr. Green would be with us shortly. We were offered coffee, which we both refused. We were in an atrium, floor-to-ceiling windows with a view of the street. Many large trucks went by.

A few minutes later, a middle-aged gent came bounding down the stairs. He was short and dressed in a sports shirt and slacks, with very fancy loafers.

"Could we speak to you privately?" Orenstein said evenly.

"You are here for a donation? I just made my round of donations for the year."

"No, we would like to speak to you on another matter."

We were ushered into a boardroom, which was off to the right of the reception area.

A big, expensive oak table took up most of the room. On the walls were photographs and another portrait of the founder of the company in a less formal pose than the one in the reception area.

Many of the photos were of our host receiving awards, mostly for golf. Others where he was formally dressed, receiving industry accolades. He sat at the head of the table. We sat on either side.

"If you are not here for a donation, what is it you want from me?"

Orenstein looked Green in the eye. "Sometimes life presents us with opportunities that we cannot foresee. In your case, you have instituted divorce proceedings against your wife."

Green got red in the face. "What concern is that of yours? That is a private matter that I really do not wish to discuss."

"The issue at hand is one which affects the community."

"How so?"

"It would be appropriate to offer your wife a *get*."

"Appropriate, says who?" He was drumming his fingertips on the table. "I do not see what difference it makes."

"That's just the point; it is really a small matter."

"I do not want to give her any more than she deserves, which in my case is quite a lot."

"That I leave to others. You wish to remarry?"

"That is not your concern."

"And should your wife choose to remarry?"

"She will do that without my help."

"She is the mother of your children?"

"They are both useless, spoiled brats. We had arguments about how to bring them up."

"You are estranged from them, are you not?"

"Again, that is none of your affair."

Just then the receptionist came in carrying a plate and holding a juice glass. No knock; no apology for interrupting. "Time for your pill."

She put the plate and glass down in front of him.

He took a bite of a biscuit and drank the juice with his pill. She left the room.

"Where were we?"

"Discussing or not discussing your children."

"The boy quit college to join a rock band. And my daughter went to art school and has adopted, what do they call it, an alternative lifestyle. Rubbish, both of them."

Just then I decided a bathroom break would be in order. I asked our host if there was a bathroom nearby. "Go out and ask the receptionist."

She eyed me as I came out of the room.

"Bathroom?"

"Through the door into the warehouse on the left."

I did as I was told; the bathroom was on the left. Ahead was another door that I opened into a warehouse filled with racks. The racks were empty. There was no one working. Back I went into the reception area.

Just then, the mailman arrived and handed a bundle to the woman with a bit of a flourish. In French he told her how attractive she looked. She told him to knock it off. And he left with a laugh. Daily routine, no doubt.

I stood in front of her as she was sorting through the mail.

Looking up, she asked, "Can I help you?"

"Yes." I paused.

"You walked into a private meeting without knocking or excusing yourself. It would appear you have special access to Mr. Green."

"My relationship with Mr. Green is none of your affair."

"Not many receptionists provide nursing care."

"I would appreciate it if you left me alone."

"I will. You might want to encourage Mr. Green, when you are alone together, to give his wife a religious divorce."

"You have your nerve. That's the reason you two are here?"

I went back into the boardroom. Both men were standing. Shmully was talking to Green in Yiddish. Green was standing with his hands in his pockets against the back wall. Orenstein finished whatever he was saying. Green saw me and stopped what he was about to say. His face was red. Orenstein never raised his voice or changed his demeanour in any way. Remarkable, really.

"Time for you two to leave. You have made your point. I will do what I do."

Shmully walked out and headed directly to the receptionist's desk. "Please, I would like to leave you my card."

She took the card and placed it in front of her. "I am not sure this will be needed."

With that, we left the building, got in the van, and drove off. Around the corner, the thing died. I looked under the hood; the fan belt was broken. Usually, I kept some spare parts in a box in the back. Not this time.

Shmully got out of the van to take a look. "It's Friday afternoon. Need to get going."

I looked up and a white Mercedes drove by with Green at the wheel and the receptionist in the passenger seat. They did not stop to help. At least they did not give us the finger.

But some fellow dressed like Shmully, in a Japanese van, did stop. He offered us a lift. I called the parts place that I hoped had a location nearby. They did not, and it would take over an hour to get here on a Friday. I asked them to leave the thing at my house, and I would settle up next week.

Our rescuer was Zev Engle, and he and Shmully were having a gay old time talking in the front seat. I sat in the back and took in the sights. The traffic was heavy, but somehow Zev managed to avoid any real snags. We arrived home at a decent hour so that Shmully had enough time to prepare for the Sabbath.

On my stoop was a package containing the fan belt. I now had to work out a way of getting back to Ville Saint-Laurent. That would have to wait until Saturday night or Sunday morning.

In the meantime, I phoned the hair salon to arrange an appointment. A very pleasant young woman told me she had an opening at four forty-five.

Friday night in our area was a solemn affair. I could walk down any street and peer in windows to see families gathered around tables celebrating the Sabbath. I, on the other hand, decided to cook some fish that had been lying in the freezer since the summer.

A baked potato and some frozen peas rounded out the meal. There was an exhibition hockey game on the French cable channel. Several young rookies were playing for the Habs. There were also several veterans mingled in to make the play somewhat interesting.

I watched the first period and singled out one or two young players who might make the team. The two announcers talked about a lot of things; calling the action was not big on their agenda. After the first period, I switched to one of the all-news channels.

There was a report from Israel about preparations for the New Year celebration. The Israeli Military was on full alert. There was also a piece about how tablets were aiding in special education. Programmes had been developed to aid those with language difficulties. Kids with autism and the like could communicate using these devices. Thinking of Molly, I went to the computer to get more information. This stuff was interesting. There was scads of information on the subject and really too much to choose from.

Surely Martha Lang or one of her colleagues would know more about this.

CHAPTER SEVENTEEN

Another semi-sleepless night. I got myself out of bed at six. I had been reading for a couple of hours before that. It was getting light much later. I decided to take a walk.

I meandered down to the Main and found myself in front of the movie theatre.

Work was continuing on the place to get it back in business. Coming out of the front door were two men in hard hats. One of them was none other than Mike Green.

So Green owned real estate as well as the knitting company. When he spotted me, he stopped short.

"You checking up on me?"

"I do not think so."

"Where's your partner?"

"You know the answer to that."

He and the other man walked away, around to the back of the building.

I was left to stare up at scaffolding covered in tarpaulin. It didn't look like the repairs were going to be finished anytime soon.

The white Mercedes was parked across the street. On the passenger side, the receptionist sat waiting for her boss. I wondered if she had torn up Shmully's card.

I decided not to engage her in conversation and walked back to the apartment. The Orenstein men were coming out to go to early morning services. The women would join them later.

Back in the flat, I made some coffee and began perusing the Internet. I found a real estate site that listed the movie theatre and an adjoining building as being owned by a numbered company. Looking up the numbered company, I was able to find that the property was owned by Green and his wife. So Green would have to pay her something to get the ownership transferred in the divorce proceedings. No wonder that was on his mind when we confronted him about the *get*.

I decided on a full breakfast with eggs and toast and bacon, which I ate hungrily.

By the time I finished with that, it was time to go back out to complete my wardrobe for my date. I found another store on the Main which looked like a good possibility to get everything I needed.

Saturday morning was a busy time. I tried on several pairs of shoes in the hopes of finding something appropriate. Several pairs later, I did.

And now for a dress shirt and tie. The shirt had to have some blue in it, and for the tie, I wanted some red. I was going for a power look. Again, more time to find the right combination. But the young clerk and I persevered. I paid for my stuff and left with a feeling of triumph.

I returned to the apartment with a spring in my step. Just as I was going up the stairs, the Orenstein women were leaving to go to their Shul. They marched in order, youngest in front, Mother in the rear. They were all dressed alike, long skirts, dark coats, flat shoes, thick stockings, and hats.

I went into my flat to spend the rest of the day preparing for my haircut.

I tried on my wardrobe. Undoing new shirts from the packaging is always a chore. Surely someone could develop something to improve on the dreaded pins. The shirt fit well, as did the rest. The shoes would take some breaking in, but they completed my look.

Not bad.

I went out to buy a Saturday paper. There was a lot of reading. In the lifestyle section were two restaurant reviews. One was an expensive place nearby. The menu looked interesting. The other review was a place also nearby, but less expensive and aimed at the college crowd. The first was where you might go with your folks if they were visiting and insisted on taking you out. The second would be a cozy place to go on a date. I made a mental note about the less expensive place, just in case.

I dozed off while reading the political pages and woke to my cell phone vibrating. It was Martha.

"Glasheen here."

"How formal."

"What are you doing tomorrow morning, early?"

"What do you have in mind?"

"Have to go to Ville Saint-Laurent to rescue Orenstein's van. It broke down Friday afternoon and we left it there."

"How early is early?"

"Eight."

"Well, I want to go get my hair done for the big *soirée*."

"I am getting mine done later today."

"And I have some report writing to do, and it is quiet around here."

"You are in your office?"

"No rest for the wicked."

"You betcha."

"Tomorrow early is okay."

"I want to leave Shmully out of this so he can prepare for Rosh Hashanah."

"We will connect in the morning."

"Over and out."

I was getting used to having Martha in my world. I wondered if she felt the same way about me.

I decided to do some more reading about the Jewish Holidays, since they were going to impact my schedule. After New Year was Yom Kippur and after that was Succoth. I wondered where the Orensteins would build their tent . . .

My cell phone rang: it was Martha.

"What is up?"

"Are you sitting down? Molly took off!"

"Excuse me? I thought she was not coming until next week."

"Well, she was deposited on our doorstep on Friday; she was here with two others, and they took off."

"Do the others at least know the city?"

"I don't think so."

"Are you still at the hospital?"

"Yes."

"I will meet you at the front door."

I ran up to Parc and hailed a cab.

When I said Children's Hospital, the guy took off. Luckily the traffic was thin. Nevertheless, he did not take his foot off the accelerator. With brakes screeching, we arrived at the front door where Martha was waiting outside.

"And you thought you were going to have a relaxing Saturday morning?"

"You, too? Beats doing reports."

"I don't think so."

Just then Marc Beaulieu, from the juvenile squad, and a bunch of his fellow officers showed up. Beaulieu came over to me. "You might want to stay out of this."

"I might not."

"You know the taxpayers pay us to look after things like this."

"Not enough in this case." Martha came forward to introduce herself, or reintroduce herself.

Beaulieu wanted a picture of Molly. Martha produced written descriptions of the three escapees, which she passed out to the police. Around the Hospital were a lot of side streets and alleys. And more ominously, the campus was smack downtown. The police took off.

Ferguson the chaplain showed up. "Well, let's get going on this. Did you bring your cross with you? Could come in handy."

Martha would go back inside to handle the unit. She needed also to brief the psychiatrist in charge. "She is going to be pissed. And you guys need to call me to keep me informed."

Off we went. Across the street was a square with a number of picnic tables scattered about. At many of these, folks were sitting; some looked like they were drinking out of paper bags.

Two were Inuit. We walked around. A picture would have been handy.

At the far end of the square was an entrance to the Metro. Into the kiosk we went. On the landing was a small group, one of whom had a bottle in a paper bag. A woman came up to us and put a paper cup out for a donation. I was tempted. Ferguson waved her away.

Down the escalator to a long tunnel where a fellow was playing guitar with a blanket in front of him. He wasn't bad. Ferguson went over to him. We had to wait for him to finish. "Seen a little girl about five feet, black hair?"

"No, man."

I put some coins on the blanket. Business looked brisk judging from the number on the blanket. He should be careful. Coming out of the tunnel, we entered the mall itself.

We started going store to store. No luck. We checked the washrooms. Nothing.

Up to the second floor, same result. The third floor. Still no. Above was a garage. We started going up the ramp, checking each car. It was a large parking area with several levels.

We split up. The guards went down and we went up. We were to meet back at the entrance to the mall. Up we went to the third level; nothing. And coming back down, we checked each car again.

Martha called, "Any news?"

"Nothing so far."

"Well, everyone over here is in panic mode. Dr. Ross was at her house in the Eastern Townships for the weekend. She is driving in. We are going to review security yet again."

"Needs to be done. Call you later."

On Atwater across the street was the old Montreal Forum, which now housed a bunch of movie theatres and restaurants. We both shrugged as if to say we had nothing to lose by going over there. Inside on the main floor was a shrine to the hockey team that for so many years had occupied this hallowed ground. To the left was the movie theatre area. Lines of people were waiting to buy tickets. Above the ticket windows was the list of films playing. Ferguson, who was wearing his dog collar, went over to the ticket taker. "We are looking for someone." He handed the sheet to the young man who looked at it.

"Haven't seen anyone like these three."

"Could we speak to the manager?"

"Look, it's Saturday afternoon and we are pretty busy."

I was reading the offerings. Where would an eleven-year-old Inuit girl hide out? There was a cartoon feature. I went to stand in line. Ferguson was having a heated discussion with the supervisor. "Two senior tickets for the cartoon."

"It has already started. The next show will start at 3:30."

"I would like to go in now. I am looking for my granddaughter."

"Suit yourself."

I went back over to where Ferguson was arguing with the manager.

"Here are two tickets. Now let us in."

We were waved through. Two demented old lunatics who want to see a cartoon. Hiding out in a movie theatre, one could live on stale popcorn and the dregs of soda. And there was a bathroom nearby.

We were to go to theatre number five, which was down the escalator. In we went. It took a second or so to get accustomed to the

60

darkness. The theatre was filled with children and there was a lot of noise coming from the screen. We split up. I took the right-hand side and started walking up the staircase. Looking down the rows as carefully as possible, I could make out very rapt young faces, but none were the ones I wanted. I started down the stairs past the entrance aisle.

In the first row below the screen in the middle, children and parents on either side, was Molly. I could not tell if she was with anybody. There was an adult on her left. And on her right were a couple of kids. Were these the kids she went AWOL with? I could not tell in that light. I sat on the stair on the aisle. Ferguson had made his way to the front row on the other side of the theatre. Just before he reached the bottom, he tripped and went head first into the wall. People jumped up to come to his aid. My attention was diverted. Through a door marked "EXIT" darted three young people. Off I went down the stairs. Several floors down I came out on the street. No sign of the runaways. I tried to get back in the building. The door, of course, was locked.

Around to the front I went. Ferguson was sitting on a chair by the entrance; the paramedics came in from the other door. He had quite a lot of blood on him. My cell phone rang. It was Martha. I turned it off. Ferguson was woozy; he had gotten a real jolt.

The manager was standing off to one side with his arms folded across his chest looking none too pleased but saying nothing.

Someone had produced a towel to wipe the blood away. The two paramedics worked quickly to put the patient onto a stretcher. At the same time, they were asking questions. Ferguson had trouble answering. I stepped forward to fill in as much information as I could.

I had no choice but to go with them to the hospital. Into the ambulance we went. I sat in front.

On the way, I called Martha. I left a very curt message about calling later and turned off my phone. There was room at the Montreal General, so up the hill we went. At the ambulance entrance, the paramedics took Ferguson in. He went off one way behind a curtain and I was left to answer more questions. A nurse came out to ask me the same questions as the EMS guys. I was told to stand over there out of the way. I obeyed.

Several staff went in and out of the curtain. They were going to send him for a CT scan. A nurse appeared with a thick blue binder with the name Ferguson printed on the spine.

He had a history here. In the middle of all this, I remembered my hair appointment. It was now three thirty. There was no way for me to make it. I went into the hall outside of emergency to call to cancel. I had a message from Martha. I phoned the hair salon to cancel.

The hair stylist was very understanding. She offered me an appointment on Sunday at eleven; she was taking one or two appointments. I agreed. Next, I phoned Martha. This was going to be a longer call. She answered on the first ring. "Where the hell are you?"

"I am at the Montreal General. Ferguson took a fall. And I think he has a concussion."

"Oh, no."

"Oh, yes."

"You know he has a fairly lengthy medical history."

"Yes. I saw them wheel out the binder."

"In the meantime, Beaulieu and his troops appeared with two of the three kids."

"And Molly?"

"One of the two."

I think I exhaled. "You are going to call in your regular staff and not have the amateurs, right?"

She ignored the jibe.

"Keep me posted. I need to stay here."

"We'll speak later."

Just then, I was paged. I went back into where they were keeping Ferguson. A nurse came out from behind the curtain. "The doctor wants to talk to you. Please wait over there."

A few moments later, a very tiny, very young woman appeared with a stethoscope around her neck. She had a badge with her picture pinned to her gown. Dr. Shaheen, it said.

"We are going to keep Reverend Ferguson overnight, at least. He got quite a jolt and he has some other issues we need to deal with."

"Can I go in to have a word with him?"

"As you wish, but do not stay long."

I went around the curtain. Ferguson was lying there with intravenous fluid going into his hand.

He opened his eyes. "What a pain. I am going to miss Sunday service at the old age home. Do me a favour and call there to tell them I am indisposed, dammit."

S. John Diamond

"And I speak to whom?"

"Whomever answers the phone, I do not remember who is on, on Saturday afternoon. Is it still Saturday afternoon?"

"Yes, and I will come back tomorrow to visit. Get some rest. You took quite a fall. By the way, they found Molly and one of the others."

He smiled and then appeared to doze off.

I left the hospital by the doors nearby. I walked down the ramp to Côte-des-Neiges.

My phone rang; it was Martha. "Where are you?"

"I just left Ferguson. I am on the street outside the hospital."

"Wait there; I will pick you up. I am finally able to leave here."

"I will be on the corner by the bus stop next to the emergency entrance."

"Ten minutes."

"Ten minutes."

As promised, there she was. I got in. "Quite a day."

"Yup. They are keeping Ferguson overnight."

"I am not surprised. He has heart issues, and I think he has diabetes. He doesn't talk much about his medical situation, but over the years little bits of information have seeped out."

"You driving me home?"

"That was the idea."

"And Molly?"

"Back in the unit safe and sound. She desperately needed a bath, which took some encouragement from staff. She was also starving. We gave her some hot cereal and toast. She is sleeping. And of course, not a word about her escapade."

"What is going to happen to her?"

"We have group homes around the city. She most likely will end up in one of them."

We reached my house. "What are you doing now? Do you have plans for the evening?"

"I have no plans other than cleaning my apartment and doing the laundry. What's on your mind?"

"Fixing Orenstein's van. I have the part and a flashlight and a toolkit, and I will buy you supper. That would free up tomorrow morning."

"Sure."

"Good. Stay here. I will be back in five minutes."

When I came back, Martha was standing on the sidewalk talking with Orenstein. It was very much a one-sided conversation. Martha was lacing into him about the fact that we still did not know who abused Joel, and, for all his knowledge about the community, nothing had been resolved. Orenstein for his part let her know that at the right time the culprit would be found. Martha shot back that this was far too metaphysical for her. Orenstein smiled and told her to be patient.

She then turned to me and said, "Are we off?"

Orenstein nodded to me and went into his house.

Away we went. There was very little traffic, and we reached our destination in twenty minutes. I think I dozed off.

The van was where I had left it on Friday. There was a Ville Saint-Laurent security van parked behind with its light on inside. There was already a ticket on the windshield.

I went to the window of Security to plead my case. He rolled down his window with no great enthusiasm. I told him my car was *en panne*. He got out of his marked car and with somewhat of a flourish placed the ticket on the windshield alongside the first one. Before getting back into his car, he managed this explanation: "*Stationnement pour un maximum de quatre heures*—four-hour parking," he said, and drove off.

Martha held the flashlight while I replaced the fan belt.

While I was working, Martha talked about the old days of her social work time; she made house calls and she thought she had been in this area before.

"Oh, really. Do you remember anything about that?"

"There had been a school complaint about two children belonging to this one family. The girl was extremely withdrawn and the boy was the opposite, very hyperactive and rambunctious. We interviewed the mother, who was sensitive and understanding but a little overwhelmed. Then we tried to interview the father, whose factory was out here. He could not see us the first time. On the second try, we found him condescending and bombastic. Essentially, he blamed the school for not doing its job."

"Can you describe him?"

She described Mike Green. He had not changed one iota.

"You and Orenstein wouldn't have had a meeting with Mr. Green? That would be too much."

S. John Diamond

"I plead the fifth."

"I know he is going through a messy divorce."

I finished with the fan belt. I had taken a cloth to wipe as much grease off my hands as I could.

"You can follow me back to the apartment?"

"Just drive slowly around here. Once we get to Décarie Boulevard, I am okay." The van started, and I waited a bit to let it warm up.

She followed me; this industrial area on Saturday night was deserted.

Once on Décarie, she took off and was waiting for me at Orenstein's. I parked the van in the lane off to one side. In the morning I would get it washed.

I joined her in her car.

"Now what?"

"Dinner."

"Any ideas?"

"Two. There were two reviews in the paper this morning. Both around here. One is expensive and the other less so. Both menus looked interesting. The second one is a Bring Your Own Wine and has Middle-Eastern fare."

"The second one and no wine for me."

It was close enough that we could have walked. We found parking, and I put money in the meter. I had learned never to leave home without a pocket full of change.

The place had been a house that was converted to a restaurant. We went in. Ahead of us was the kitchen area. To the right, in what had been the front parlour, was the dining room. There was room for two. There were not many tables. And they were nicely spaced out.

Better still, the lighting was subdued. Martha sat while I went downstairs to wash my hands.

I had a theory about restaurant washrooms. There is something about cleanliness and the quality of the food. This one passed, and I was able to properly clean my hands after fixing the car. Now, if the fare was as good as the washroom was clean, we would be in luck. I was starving.

I joined Martha at the table, where some appetizers had been placed. That was a good start. The heading on the menu claimed that the food was North African. A lot of the dishes required an explanation. I did notice a section that said "Soup."

"Anything speak to you?"

Lang looked up at me. "I think I am going to enjoy this. Good choice. By the way, no talking shop here in a public place. Compliance."

Looking around, I could not see what difference it could make. The place was filled with college-aged people, and besides us there was one table filled with our contemporaries. "Do you know those four over there?" I whispered.

"Do not," she said. "I think over in the corner there are two who were students of mine a while back. I wanted to hire the woman, but the position was part-time. She got a full-time offer from the Institute for the Blind. The fellow she is with, I believe, is still not working in the field. I do not know what he is doing."

The young server came over to take our orders. She turned out to be the part-owner with her husband. She explained the various menu options and we made our choices.

I did start with the soup, which came immediately and was delicious. Martha opted for a salad, which looked very tasty.

"By the way, I spent a lot of time and some expense putting together an outfit for tomorrow night."

Martha looked up. "So did I."

"We will be the belles of the ball."

"You know, I did not go to my high school prom. A group of us decided it was just so ridiculous. So we held an anti-prom in the parking lot of the school. We all dressed in ratty jeans and torn sweatshirts. We could not light a bonfire so we shone flashlights. By the end of the evening there were more of us outside than in the gym. We started a revolution. The principal was not amused. Anyway, we pulled it off and we were home by midnight. No renting limos and staying out until dawn."

"There was conformity in your revolution."

"There was a purpose to it all. We were very serious about it."

Next came the mains. I had ordered fish. It was a white fish bathed in a sublime sauce.

Martha had ordered the lamb, which looked like a ragout. Both dishes came with couscous and marinated vegetables. Delicious.

Unprompted, Martha started to talk about her relationship to Judaism. "My mother got angry one day. Took me out of school, and we went to Israel!"

"You and your mother both take issues personally?"

Martha laughed. It was the first time I had ever seen her just laugh. I smiled.

"She was angry that Israel could not defend itself without a lot of world condemnation and that as Jews we had a duty to stick up for the good guys."

"You are Jewish?"

"Yes, but unlike Orenstein, I come at it from the left-hand side of the ledger, if you get my drift."

"Not entirely."

"My parents and all of their friends and relations were non-religious Zionists."

"Just like there are several kinds of Catholics."

"Yes, exactly. The only time I go to synagogue is for a wedding or a bar mitzvah. And some years, only funerals. My contact with the Jewish community is through work. Anyway, we stayed in Israel for about two years. I was enrolled in school and learned Hebrew. My mother started off volunteering at the hospital in Jerusalem, and eventually they gave her a job as a coordinator. She was very good at bossing people around and organizing files. This was before computers. We lived in a nice little apartment, made friends, and enjoyed life."

"Why come back?"

"Mother did not want me to go into the army, which, had we stayed, would have been a given."

"You could not have it both ways."

"Exactly. We came back here, and I started high school. Mother got a job at the Montreal General doing more or less what she had learned to do in Israel. She kept at it past retirement age; they did not want her to leave."

"My mother also remained a teacher well into her sixties. In fact, she was close to seventy when she left teaching. She thought that retirement was death; she managed to keep busy until the end. She taught herself to use the computer and kept up a correspondence with many of her former students. And she volunteered in various places around town. She did not drive or own a car, but she managed to get around on public transport.

"She taught English in the prison. A priest she knew encouraged her to get involved in the programme. Actually, I think he begged her.

Anyway, she would trek out twice a week and spend all day tutoring. They graduated more inmates than ever before. When she left, they gave her a plaque, which I have in my bedroom."

"We come from interesting stock."

Too true. To change the subject slightly, I want to go visit Ferguson in the hospital. I suspect they will keep him through tomorrow."

"Yes, I do, too. Maybe on our way to the dinner we could drop in."

"Good, I will make sure he is still there. Next topic. I was watching one of the news channels and they were talking about using tablets with language-impaired children. Do you know anything about that?"

"In general, yes; in great detail, no. But a lot of work has been done at our place. I could introduce you to the person who runs that if you are interested."

"I am."

"Are you thinking about our mutual young friend?"

"I guess so."

"To be continued."

"Yeah. Some other time."

"Dessert?" The young woman had come over to clear our plates. "We have several choices all with lemon as a theme." After fish, this was a great set of options for me.

Martha opted for a lemon tart with tea. I chose lemon cake and coffee.

The young couple approached our table. Introductions all around. Martha asked the young man, whose name was Seth, what he was up to. "I am working at the French Children's Hospital setting up a special needs summer camp programme. My camping experience is finally paying me dividends."

Martha said that she had been trying to organize a similar programme for years, with no success. "Please put me on your mailing list—I want to know all about what you accomplish. I am so pleased that you are doing this."

"We are in the process of setting up a website; I will send you details when it is up and running."

The young woman, whose name was Alexis, looked a little forlorn. "I am not enjoying working with old blind people. Please, if you have anything full-time, even at three-quarter time, I would take it in a heartbeat."

"You know as well as I that may be next to impossible. However, miracles have been known to happen."

They said their goodbyes and off they went.

Dessert came. The cake was excellent, and the coffee was superb. Martha left most of her tart uneaten. She was enjoying the tea.

"Was everything to your liking?" Sara, the server, appeared at our table. "And you want me to package the tart to take home for a late-night snack?"

"Sure, why not."

She came back with the package and the bill, which she put in the middle of the table.

I grabbed the bill. Martha put a twenty-dollar bill on the table. I did not know what to do. What was the etiquette?

I put a twenty on top of hers and another five for the tip. That seemed to do the trick.

We got up to leave. Sara met us on the way out the door to thank us. We thanked her for a lovely evening.

"You know, I could walk home from here."

"No, I insist on driving you home."

"Not necessary."

"I know. But really, don't be so stubborn."

"How about you?" She laughed again.

I got in the passenger side. The five-minute drive was silent. Neither one of us was prepared to risk saying anything that would detract from the mood of the evening. I was about to get out of the car. She leaned over to give me a quick, chaste kiss on the cheek. "Thanks for a wonderful time. And happy haircut."

"You, too."

"Tomorrow, then. I will call you."

She drove off slowly.

I went to my front door and was about to undo the lock when Shmully came out in his shirt sleeves and black vest. "Thanks for fetching the van."

"You know, you might consider getting rid of it. The thing breaks down too regularly."

"Yeah, yeah. My wife and boys feel similarly. Soon."

"Not soon enough for me."

"They want me to get an even bigger truck. We shall see."

69

"By the way, I am invited to a Rosh Hashanah party in Westmount." I thought I detected a frown even in the dark.

"Really. My, you get around."

"Martha, the social worker, asked me to accompany her. The hostess is one of the major fundraisers for the hospital. She and Martha are friends."

"How ecumenical."

I ignored the dig. "I will get the van washed first thing in the morning."

"Yes, and thank you. Oh, I heard about your friend Ferguson, the pastor."

"How is that?"

"A young doctor who attends our minyan to make our quorum. You were involved, yes?"

"We were chasing after some runaways, and Ferguson tripped. I think he has a concussion. I will be visiting him tomorrow in the hospital."

Orenstein nodded.

"And the runaways?"

"Beaulieu and his posse found two of the three." Again, a nod.

"And your connection to these children?"

"I knew one of them from the north."

He gazed into my eyes for the first time. "Something special about this child?"

I looked down. "Yes."

He made no comment.

"'Night, then."

"'Night."

CHAPTER EIGHTEEN

I went into my apartment. For the first time, the place seemed especially empty. I went around watering plants, all of which were relics from Mother. I thought they were doing rather well. She would be proud.

I puffed up sofa pillows and put dishes from the drain into the cupboard to the right and above the sink. I thought I heard a cat on the back landing.

Nothing there. I felt like I was filling up the apartment with activity, buzzing around doing stuff.

How did Orenstein find out things so quickly? It's as if he had a big scanner tuned in all over, including the police. He must have spies everywhere.

Time for bed. Putting on my night attire, light blue pyjamas with a crease in the pants, I lay down with my glasses on. I turned on the radio to hear the repeat of a radio documentary on modern Judaism.

Mostly, the programme was about the divisions among the various shades of religiosity. And how it was all a question of interpretation. One of the speakers was a young Rabbi, who, in discussing the role of women, spoke about a passage he had read that does not prohibit involvement as long as it does not offend the community. I wanted to find that reference and I wondered whom I might ask to find out. Both Orenstein and Rabbi Shinder might be too dismissive to permit a sincere discussion on the issue.

At the end of the programme, there was mention of a website, which I decided to access to find out more information. Something to do over Rosh Hashanah when everyone around here would be preoccupied with celebrations.

Sleep came fitfully: tossing and turning and running the day through my mind. I got up to get a glass of water. I turned the radio back on to listen to recorded programmes from around the world: documentaries from Germany, France, Australia, and elsewhere.

Eventually, I dozed off and woke with a start at five. The radio was still on, playing the National Anthem. The news was next, and after a couple of items, I turned it off. I lay in bed staring at the ceiling. The next thing I knew, it was eight thirty. I had a quick breakfast of a stale roll and orange juice.

I would grab coffee later. I took the van over to Nicolet, where there was a car wash. On Sunday morning, it was not open until ten. I needed to find an alternative, and again, time was getting tight.

Across Saint-Denis Street was a net-café. I went in, got coffee, and paid to use the computer for five minutes.

There were two other car washes in the area, which I decided to forgo until after my haircut. After parking the van in the alley, I walked down to the Main and up to the hair salon, which was on the second floor of a loft building. I was rung in and I walked up the stairs. I was met by a young woman who introduced herself as Julie. The place had high ceilings and large windows facing the street.

"Coffee?"

"Yes, that would be very nice."

I sat on a sofa in the middle of the room. The coffee was excellent.

"Take your time; I still need a few minutes."

A young woman came out of the washroom and sat in the chair by the window. The blow dryer came out to finish off what looked like a very nice do. A few minutes later she was finished, paid, and left.

My turn. I was outfitted with a black gown and led to a chaise by a sink to have my hair washed. The experience was so relaxing that I dozed off briefly.

I was then led to the chair by the window. "And how would you like your haircut?"

"Like it was not cut."

"No problem. How did you hear about us?"

"Through friends."

"It's always interesting how that works."

"Do you usually take clients on Sunday?"

"Not usually; but it is Jewish New Year, and there is always someone who needs a last-minute haircut. I am not working again until next Wednesday."

"Well, I am invited to a dinner party tonight and I thought I should show up neatly shorn. Actually, the hostess was the person who told me about you."

"And her name?"

"Elyse."

"Oh, her. She is quite the maven. She seems to know everyone in town. She does a lot of community work. Her husband is a lawyer and someone in his firm did the legal work for our lease and generally guided us on how to set up."

"How long have you been open?"

"Just a few years. There are three of us here; we met elsewhere and decided to strike out on our own. So far, so good."

"It is working well for you."

"Yes, thankfully."

Julie was working quickly and efficiently. Her hands were so soft I almost did not feel anything.

"My sisters and I are hosting our family this evening. There will be fifteen around the table. Potluck. We all bring or make something. It is always a fun time. We alternate houses every year, and this year it is my older sister's turn. I am leaving here after I finish with you to help her out."

Finished, I looked in the mirror and was very pleased with the result. It looked neater but not obviously cut. I paid and was about to leave when Julie asked, "Are you walking down the Main?"

"Why, yes."

"We can walk together, if that is okay?"

"Sure."

The weather had turned sunny and warm. The street had filled up with walkers. Julie seemed to know many we passed.

"My, you are popular."

"I have been living and working around here for quite a few years."

"How did you become a hairstylist?"

"Well, I was in between things and a friend of mine was working for a salon as a student stylist. She was getting a small salary, and the salon was getting money from the government to train her. I thought that if she could do it, so could I. I found another salon on the Main which offered the same programme and was accepted."

"You enjoy what you do."

"Yes, and now I enjoy running my own business."

As we were walking, we passed several shops and restaurants. "Anyplace around here where I could buy some decent overstuffed chairs for my living room?"

"Well, yes, but these shops make to order and they are expensive. How many do you need?"

"Two. I need to get rid of two shabby heirlooms."

"Do you have a moment?"

"Just."

A few doors down, one of the shops was opening for the afternoon. We went in. Julie was warmly greeted by the young couple there. "My friend here needs two overstuffed chairs."

My eyes had adjusted to the light inside. There were examples of their handiwork on the floor. Very impressive. Tables, chairs, and sofas. Very good-looking wood, very modern, and very expensive looking.

"We can manage that. If you go to the back of the shop, there are some for you to take a look at. I'm Jack, by the way." In the back were three finished chairs, each slightly different.

"Have you measured the space you have available?"

"No, I am replacing two raggedy things which should have been thrown out years ago. These chairs, each one of them would fit perfectly. Would I have a choice of material to cover them?"

"Oh, yes, and if you do not see the colour or pattern you want, or the kind of finish, we can order it for you." He produced a catalogue.

I sat in each of the chairs. One had wider arms than the other two. Perfect for watching hockey with a libation on the arm. And it was comfortable; good for the back.

"This was kind of spontaneous, and I really need to go do some errands. Are you open this week?"

"Yes. We are closed Mondays, but if you call, we can arrange to meet you."

He produced a card with two phone numbers and a web address.

We walked to the front of the store. His partner, who was on the phone, smiled and mouthed, "Thanks for coming in."

Jack opened the front door. "Hope to see you again."

"Thanks for your time. You will."

Julie had remained quiet during the visit. "Well, what did you think?"

"I think I would like to do business with those folks. I was impressed with their handiwork."

"Be prepared to spend a few dollars."

"I think I need to do this."

"I am going into the flower shop, here, to buy flowers for this evening."

"Well, thank you for your time, and Happy New Year."

"Nice meeting you. Enjoy your dinner party."

"I am sure we will meet again. I am very pleased with the haircut."

With that, we parted. I had just enough time to get the van washed before the witching hour.

As I set off up the street, I saw Rabbi Shinder walking toward me. He was walking quickly with his head down. I stopped. When he got to where I was standing, and he looked up. "Mr. Glasheen, I am in a hurry to visit the sick wife of an old friend."

"Do you mind if I walk with you and ask you a few questions?"

"What do you want to know?"

"Where were you when your grandson was attacked?"

He stopped, turned to look at me. "I was at home, in my study, I think."

"Did you visit him in the hospital?"

"I had been there earlier that evening."

"Do you remember what time?"

"Do you need to ask me all these questions? I guess you do. Between seven and eight. I include Yoel in my prayers every day."

We had stopped in front of a long staircase, which the Rabbi started up. "Visiting the sick needs to be done. I am sure you did the same."

"Yes, often. You know, it surprises me how nonchalantly you are taking this whole episode. Your grandson was attacked, after all."

He had mounted a few more steps. He turned to look down at me. "You know that at the right time, the attacker will be revealed."

With that, he turned to finish his climb.

I turned to continue my walk home. I was feeling very uncomfortable.

People pushing strollers, carrying packages with last-minute purchases before the holiday, passed by. I went into the alley to get the van, and—lo and behold—the thing was clean. I stood staring in disbelief. Through the fence, I could see Orenstein sitting outside on that rusty chair praying. He was alone. I went into the apartment and out the back staircase. As I approached, Orenstein put down his prayer book. "Beat you to it."

"What's gotten into you?"

"Nice haircut."

"Listen, I have been wondering a couple of things."

"Such as?"

"What you were talking to Green about when I came back into his boardroom?"

"Doctors."

"Doctors?"

"He was dissatisfied with the one he had."

"Nice touch."

"We shall see."

"I suspect none would please him."

"Perhaps."

"I looked into the warehouse. The space was empty and there was no one working."

"Not surprising . . . nothing which could be seized. I am sure it is elsewhere."

"I took a walk yesterday morning down to the movie theatre."

"Yes, he owns it along with his wife and her family."

"Messy."

I got another nod.

"We really have not solved anything."

"You know, some things take time. And especially the delicate issues we are involved in. It took the Jews forty years to reach the Promised Land."

"Neither one of us has forty years. I have been wanting to talk to you about another issue."

"And that is?"

"Do you want to buy my apartment?"

He started to rub his beard. He looked me directly in the eye. "You want to sell?"

"My mother has been gone a year. The mourning period is over."

"It never is. You know, your mother was a really interesting person. She was genuinely curious about everything. One time, when the weather was bad, I drove her to the prison so she could teach. She was devoted to her students. She saw them as human beings, not as monsters. Not everyone could work in that kind of situation. She was to be admired.

"As for buying your place, I will think it over during the holidays. Yes, I could use the space. You would stay in Montreal?"

"I do not know. Probably. I like it. I could not see myself living in any other city in Canada. There is energy here. Plus, I would miss my hockey team too much."

Orenstein stifled a grin and nodded again. Two people who rarely smiled in less than twenty-four hours exhibiting something I thought impossible. There was hope for humanity. He got up. We shook hands. "Good health to you."

He nodded again. "Enjoy your dinner party."

With that he walked up the few stairs to his flat and disappeared behind the curtained door.

CHAPTER NINETEEN

I looked at my garlic bed and decided it needed more mulch. Some of the leaves had blown off.

Not a chore for today. but on the to-do list. I climbed the stairs to my flat. Just as I got to the top stair, my phone rang. It was Martha. "Pick you up at four. Ferguson is still in hospital. They are doing tests. We can visit before going to the soirée. Okay?"

"Sure. Should we stop to buy him a plant or something?"

"Already done."

"My, we are efficient."

"You betcha."

"See you later."

We rang off. I forgot to ask if she had bought anything for the hosts tonight.

I decided to take a shower. After towelling off, I tried to nap. No luck. I made a tuna sandwich and found some stale potato chips to round out the meal. I threw out the rest of the bag of chips. Buying for one had its drawbacks.

What next? Perhaps a short walk and some fresh air.

The day had remained sunny and warm. The end of September in Montreal could often be really nice.

Turning the corner, I ran into young Joel walking alone. He was dressed in a new-looking black suit with the same fedora he had on at the interview. "Happy New Year."

He looked up and smiled.

"How are you doing? Bet you are excited about the holidays. And that hockey team of ours starts the season in about a week or so." I just kept talking; he was not moving. He looked down; he looked away.

Finally, I said, "Tell me how you are feeling." I waited.

He looked up, "Okay, I guess." Very quietly, almost conspiratorially.

"Does it still hurt?"

He shrugged.

"Is that a 'yes'?"

He shrugged again. He was not moving. I put my hand on his shoulder. "You know we are going to catch the bad guy." He mumbled something about being late and left.

I stood in the middle of the sidewalk, watching him disappear down the block. He did not turn to look back. I considered that conversation a triumph, albeit a painful one for him.

I still thought that we spend too much time searching for the criminal and not enough time on the victim. We protect him by ignoring him or, at best, asking a few questions in order to fill out a report. It is as if we form a protective circle with our backs turned to him. We do not know how to talk to him. He has been violated and numbed by the experience.

Orenstein was right, in a way; these things did take time. I would put the emphasis in a slightly different way. Joel's silence was in fact a statement. I would have loved to better interpret it; I would also have liked to know if the trauma expressed itself in other ways: sleep pattern, eating, and relationships with people in general. Joel was obviously shy and appeared to keep to himself.

What was he really interested in? Would visiting his room provide clues? And just maybe, he really wanted to be left alone to figure it all out for himself. Twelve-year-olds have a slightly exaggerated view of their abilities. And just maybe, sometime in the future, he would start asking his own questions to which he had no answers. And just maybe someone would be around, someone he trusted to help answer some of those questions. Yes, but the first thing to go in Joel's case was trust. His father was supposed to be in the room and was not. Would that fact hinder their relationship now or in the future? I did hope that someone was keeping an eye on him.

I had resumed walking and was oblivious to time and place. I had left my cellphone at home, so if Martha called, I would not know. I thought she was as giddy about our date as I was.

I slowly returned to my street, which was now much quieter than before.

Going into the apartment, I was not astonished to see missed calls on both phones. Martha was one, and the other left no message and the phone number was blocked. I was most curious about that one.

I took another shower; the walk had made me clammy. My phones rang again. There was no message and again the number was blocked. I ran through the likely candidates only to come up blank. I decided to call Ferguson. Someone answered, "Yeah."

"Reverend Ferguson, please."

"Hey, Rev, it's for you."

I heard shuffling and muffled sounds. "Afternoon, Ferguson here."

"Glasheen here."

"Ah, Nurse Nightingale."

"Hardly."

"Are you coming to spring me out of here?"

"Not today. And how are you?"

"Reasonable. Coming later? Bring me some food."

"What about your diet?"

"The dietitian is anorexic, hardly a good ad."

"How about salt-free crackers?"

"Is that the best you can do for a friend in need?"

"Martha and I will be along later. And did you call me before?"

"Negative. And don't bother coming without sustenance." And with that he rang off.

I decided to bring him a chopped egg sandwich on white bread. That should not offend anyone, except the patient.

I finished dressing, looked in the mirror, and decided I would have felt more comfortable in my former uniform. The new shoes needed to be worked in. I hard-boiled two eggs and quickly made the sandwich. I hoped the salt content of the bread would be acceptable.

Martha called. "Running late, meet me on Parc Avenue and Saint-Viateur."

I left the house immediately, the day still warm in the late afternoon sun. Mrs. Orenstein was on the porch. She was wearing a beret and had on one of those old frilly aprons my grandmother wore. She was drying her hands with a hand towel. She smiled at me and I wished her Happy New Year. She nodded. This exchange was more evidence of a thaw in our relationship. Or maybe Shmully had mentioned my offer to sell. Off I went, west on Saint-Viateur, carrying the sandwich in a paper bag.

Standing on the street corner, I looked at the YMCA building, thinking I should probably join, if only to go for a swim now and then. Martha's car came to a stop in front of the Parc Avenue bus. The driver let it be known that this would not do. I quickly scrambled in.

"Greetings."

"You look eminent."

Martha was wearing black slacks and a brocade jacket which had hints of several colours, mustard being the base. Her hair had not so much been cut as arranged neatly. "You do not look half-bad yourself."

"What's in the bag? Have you yourself a snack just in case?"

"Food for Ferguson. Otherwise, we are disinvited to see him. It is a bribe."

"I suppose that means he's feeling better?"

"Speaking of which, your tentacles reach into this hospital as well?"

"Meaning who can we pump for information about the Reverend?"

"Yes, something like that. A couple of my friends' kids are now in med school. But I no longer know any of the doctors. Most of the old crowd have left or retired. There is a whole new crop."

We were coming up on the General. Parking in front of the upper entrance required meter money. Luckily, Martha had some change. She put in enough for two hours. She had a plastic bag with the logo of a local bookstore on it. She looked at me conspiratorially. "He loves mystery novels."

"Figures."

We took the elevator to the fourteenth floor as instructed. The room was down the hall to the left; three beds occupied the space. In one was a younger man who had two women doting over him. Ferguson was napping in the bed opposite. He looked serene. There was one unused chair, which Martha sat in. I sat on the third bed, which was empty.

A nurse came in and woke Reg up to give him a pill. He was a good patient; he smiled at her, thanked her, and took the meds, then turned to us and said, "I cannot sleep here at night. I try to catch up during the day. Food?"

I produced the paper bag.

"Bless you." He devoured the sandwich without taking a breath or chewing much.

"How do you feel?"

"Truthfully?"

We both nodded.

"Like shit. They want me to lose weight and are feeding me accordingly. I still have headaches, but milder than before."

"You did slam into that wall with a lot of force."

"I remember tripping and then I was here."

Martha stood and went over to his bed. "Terry, come help me lift him up in the bed. He does not look in the least comfortable."

We each grabbed him under a shoulder to move him up the bed. He was not as heavy as I would have thought. Martha fussed with the blankets to get them just right.

I noticed get-well cards on the night table and windowsill. There was a flowering plant from the old-age home. Nothing I could see from the Children's. Martha produced her present, which Ferguson removed from the paper bag. "If you have read it, there is a return sticker."

"I know his work and I have not read it. I get a vicarious thrill from reading this stuff. Raymond Chandler was the best."

"Still is. And Bogie's was dead-on. Just the right combination of world-weariness, with a touch of optimism."

Martha chimed in, "No wonder you two have hit it off. You are both romantics at heart."

We stared at her. Ferguson, who by now had put on his glasses, peered over the top of them to suggest that she was too young to be so cynical. "Listen, I think we need a little balance, here."

"Did you ever read Nancy Drew?"

"I was not encouraged to do so. I was breast-fed on Dostoevsky."

"What deprivation," Ferguson bellowed. With that he had a coughing fit between bouts of laughter. He drank some water from the side table and appeared to right himself.

A tall young man with a name tag clipped to his white coat came in. Martha looked at the tag.

"Your mother wouldn't be Betty?" The fellow looked away from the binder to give a nod.

"I went to graduate school with her. How is she?"

"Well, she is fine. Living in Florida. And you are?"

"Martha Lang. We did social work together. She came back to school after you and your sister were born. She was a mature student and her perspective was entirely different from the rest of us. She was refreshing."

"I will tell her I ran into you. Now, if you'll excuse me, I need to spend some time with your friend."

Martha and I went out into the corridor.

S. John Diamond

A few minutes later, the doctor came out. "In a funny way, it was a good thing Ferguson took a fall."

"How so?"

"He was not looking after himself. His blood pressure was sky-high. And more importantly, he has become seriously diabetic. So mostly what we are doing is trying to regulate both those issues. He will need to come to the diabetes clinic to teach himself to inject insulin, watch for warning signs, and do something about his diet. Right now, he is pushing for heart failure or a stroke."

"Well, thank you for that. I will be on his case."

I interjected, "I can speak from personal experience; the poor man has not got a chance."

Martha elbowed me as we all laughed.

The young doctor took his leave.

"At least we know why they are keeping him here and subjecting him to all those tests."

We went back into the room. Ferguson was asleep with his glasses still on. Martha went over to remove them and kissed him lightly on the forehead.

We left. Walking down the corridor, I put my arm under Martha's elbow. Very quietly, I said to her, "That is the first time you called me Terry."

"Really?"

"Yes, really."

We reached the elevator and had to wait for what seemed like forever for the car to come. I interrupted the silence by asking, "And who is likely to be at this shindig?"

She paused for a second. "Surely I have called you Terry before."

"I do not think so."

The elevator came. We got in. By the time we reached the Cedar exit, the car was full. There was no further conversation. When we were seated in Martha's car, I had moved the seat as far back as it could go, so I was looking into her shoulder.

"The likely guests will be a couple of guys with no known occupation. Elyse's husband, if he behaves, can be interesting. He wants a judgeship. So far, no luck on that score. Some of Elyse's women friends are far more interesting than their husbands. Present company included."

"Sounds like I need to be on my best behaviour."

"You will manage just fine. Elyse and Martin, her husband, will carry the conversation, initially."

"What have you told them about me?"

"Just enough. By the way, you and Reg really have a lot in common. You could do yourself a favour and get to know him better."

"I sense he is a decent man. And is there anyone to look after him? He is going to need care when he goes home."

"No, he lives alone. Something will have to be arranged."

"This is going to be like dining with the bishop or several bishops. My best behaviour will be required."

"I have faith in you," she said with a bit of a chuckle.

We were driving west into the sunset. At a light, she turned left down a tree-lined street to the middle of the block. We passed a number of large homes, all distinctly different. She turned the wheel of the car toward the curb and applied the parking brake. We walked a few doors down, turning right into the walk-in front of a large red-brick house. Judging from the height of the windows from the ground, I would place the date of the home at around 1920. To the left and down a laneway was a garage that must have been a recent addition. On a ramp to the left, a newish SUV was parked. We walked up a few stairs, and the large front door was opened by a young woman in a maid's uniform. "Good evening."

We walked into a large foyer with high ceilings, where some men were standing clutching glasses and talking.

"Hello, Martha. Nice to see you. And this is?"

"Martin Gold, this is Terry Glasheen."

"Terry, nice to meet you. I am Elyse's husband. Would you like a drink? I have really interesting malt."

I must have nodded.

"And Martha, your pleasure?"

"Half a glass of white wine."

"Terry, ice?"

"No ice, thank you."

"Oh, we have an expert here." Martin's cell phone rang, and he disappeared to the kitchen at the rear of the house. I noticed that neither of the other two men was wearing a tie. The walls bore some interesting art that I could see only peripherally. One of the men was Steve, and the other was Stan. They had been talking golf. Stan looked at Martha. "Well, how goes the battle at the hospital?"

Martha looked up at them both. "Maybe I'll take up golf."

"That good, eh?" And they both laughed.

The young woman appeared with a tray and handed Martha her half-glass of white wine. I tasted the scotch; it was good. Not too peaty.

Martha led me into the salon, which was to the left of the hall. Three women were standing and talking. All were much more formally dressed than the men. I quickly noticed more art on the walls and a couple of Inuit carvings placed strategically around the room. Through the doors toward the rear of the house was the dining room. A tall, dark-haired woman was fussing with the table: this finally must be Elyse. I was introduced to the others. Sarah was Martin's sister. Claudette was Steve's wife, and Iris was with Stan. Martha was lauded for how well she looked. "It was nothing."

I noticed a portrait of our hostess above the fireplace. She was sitting slightly forward in a high-backed chair. A brooch was pinned to her white blouse. The skirt was a checked affair with black and white. Her legs were slightly crossed, and she was wearing dark high heels.

Just then, she made her entrance into the room. She walked right over to me, stuck her hand out: "Terry, it is so nice to meet you. I have heard so much about you."

I think I blushed. Her handshake was firm, and she was at least my height.

"Nice to meet you, and thanks for the recommendation for the haircut."

"Julie really did a good job, didn't she? It does look good."

Speaking to the others, she announced, "Terry here spent time in the north working with our Native population."

"And others," I interjected. The women nodded. Their eyes did not exactly glaze over.

Claudette asked, "Then how did you meet Martha?"

"We met at the hospital. I am retired now and living here."

Claudette interrupted, "So you are a volunteer?"

"In a manner of speaking." The young woman came around with a tray of hors d'oeuvres. They were tiny meatballs with a very tangy sauce. I ate two. I was starving and hoped the meal would be soon. The scotch was creating a bit of a buzz; I was not used to this. I was a beer and wine guy.

"Martin is on a long-distance call which he 'needs to take.' When he is finished, we will move to the table," Elyse announced.

More *hors d'oeuvres*, this time tiny egg rolls. They were good, if a touch salty. Iris wanted to know if I missed the north and the cold. "This will be my first winter here in many years, and I miss the people I worked with."

"What exactly did you do, work for the government?" Iris followed up.

Just then, Martin came into the room, his face slightly red. "My phone is now off."

Elyse took my arm and escorted me into the dining room. Martin did the same with Martha. Nice touch.

Martha was seated to the left of Martin, who was at the head of the table. I was beside Martha.

Sarah was at my left. Elyse was at the other end of the table with her back to the salon, whose doors were now shut. The tablecloth was very white and intricately designed. The cutlery, and there was a lot of it, was sterling silver. Not since I had lunch with the bishop had I seen the like. In fact, the formality here reminded me very much of dining with him. After we were seated, Martin stood to say a few words. "Welcome all! Elyse and I are very pleased that we are all together at this time. I would like to acknowledge that Martha, who actually works, has finally chosen to be among us. And she has brought along a very welcome guest. I offer a toast to our continued good health and a Happy New Year."

Steve said, "Hear, hear."

Glasses were lifted. Mine held the rest of the scotch. I dared not drink any wine. I looked to my right to see if Martha was blushing; I very gently elbowed her. She looked my way and winked. Sign language.

Martin asked Elyse if she wanted to make any remarks. From her chair, she announced, "Dinner will be served." I think she buzzed the kitchen; two seconds later, a cart appeared with a tureen of soup and bowls. A separate bowl was placed in front of Sarah. She mumbled in my left ear that she was vegetarian and did not eat chicken soup. The soup was superb; just the right amount of salt. Next came a mixed salad with a very light vinaigrette dressing.

Martin, seeming more relaxed now, looked at me. "So how do you occupy yourself these days? You are retired, aren't you?"

"I sort of volunteer around the neighbourhood. From time to time, I volunteer at the Children's Hospital."

"You are retired from what?" Stan asked.

The whole table was listening.

"Well, I was working for a large multinational and I disagreed with their orientation. So I cashed in my chips and left."

Elyse looked down the table at me. "That's the biggest bunch of hooey I ever heard."

Martin came to my defence. "Makes perfect sense to me."

Martha was laughing.

Sarah said, "I thought you were working for the government in the north."

"Not entirely. Dealing with the government was part of what I did."

"So what exactly did you do?"

I took a breath. "I was a priest."

Silence.

Elyse started to laugh. "A large multinational corporation . . . that was rich, very creative."

"You were not thrown out?" Iris suggested.

"No, no, not at all. I left of my own accord."

Martha, in a very serious and authoritative tone, said, "Can we stop the inquisition and let the dear man alone?"

Elyse: "Hear, hear."

The cart came back to deliver a plate with a cake of something I could not identify on a bed of lettuce. On the edge of the plate was a red sauce and a white sauce. I must have stared. "Gefilte fish," Martha whispered. I noticed that Sarah did not have this concoction in front of her. She had, instead, some melon, which looked far more appealing.

I chanced it. Mixed with the sauces, it was not bad—an acquired taste maybe, but definitely not bad. Claudette: "Who made this? It is the best it has ever been."

"Secret herbs and spices," Elyse laughed. "Actually, Irma and I made it together. I found a recipe online, bought the fish already chopped, and away we went. I refused to buy commercially."

Stan did not touch his portion and, since I had made my announcement, he had been eyeing me in a way I could not interpret. Plates were cleared. I was working my way through the cutlery.

In the lull, Stan cleared his throat and looked directly at me. "I hope you do not misinterpret what I am going to say, but the Church acts like a large multinational which has lost touch with its market. And I am glad that we have finally been absolved. It only took how long?" With that, he sat back in his chair.

"I agree with you." I paused. "And I would add the shoddy treatment of women."

Sarah turned to me, "You mean that. I do not believe what I am hearing. Do you think there will ever be women priests?"

"Yes. Perhaps not in my lifetime, though I am not so sure."

"You know I refuse to attend the 'Family' synagogue for just that reason," Sarah was just getting warmed up, it appeared. "Father was president of the board and no way would he and his cronies change one thing about the involvement of women. Tradition."

A plate appeared in front of her with stir-fried vegetables in a black sauce. She had been kneading her napkin in her hands as she talked. It now rested on her lap.

"Nice-looking dish," I said.

"Yes, it does look tasty. You know, I do not think that the treatment of women is divinely inspired. It is a man-made construct."

Nobody else at the table looked the least bit interested in this conversation. Martha and Martin had been whispering about something. The two men were talking through Iris. Elyse and Claudette were discussing something else.

Martin looked at me. "I see Sarah has caught your ear about one of her favourite topics. She attends some new-age service in Hampstead."

"Oh, Martin, stop being so patronizing."

A very attractive plate appeared: on it was a cut of meat I did not recognize, a sweet potato concoction, and steamed broccoli. Colourful, anyway.

"Tzimmes," said Martha.

"Yes, time to bring back this old chestnut of a dish." Elyse looked very pleased.

The others were served, and we started to eat. "Where did you buy the brisket?" Claudette asked.

"My old friend on Van Horne; he is still in business, and I am loyal. He always does a good job."

"I have not been in there in years," Iris interjected.

Sarah leaned over to me. "This is boring. I hate when they start talking about stuff like this. It becomes a competition. This butcher, that butcher, my butcher, this restaurant, that restaurant, on and on."

I started to laugh.

"What do you do?" I asked her.

"I teach art."

"Oh, I ran into someone the other day whose daughter was sent to the US to study art."

"And her name would be?"

"Her last name would be Green."

Sarah turned to me full-faced and put her hand on my arm. "I know her. She calls herself Greengarten to separate herself from that rotten father of hers. She has talent. I got scared for a moment: I thought you were going to tell me something horrible about her. Angela, that's her first name. Nice girl."

Just then Martin stopped his conversation with Martha, sat up rigidly in his chair, looked at me, and said, "So you know Orenstein and you went to visit Mike Green last Friday!" There was agitation in his voice, and he got red in the face. The table went silent. Elyse broke the silence, "Martin, please! I do not want you to discuss business at this table, and especially that awful client of yours." He sat back in his chair, continuing to look at me, and his face relaxed a little.

"You and Orenstein, now there is an interesting couple. How did the two of you ever get together?"

"We are neighbours and I know how to keep his van on the road. So I chauffeur him around. That is how Martha and I met."

Martha chimed in, "They make a very effective team—I can vouch for that. They ooze sincerity and morality."

"Orenstein was here in our house, well not *in*, exactly, but he provided extra security. We had some Israeli dignitaries visit for an evening reception. Security demanded that Orenstein be used to augment their detail. He had a short meeting with his fellow officers on the front steps and then spent the rest of the evening in the shadows. He does not fit the stereotype—a slight man with a white beard. On second thought, he is perfect; you would never suspect him at all. And you, quite a career shift from priest to chauffeur." He chuckled at his own joke.

"Well, I suppose I could say something banal like 'the Lord works in mysterious ways.' But I would like to think that I am open to new experiences, new challenges. When I started as a young priest in the North, I had no preparation for what I was getting myself into. The parishioners trained me. I did receive some guidance from the bishop, but most of it was trial and error."

"When I started in law, it was the same thing. I did a little bit of everything. But most of it was learning on the job. I had some guidance from some of the senior fellows around, but that only took me so far."

"Exactly."

Martha, who had been listening intently to this interchange, suggested that she, too, had the same experience. "I could tell you a lot about welfare law. I had no clue how to actually apply for welfare. I did not know how to deal with the bureaucracy. Trial and error. The best learning tool there is."

The two guys from across the table who had spent most of the time talking golf and the NFL season each weighed in on the subject of welfare. Mostly they thought there was too much of it here. Martha looked at both of them and told them to change the law. Steve said, not unkindly, "Once a left-winger, always a left-winger."

It became clear that both Iris and Claudette were teachers. Iris was still working. She said, "I have worked in special education my whole career, including a stint at the Children's Hospital, where I met both Elyse and Martha. It was really important in many of the schools to keep the lunch programmes going by hook or by crook. We fought for that. There were always rumours of cutbacks. We were prepared to lobby private industry to do their bit. The school board was really uncomfortable when they got wind of that. And we were called on the carpet by our union for usurping their power. You cannot teach a hungry child."

Claudette nodded in agreement. Stan opened his mouth to say something and thought better of it. Someone asked why Iris had left the hospital.

"The work was short-term—more of an assessment role than anything else. I preferred a longer-term relationship where I could see results."

I was totally wrapped up in the conversation and neglected to finish my plate, which I did very quickly when I saw the cart again. By now, Martin had taken off his blazer; he was wearing a vest over a very expensive-looking shirt and tie. He wore cufflinks! Did men still do that? Obviously, but where had I been? I did not think in the limited time I had been south I had ever seen cufflinks. And they certainly were not worn in the north.

Elyse orchestrated the meal by using a foot buzzer to ring the kitchen. I had spotted it as I sat down. Her command of the table was total. Next came sherbet to cleanse the palate.

I was tempted to ask Martin about Mike Green. However, it was obvious that the topic was a non-starter around this table.

Martha, bless her soul, looked at Martin. "You know, very early in my career I had a meeting with Mike Green. His kids, Richard and Angela, had come to the attention of the guidance department—the boy because of acting out and Angela because she was so withdrawn and uncommunicative. We had to see mother and father separately. The mother was overwhelmed, and Green was difficult to see; and when we did, he was a royal pain in the ass. He blamed the school system for his children's difficulties."

"Martha," Elyse burst in. "Do we have to discuss that abomination again?"

I jumped into the fray, "Funny how a situation like this affects us all."

"How so?" Stan asked.

"Well, Martin is involved, Martha is involved or has been involved, I am involved, and most others around this table have very definite opinions about this situation. This thing, it is fair to say, has infected this room. Is it also fair to say that many of you know Mrs. Green?"

There were nods.

Claudette came to her defence: "I have known her since McGill. She was bright and funny, a good person. She is still all those things; but the stress of her life has worn her down. I don't think I have seen her smile in years. Her son quit college to go on the road with a rock group. And Angela has taken up with another woman; they live in southern Vermont, and I think I heard that they adopted a baby."

Sarah couldn't contain herself any longer, "What a bunch of judgemental old coots you have become. So what if these young people are following their dreams? Is Sheila happy? Is Green happy?"

"Did anyone see the babe that Green is squiring around town?" Stan said, sitting back in his chair with a Cheshire grin. "What's to be unhappy about?"

Elyse stood. "Enough of this drivel. We will adjourn before dessert. And please, no more talk about the Greens."

I was offered a digestif; though tempted, I declined. We were in the salon. Sarah wandered over to stand beside me. Everything about her was short. Short stature, short hair, and, I thought, short-tempered, or impatient—not willing to suffer fools gladly. She had on an olive-green shift that went to her ankles. She wore sandals and she had put a shawl over her shoulders. "On the whole, the dinner conversation was the most interesting in years. I would love to hear more about your views on women in the Church. And I do not think I have ever seen my pompous brother squirm the way he did this evening."

"You know, I am more interested in talking about what you do, and about Angela Greengarten and her brother. However, one argument that recurs concerning women and the early Church relates to inheritance. Many of these early priests were rich men's sons who brought along property to the Church. If they married, the Church would lose out on succession."

"What a crock, what a fraud. You know all these institutions are simply afraid of women. Isn't that the bottom line?"

I looked at her. "You know, you are probably right. And you can save your next series of questions for another time."

"You still sorting that stuff out for yourself?"

Martin and Martha came into the salon. She walked over to me, held my hand. "I see you two have hit it off."

"And I see you and Martin have solved all the problems of the world." I squeezed her hand back. Sarah had wandered away to look at one of the paintings on the wall. Martha and I stood behind Sarah as she began to describe the painting in great detail. The artist was totally unknown to me. Both Martha and Sarah knew him personally. He was an Israeli who had lived in Montreal for many years. Two of his paintings hung on either side of Elyse's portrait. The one on the left showed a lone tree in a field; but on second glance, there was another tree behind the first. Sarah's description made the whole scene come alive in a way that I never could. We moved to the painting on the right. This painting looked like the first, but from a slightly different perspective. There were more trees and there were mountains in the background with snow on them. Again, Sarah was able to point out elements not obvious to the novice.

"Did you paint Elyse's portrait?"

"Yes."

It was only then that I noticed the signature at the bottom left: "Sarah L."

"Nicely done."

"Thank you. It took a lot of work. There were egos involved. We argued about everything. I was not the first choice for the job. It fell to me. The first choice drank himself to death or took off with one of his models or some excuse. Martin had to intervene to tell us to behave and grow up. We declared a truce and you can see the result. There are a few things I would change if I had the chance, but nothing major."

I excused myself to go to the loo, which was underneath the staircase to the second floor.

On the back wall was a framed poster warning against VD. The work dated from the forties. It showed a seductive woman with a skeletal face. This was a warning for the troops in Europe.

Many would object to the treatment of the woman today.

When dessert was announced, we returned to the table. Elyse and Martin had switched seats. Martin's phone buzzed. He got up and disappeared behind the sliding doors to the salon.

Elyse looked none too pleased. She said something to Martha, who nodded.

I turned to Sarah. "What does the 'L' stand for?"

"Lazarus. I was married once. I just kept the name. It was simpler than doing all the paperwork to change it back. I have a question for you."

"Shoot."

"I hope you do not think I am being nosey."

"Go ahead."

"How do you guys cope with celibacy?"

"It is something you get used to. It's expected, and everyone in our crowd does it."

"That's a very simplistic answer."

"Perhaps, but it was a given. It was part of the price of admission."

"You know, I once spent some time at a commune in New England—it was termed an intentional community. And the young men decided to take a vow of chastity for a month. Some went on to do it for two months. A few kept at it for three months."

"Do you fast on Yom Kippur?"

"Yes, I do."

"Do you think about it? I mean you do it every year and you attend synagogue, and all those folks are fasting as well. It is a group activity done individually. There is something about being together experiencing the same thing."

"Your comparison is interesting; I would not have drawn that parallel. That brings up other issues about group psychosis. Like, what happens if the group is dead wrong?"

"Like the Nazis."

"Something like that."

"Do you remember the fairy tale about the emperor who wore no clothes?"

"You would hope that somebody in the crowd would shout out to stop the nonsense."

"Yes."

"This is the beginning of a very good conversation that perhaps we could continue some other time."

"If you wish. Where do you teach?"

"I teach at Concordia in the Fine Arts Department."

"And your area of interest?"

"Canadian Jewish Artists."

"You have me there. I know nothing about this at all."

"The National Film Board has a film about an artist named Sam Borenstein which you can watch online for free. Highly recommended."

Martha elbowed me. "Is it time to go? I have to work tomorrow."

"Oh, sure; as you wish."

"Look, if you want to stay, I am sure you could manage to find your way home."

"It is you and me, Babe."

She grinned.

We stood and said our goodbyes and thank-yous.

Sarah especially wanted me to call her to have lunch.

As we went out the door, Martin put his hand on my shoulder. "I want you and Orenstein to come to my office on Wednesday. Come at noon."

I shook his hand and thanked him for a lovely evening. Walking down the walk, I knew what the agenda was likely to be. Still, Martin was troubled, and I was curious to know more about that.

Martha was sitting in the passenger seat; I guess I was driving.

"Where to, Ms.?"

"Cute."

"I will drive myself home."

"Fine."

"And what, ah, is wrong?"

"Skip it."

Driving over the mountain road, the cemetery loomed on the left, where Mother was buried. I stopped at the lookout overlooking the eastern part of the city.

There were few sightseers in the parking area. I wanted to leave the car if only to allow air into the car and replenish mine. Turning off the motor, I looked at her. "A penny for your thoughts?"

She was staring right ahead. "Don't patronize me."

I said nothing and continued to look at her.

"You were the star of the fucking show. And that slut Sarah. What a piece of work she is. She wouldn't leave you alone. She has been married and divorced twice and each time she divorced up."

"Divorced up?"

"She got a lot of money the first time and more money the second time."

I said nothing.

There were several seconds of silence.

She turned to look at me. "And I cannot believe my reaction to all this horseshit."

There was a pause.

"Where were you ten years ago? I know, I know; saving souls in the Yukon."

I laughed quietly and so did she. The air was beginning to return.

"I wanted a kid. There was no one around. I did not necessarily want a relationship; I just wanted a kid. And now ten years later you walk into my life, right into my office—I didn't have to go anywhere." I waited to see if there was more. I looked out the windshield and was able to see the tower of the Olympic Stadium. I returned my attention to Martha. "Let's go; I'm cold."

We headed down the curving road past Parc Avenue. On the right was Fletcher's Field.

At Saint-Laurent Boulevard, I turned left, heading toward my apartment, stopping in front. Going around to the passenger side; Martha got out and hugged me. The hug lasted a while.

It was more comforting than anything. Nothing else was said. She walked to the driver's side, got in, and rolled down the window as I was closing the passenger door. "Thanks."

"No, thank you. I had a lovely evening." She continued looking at me through the window as she rolled it up. And then slowly she drove off.

CHAPTER TWENTY

The street was empty and eerily quiet. I opened the door to my flat and walked up the stairs, which this evening seemed to be a chore. Time to move; the staircase was becoming an issue.

I sat in one of the overstuffed chairs and stared out at nothing, needing to put the evening in some kind of context. There were a number of themes running through the dinner. I made an enormous error mentioning Green by name. On the other hand, maybe some good would come from that. After all, Orenstein and I had a meeting with Martin Gold, his lawyer.

One thing was certain, the person who was calling Martin was Mike Green. And there were all the other themes which ran through the evening, which ended with Martha's outburst.

I was not used to that. After all, nobody ever attacked a priest directly.

Welcome to society.

I then wondered: If the evening had started on a different note, with some religious rite, some prayer, perhaps, would the experience have been the same? I continued staring out at the wall.

My cellphone rang. I got out of the chair; it was first light. I ran to the counter in the kitchen where I had left it. "Hello." I did not even look at where the call came from.

"I want to apologize for my rant last night."

"Oh, no, no."

There was a pause.

"I really do not know where all that came from. I mean, I do. I said it. I just did not know it was there with such . . ."

"Passion."

"That's a word I have trouble with. I can hardly say it."

"Well, you were passionate."

"Did you sleep last night?"

"In the chair in the living room, still in my party clothes."

"You are very kind."

"I sense you cannot listen to me now; I just want to say I enjoyed myself immensely."

"I—I have to go."

Outside, Orenstein and the young men were walking down the walk to go to prayers. It was seven a.m.

I stood staring out the window. Eventually I went to change. I lay on my made bed in a robe. The clock said ten thirty a.m. I had the day before me; in fact, I had two days before me.

On the National Film Board site, I sat through the Sam Borenstein film in total fascination. His paintings pummelled the senses. It was as if he were throwing paint at the canvas. There was no subtlety. I suspected that he was a difficult, temperamental man. The credits ran; his daughter had made the film. Maybe I had missed that at the beginning. How amazing; I had no idea this fellow ever existed. I wanted to watch it again. I started it over. The phone rang.

The number was "unknown."

"Mr. Glasheen."

"Yes."

"This is the nursing coordinator on the fourteenth floor of the Montreal General Hospital."

"Yes."

"We want to send Mr. Ferguson home today. He must be escorted by a family member or a friend."

"Oh yes, sure, sure. When is this going to happen?"

"Anytime you can get here. No hurry."

I hung up. Funny how stuff fills empty space. *Horror vacui*, I guess.

I showered, shaved, and stayed in the same clothes as last night, sans tie. I took off the fancy shoes to put on my runners. Far more appropriate.

I went to the ATM to get some money; luckily, the pension cheque had been deposited.

Walking south on Parc Avenue, I passed the statue where the Sunday tam-tam drumming took place. Several city employees were cleaning up from yesterday's festivities. And across the street, I noticed that what I remembered as Fletcher's Field was in fact now called Parc Jeanne-Mance.

Farther along, I went by the university gymnasium. Through the window that looked out onto the street, I could see lots of young people doing all sorts of exercise: cycling, lifting weights, stretching. Today, I felt tired just watching this display of energy.

Passing the football stadium, I recalled watching many games as a kid. If you climbed Mount Royal, which was behind the stadium, and stationed yourself on a certain tree limb, you could see three-quarters of the field. It was free.

Up the hill past the Royal Victoria Hospital, which looked like some sort of medieval castle, complete with turrets, there was a sign in support of the current fundraising campaign.

Running out of sidewalk, I crossed to the south side of Pine. I passed several buildings that were once private homes and now were part of the university. Farther up the hill was the Medical Building, which stretched a great distance back from the street. The walk had levelled off.

On my left was the Speech Pathology Department, which was housed in an old home right up against the sidewalk. Soon I would have a decision to make: go up Cedar to the front door of the General or continue on Pine and enter the Hospital through the rear doors. While weighing this choice, I passed the home of the former prime minister. I remember seeing television footage of this location when he was on his deathbed. I wondered if the family still owned the place.

The traffic light ruled my decision. Up Cedar I went. There was forest on the right, above rock outcroppings, where in winter there was a spectacular icicle show. Farther up on that side was the Shriners' Hospital. I was puffing now. The hill was quite steep. On my side was a small fire hall that had been converted into a residence. I would have liked to get inside to see what they had done.

Ahead of me on the left was the more modern, geometric General, reaching about twenty storeys into the air. As I went down the stairs to the front door, I passed several smokers. Outside the building to the left and right of the entrance, more smokers, some in patient garb trailing medical devices on wheels.

Once inside, there was much hustle and bustle. Volunteers sold books. People were milling around. There was a coffee bar on the left. Tempting though it was, I begged off. The elevator took forever, as it had on Saturday night with Martha.

Finally on the fourteenth floor, walking into Ferguson's room, I found him sitting in a wheelchair all set to go. "What took you so bloody long?"

I ignored the question. "My, you look almost healthy."

"It's the drugs. I am stoned."

Just then a male nurse came in. His name was Stefan, or so the name tag said.

"So you are all ready to go. Here are the prescriptions you need to pick up. They have been faxed to your pharmacy on Greene Street."

"Greene Avenue," Ferguson corrected.

"Yes, Greene Avenue."

I wheeled him out by the nurses' station. One of the older nurses came out to wish Ferguson well.

Ferguson really did look a lot better. His hair was combed. His complexion looked normal and not flushed.

The elevator came and we exited at the Cedar entrance. We got into a cab and the fellow drove us down the hill to Greene Avenue. Ferguson paid the driver, and we went into the pharmacy.

We made our way through the narrow aisles to the rear. Ferguson gave the young woman his name and she retrieved a large bag of medications. "Before I give these to you, the pharmacist wants to speak to you."

We waited.

She came over eventually. "Mr. Ferguson?"

"Yes."

"Some of these medications you must take with food. Some you take in the morning and some at night.

"Do you have a cuff at home?"

"A cuff?"

"A blood pressure monitor. You are going to have to take your blood pressure at least twice a day."

"Oh, this whole thing is sounding like a full-time job."

Without the slightest hint that she got the joke, the pharmacist continued, "You need to be very diligent about your medication."

I told Ferguson to sit in a chair in the waiting area beside the counter. I rounded up a notebook from elsewhere in the store. Sitting beside Reg, I took each medicine out of the bag to write notes. I jotted down which medicine was for the morning and which was for the evening. I put a star beside the ones to be taken with food. One vial was for a pill that was for three days only and was not to be renewed. I went back to the counter with the notebook and asked to speak to the pharmacist. She came over a few minutes later.

"I want to review Reverend Ferguson's medication with you."

S. John Diamond

"And you are?"

"His caregiver, Father Glasheen."

She looked at the very neat, I thought, columns I had made.

"That looks about right. Essentially, he should take his medication at mealtimes."

"There are some vials which have different names than the ones on the sheet from the hospital."

She filled in that information. "That should be clearer."

I thanked her; there was almost the hint of a smile.

We went to the front of the store to pay for the notebook and then walked into the warm September sunshine.

"To home, I think."

"Home is?"

"Around the corner."

We slowly walked up Greene Avenue. Gazing up the Westmount side of Mount Royal, I could see houses perched against the clear blue sky. Every few paces, I had to wait for my patient to catch up.

He stopped. "I have no food at home and I'm famished."

"Is there a grocery store nearby?"

Pointing to the new building on the corner, he said, "They will be reopening this one soon, in about a month or so, the local paper says."

"That does not help us now."

"There is a diner on the corner."

"You have the number?"

"Somewhere."

Several people passed us as we walked. Some nodded at Reg as we lumbered up the street. At the corner of Sherbrooke, I crossed to go into the diner to get a card with their coordinates and to make sure they would deliver to a home address.

They asked me who for. "Reverend—"

"Oh, Reg, sure, no problem."

We laboured across Sherbrooke Street. At the far corner, we turned left. The next block was a small street lined with trees. On the west corner stretching back from Sherbrooke was an apartment building.

"This is where I live."

The building was nondescript: dark brick, otherwise faceless. As we came to the front door, a woman with a shopping bag was coming out. "Reverend Ferguson, where have you been? Your newspapers were

101

piling up at your door. I have them in my office. When I get back, I will bring them to you."

"Flo, you are a dream; you spoil me. This is my friend Glasheen. Glasheen, Flo Jones."

We exchanged pleasantries. She went on her way, and we entered the building.

Ferguson went off to the left to check his mailbox. It was full mostly of flyers of one sort or another. There was a news magazine. And there were a couple of letters.

"I really should cancel this magazine; but I have been receiving it for so long, I just haven't bothered."

Exiting the elevator on the third floor, we walked down a long, not terribly well-lit corridor.

"Flo is the concierge . . . she runs the place. If she leaves, nothing in the building will work properly."

His apartment was on the left. He found his key and opened his door into a large room filled with overly large antique furniture. Sunshine lit the room.

He immediately went to the sofa under the window and sat down. Actually, he collapsed into the seat.

"I guess you should take it easy."

He had closed his eyes as if fighting pain.

"That was a bit more than I had thought."

"Are you still hungry?'

"Maybe some soup."

The kitchen was off to the right. I looked in the cupboards above the stove to see what was there.

I found two cans: pea soup and tomato bisque. I brought them both out to show him.

"Either one of these do?"

Through half-closed eyes he motioned to the tomato. I went back into the kitchen, found a saucepan, and heated the soup.

I found a bowl. "Do you want to sit at your dining table?"

"No. Go into the den—there is a small table you can set by the sofa so I do not have to move."

I placed the bowl on the table and he manoeuvred himself so that he could eat the soup.

He finished rather quickly. He leaned back on the couch; he had no energy.

"I want to go over your medicine again. I think there is something you are supposed to take now."

He was asleep. I found a blanket to cover him, even though the house was quite warm.

I reviewed the medications and, in as neat a script as I could muster, I printed out the directions. He also was supposed to go back to the hospital at seven thirty in the morning to the Diabetic Clinic.

There was a knock at the door. Flo was standing there with a pile of newspapers in her arms.

"What happened to him?"

"He took a bad fall."

She grunted. "Happens a lot around here. We have a lot of older tenants. Listen . . . if you wish, Doris could come mind him."

"Doris?"

"She is a caregiver who has worked with people in here on and off over the years."

"I am okay today, but for tomorrow afternoon and night, I might call Doris."

"I will be back with her phone number later."

The phone rang. I answered it.

"Hello, I am looking for Reverend Ferguson."

"My name is Glasheen, Terry Glasheen, and you have found him. And you are?"

"I'm Carol Simpson, executive director of Le Manoir, where Reg volunteers his services. How is he? He is home, right?"

"He is here and he is taking a nap. When he gets up, I will have him call you."

"That would be wonderful, thank you."

I sat down with the newspapers and started to go through them. I put them in order, latest to earliest.

Ferguson stirred. He awoke and looked around, putting on his glasses.

"Nice to be home."

"You need to take your pills."

"Yes, sir."

I went into the kitchen to see if he had any crackers to take his medication with. I found a package that had not been closed properly; they would do. I set him up at the small dining table against the wall halfway down the room.

"Now we are going to have Pill 101."

He grunted and moved slowly to the chair facing his front door, his back to the window.

I found some water in the refrigerator.

"Let's go. Eat a cracker. This pill goes with food."

And so it went.

"Tomorrow you have to go to the clinic."

He looked up at me. "I feel like shit."

"Do you want to lie down in your bedroom?"

"The couch is good enough."

"Do you want to change your clothes?"

He gave me a pained look.

"I will help."

He was looking drowsy. I walked him back to the couch. I lifted his legs up and covered him with the blanket. I put his glasses safely on the table. I sat in the chair next to the sofa and started to go through the newspapers again. I phoned the diner, and they agreed to send me a tuna sandwich and a small salad.

There was a knock at the door. The concierge was standing there, and she handed me a note with some names and phone numbers.

"In case Doris is not available, I consulted some of the *yentas* around here to get some more names. You know what a *yenta* is?"

"I do," I said with a smile. "Sometimes *yentas* are useful."

She smiled and left.

I was about to close the door when the delivery fellow showed up with lunch. I paid and he left. This caretaker business was labour-intensive.

I sat at the table looking out toward the street. I had a magnificent view of the top of the ancient apartment building on the other side. I started looking through the Saturday paper. There was a little sidebar item that caught my attention: "Fire at adult movie theatre, arson suspected."

Underneath the headline: "Fire officials are calling the origin of the blaze suspicious. The theatre on the Main remains closed."

There were no other details. The meeting with Martin Gold on Wednesday was going to have a very interesting agenda.

Ferguson stirred. "What time is it?"

"Three in the afternoon. You have a date? By the way, a woman named Simpson called to find out about you. Regards."

"She runs the old age home I spend time at. She does a masterful job. How long are you staying around here? And thanks for your help."

"I will stay until tomorrow afternoon. I am going to arrange for someone to stay with you for the rest of the week."

"I won't fight you on that. I really resent this. All I want to do is sleep. My phone book is around here, somewhere. I have a special number for the nursing service at the local health centre."

"And that would likely be?"

"Around, in the den. It's green."

"I found it. And in fact, it is red."

"Whatever. Where are my glasses?"

I had put them safely out of harm's way on the dining table. He started looking through the book. "I cannot remember how I listed it."

I took the book and started looking under "N" for "nurse." No luck.

Health Centre—*nyet*.

"Look up 'Yolande.'"

"Before I do that, you need to drink and eat something."

There was a bagel in the freezer and some frozen orange juice, which I quickly organized for him.

He drank the juice and ate the toasted bagel *au nature*. "You make a good caregiver."

I phoned Yolande. There was no answer, so I left a slightly convoluted message. A few minutes later, she called back.

"What happened to my dear Reverend Ferguson?"

"He took a fall a few days ago and was kept at the General for observation and tests."

"They no doubt found something, right?"

"Yes, his pre-diabetes is now full-blown. His head still hurts from the fall. And his blood pressure, we hope, is now under control."

"I have a list of caregivers, but, unfortunately, I have no one available on such short notice."

"That much demand."

"When does he go to the clinic?"

"Tomorrow morning."

"Call me if there is a problem. Maybe I can do something; no promises. And yes, demand is high and supply is low. By the way, wish him well. He is a good man."

She rang off and I made a note of her number. I walked Ferguson back to the couch.

"Bring me today's paper if you have it handy. I have lost total touch with the world."

Within a few minutes, he was sleeping sitting up. I took off his glasses again and put them on the table.

After removing the paper from his hands and gathering the rest of it off the floor, I sat back on the chair to the right of the couch. I, too, fell asleep sitting up.

The ringing phone woke both of us. I went into the den and took the phone and the phone table back to the chair.

"Hello, Ferguson residence."

There was a pause.

"What are you doing there?"

It was Martha.

"Playing nursemaid."

"How noble. You received the phone call from the hospital so Ferguson could be released. And since you had nothing better to do on Rosh Hashanah, you obliged."

"Correct."

"How is he feeling?"

"You can ask him yourself."

I handed the phone and glasses to Ferguson.

"Afternoon, ma'am. Like shit. And all I want to do is sleep . . . I go to the clinic tomorrow at the crack of dawn . . . I guess Glasheen will go with me but I haven't asked him yet, and he has not volunteered."

He gave the phone back to me.

"Must be nice to be retired. You going to sleep there tonight?"

"I guess so. I really had not thought about it."

"He needs a caregiver for a few days. Not you."

"We have names but no actual person yet."

"Good start. I will come over with food around six, and perhaps we can sort this out together."

"Fine with me. Reg, okay if Martha comes over with food and to spread cheer?"

"Food, yes. Cheer? That's subjective."

"See you, then."

I sat back down.

"You anywhere near solving any of the various mysteries that you and your partner are involved in?"

"That is a great question, and the answer is also subjective."

He laughed. Good sign.

"You and Orenstein have a difference of opinion."

"In a manner of speaking. He feels that all our various mysteries will solve themselves in due course."

"And you, of course, do not see how that is possible."

"Something like that."

"I agree with Orenstein."

"Both of you have a kind of faith that obviously I lack."

"Perhaps. What are you going to do about Molly?"

"I do not know."

"You realize that situation will sort itself out, too."

"I would like to know what Molly wants. She could be homesick and simply wants to go back to her village. That is what I want to attend to tomorrow afternoon."

"I assume you do not have a plan."

"I assume I have one that I have as yet not articulated."

"How is that different than Orenstein?"

"You are a perceptive old bastard."

"At your service."

There was a pause in the conversation. His energy was noticeably better. I checked my watch.

"Where is your blood pressure monitor?"

He made a face. "Somewhere around here. I think on top of the closet in the den. I have not used the thing in a while."

I found the box and brought it out to the table.

"Come on over here. You have to do this." He sat down, and I put the cuff over his right arm. "Wait a moment or two to get yourself relaxed."

"Maybe I should think of green garbage bags."

"Great idea."

He took a reading. The results were not great.

"Okay, let us wait and do the other arm."

We waited a few minutes and tried again. The results were more encouraging. I found some paper and made a note of the times and the results.

"We will do this again in a few hours."

He ambled back to the sofa. "You know, my wife and I fostered two Native children. One was a success and the other was not."

"How so?"

"Thomas finished high school, learned a trade, went back to his community, and became a model citizen."

"And the second?"

"Tore us up. He ended up in prison and died there under mysterious circumstances. We never did get a straight story."

"It affected you."

"It affected us both terribly. We experienced so much joy with Thomas that we took a chance with Jay. We blame ourselves, as one does. But really, he was very self-destructive."

Martha called. "I am going to be later than six. Is that okay?"

"Reg, Martha is going to be later than six."

"Fine with me. I have nothing to do but heal."

"Okay with us."

I looked at Ferguson. "In the grand scheme of things, fifty percent is not bad."

"It still haunts, and I know that my late wife took those feelings of failure to her grave."

"What was her name?"

"My wife? Everyone called her Betty. Her name was Beatrice."

"She was an asset to you in your work?"

He nodded. "Could we change the subject?"

"Do you want to call the woman who runs the old-age home?"

"Oh, yeah, Simpson. Carol is her name."

I placed the phone closer to where he was sitting. He dialed the number and found out she was busy. He left a message for her to call back.

"Maybe she has someone who can come in to give you a hand?"

"I had the same thought. They had to reduce staff; I am sure one of those folks would be interested in helping out an old diabetic man of the cloth."

"How dramatic."

He sat back on the sofa and struck a pose.

Martha called again. "I forgot that the grocery store on Greene was under construction and still is not open."

"Come over; we will order in."

She rang off.

"You have struck a pose. What is on your mind?"

"You and Molly. You and Martha."

"They should switch roles?"

"Great idea. You take in Martha and Molly runs the Social Work Department."

We chuckled.

The buzzer rang from downstairs. I was instructed on how to use the phone to let Martha in. The doorbell rang.

"Door's open," we said in unison.

"And how is the odd couple?"

"Hungry."

"Let's order dinner. BBQ chicken okay?"

"Fine."

I found one of those small local phone books and called. "Everyone but Reg want frites?"

"Damned diet."

"Sure, sure, and coleslaw," Martha chimed in.

I finished the order and rang off. The food was going to be delivered "within thirty minutes."

There was a message on the line. Carol Simpson had called and gave her cellphone number to respond back. I gave the phone to Ferguson. "Your girlfriend called back."

I gave him the number, and he called. "I am fine for someone with diabetes, a concussion, and high blood pressure. I have two guests here and since I never entertain, I do not know what to do with them. They seem to be managing on their own, bless them. And how are you? Is the place getting along without me? Please say no; my ego needs a boost."

He took a breath. "You are very kind. Look, my nurse here wants to talk to you."

I took the receiver. "Glasheen here, nice to meet you on the phone."

There was a giggle on the other end. "Likewise, and how does nursing suit you?"

"So far, so good. Reg here is going to need someone to be with him over the next few days. Would you know someone who could give us a hand?"

"This is not an inexpensive request. The short answer is yes. A couple of our former nurses have a short-term care business."

She gave me their names and a phone number. "And more importantly, how is he?"

"He seems a lot better. And after that oration about his situation, he is positively cured."

"Tell him to behave himself so he can come back to us soon. We miss him around here."

"Will do. Thank you." Ferguson had sunk back into the couch. "You are missed at the home. They want you back soon."

"At the moment, that feels very far away. I am hungry . . . where is my *frite*-less supper?"

"Martha, do you have anything to add to the discussion about who might tend to Reg, here?"

"The simple thing would be to call the woman the concierge recommended."

I took the phone and called Doris. She answered on the first ring.

"My name is Glasheen. I got your name from Flo Jones."

"And how is she? I have not been in her building in a while. What's up?"

"Well, Reverend Ferguson needs some help for the next little while. He took a fall and his diabetes has been acting up."

"When would you need me?"

"Starting tomorrow afternoon and continuing for the next week or so. Do you feel comfortable making sure he can take his insulin correctly?"

"Taking insulin these days is really simple. When do you go to the clinic?"

"Tomorrow morning. So are you free?"

"For the next week, yes. I am busy after that with a previous engagement."

"How much do you charge?"

She told me her rate. I blocked off the mouthpiece and told Ferguson the rate. "What does that sound like?"

"Nice, reasonable. Hire her."

"I think you need to do this yourself."

"I am Reg Ferguson. These do-gooders here think I need a babysitter."

He started to smile, "Well, my dear, if you can start tomorrow, that would be fine. It will be only for a week, so perhaps we can get along."

He gave me back the phone. "So that's settled, then?"

"You call me when you are back in the apartment. The timekeeping at the clinic is not exact."

"Will do. And thank you."

Martha looked at Ferguson. "What did she say to you?"

"I could not afford not to hire her, or words to that effect."

The buzzer rang. Our food had arrived.

The delivery man came to the door with a very large bag. Martha and I paid and tipped him.

We went into the kitchen to organize the meal. I turned to her. "Thanks for coming over. I want to see you tomorrow afternoon in your office."

She looked at me. "Molly?"

"Molly."

Reg was already sitting at the table. I guess we were all pretty hungry. Not much was said as we devoured the very tasty meal.

"Napkins?"

Reg thought for a moment. "Not sure where they are. Have some good cloth ones in the breakfront over there."

"What a waste. Paper towel okay?"

"Any port in a storm," Martha said, laughing.

Ferguson excused himself to go to the loo.

"You okay to do that by yourself?"

"I certainly hope so; I have been doing it for years."

I turned to Martha. "What were you and Martin Gold whispering about at dinner last night?"

"We were eviscerating the board of the hospital."

"How cruel."

"Yes, but what fun."

There was a knock at the door.

"Door's open."

Flo looked in. "Everything all right?"

"We are managing nicely."

"You want me to stay with him tonight?"

"Not necessary. He has a very early appointment at the General tomorrow. I'll stay with him."

"Did you get ahold of Doris?"

"Yes, and she is available for a week, which is perfect. Thank you for suggesting her."

"You know the Reverend is a good man. His wife, Betty, was also a good person, I know he misses her terribly. If you need anything, call."

"Thank you again."

Reg came back into the room and sat on the couch.

"Evening, Flo. Checking up on me?"

"What's it to ya?"

She closed the door and left.

"Reg, pill time."

"Crap."

"Nice talk for a man of the cloth."

He slouched back to the table. In between the dishes, which had not been cleared, we went through the pill ceremony. I tried to turn it into a game. "We have zee white pill. We have zee orange pill."

He took the nonsense with humour.

Martha offered to drive me to my house to pick up a change of clothes. "Or I will stay here and you drive my car to pick up your stuff."

"Thanks, but I think I will just go to the pharmacy to pick up some toiletries. What time do they close? Anybody know?"

She whipped out her tablet and glided her fingers over it. "Eight."

"I had better get going."

Ferguson had returned to the couch.

Martha started to clear the dishes from the table.

From the kitchen, she called out, "Please buy some dishwashing soap."

"Yes, dear."

"Knock it off."

From the sofa came a giggle.

"Ferguson, you knock it off, too."

I put on my ball cap. "Anything else?"

There was no response, so I left.

The evening was mild. The diner was closing up. I glanced into the coffee shop to see that it was open and empty. Picking up my pace, I reached the drugstore just before eight.

I quickly picked some shaving cream, a throw-away razor, a toothbrush, and travel-sized toothpaste. Then over to the last aisle to find the dishwashing soap. Would the no-name brand do? I chose a name brand for two dollars more. Nothing but the best.

On Greene, it was now fully dark. Someone called out from the curb across the street, "Terry, good evening."

It was Sarah Lazarus. I crossed to meet her. "Out for some air?"

"No, I am walking home from yet another New Year's do."

"Listen, I would love to chat, but I have to get back to tending a sick friend."

"Let's lunch—maybe Wednesday, somewhere around here."

"I have a meeting at noon. Is two too late?"

"No, that's perfect. Give me your coordinates and we will work out where and all that."

I told her my email address. I had yet to master typing with my thumbs.

She repeated it back and away she went.

I re-crossed the street to head back to the apartment. The street was empty and there was a slight chill in the air. I passed one dog walker with two small, white dogs. She was talking to one of them as though to a child, "Mind your manners and no barking." The animal immediately started to yap. Well trained.

Rounding the corner to the little street, I saw the concierge standing outside talking to a portly, middle-aged man. She turned when she saw me.

"How is the patient?"

"Sleeping, mostly. He really had a nasty fall."

The fellow chimed in, "Tell Reg that Will wishes him well."

"Yes, of course, and thank you."

The apartment door was open. Martha was sitting in the chair next to the sofa reading the newspaper. Ferguson was stretched out, his eyes closed with his glasses still on.

Martha looked up over her reading glasses. "Did you meet someone?"

"Yes—Sarah."

"Oh, really, I was wondering why you were taking so long. What did she have to say?"

"We are going to have lunch on Wednesday."

"Boy, oh boy, she moves fast."

"Here is the detergent."

"Did you have to get the expensive brand? The no-name would have done."

"Not for this crowd. I'll finish in the kitchen and then Reg, here, has to take some more pills."

"I need to leave soon."

In the kitchen, what was left of the chicken had been neatly put in the fridge. The dishes were neatly stacked in the sink. In short order, the clean dishes were in the drainer.

"Reg, Reg, pill time."

"I am not deaf yet."

He swung his legs to the floor and stood a bit unsteadily.

"Dizzy?"

I walked him over to the table. I had organized the pills in a sewing box which I had found in the cupboard in the den. On top, I had put the list of meds and the times they were to be taken.

"I am turning into a dope fiend."

"I want you to relax so we can take your pressure."

"I am trying hard to obey my very demanding nurse."

Martha laughed.

"Now sit up straight, put your feet flat on the floor, and think wonderful, relaxing thoughts."

"I am thinking of steak and kidney pie, washed down with a very good European beer."

He was able to manipulate the machine himself, and the reading was not bad. He wrote down the result on the sheet I had started. Next, he counted out his pills and took them all at once with a very small sip of water.

"Well, folks, it has been a scintillating evening."

Reg, not looking up, said, "Glad we could oblige."

"I am sure the two of you will cope with the sleeping arrangements. Call me tomorrow after the appointment to keep me abreast of the results."

She leaned down to kiss Reg on the top of his head.

She came over to me, put out her hand, which I took in mine, and reached up to kiss me on both cheeks. Her hand lingered. "If I ever take ill, I want you as my caretaker."

"Thanks. You are not planning anything, are you? I am kind of booked at the moment."

I saw her to the door, which was still partly open. She let go of my hand and walked out. I gently closed the door behind her. Reg, who had not moved from the table, made a clearing sound in his throat, but did not say anything.

"I want you to take your pressure again." It was even better this time.

"Are you going to have me doing this all night?"

"If you wish."

"I do not."

He moved back to the couch. I went to sit in the recliner next to where he was.

"You know, several years ago, she had a relationship with a young doctor, a surgeon. He was an arrogant, narcissistic prick and he treated her, I thought, abysmally. I do not know what happened, exactly; but I think they lived together.

"It was around the time my wife was sick. The fellow got a job in the States; he was a real go-getter. And their relationship ended, or maybe it ended before he left town. He was mean and he was self-centred. He was going to revolutionize surgery. She never talks about it. I suspect it plays a role in her life, still."

"Was this about ten years ago?"

"Around. Yes, that is about right. Why?"

"Something she said to me last night."

"Changing the subject, I am going to sleep on the sofa, here. You can have the bed in the bedroom."

I went to test the bed. Too soft. I needed a slab.

"If it is all the same to you, I will sleep on the recliner here."

"Suit yourself."

"I will try not to snore too loudly."

"Likewise. Come to think of it, maybe fifteen years ago."

"What?"

"Martha's boyfriend. I still had my church and I only occasionally came to the hospital."

"How did you meet her?"

"We both had an interest in the same child. She was the daughter of one of my congregants. A single mother. Back then, she would have been checked out. Martha wanted some background information. We hit it off.

"You know, she spent some time in Israel. And I think she would have stayed there if she could have. Anyway, the young girl did not make it. Very sad. Very tragic.

"The mother went through a very bad patch. But over time, she rallied. Her family owned a business and she became very involved in running it. I have lost touch with her."

"You need to take your last pill of the day." I went to get some water.

"Bah, humbug."

"You will get the hang of it."

"This is not something I want to get the hang of."

"Nobody does. But this is the way it is."

"It's not written anywhere that I have to like this."

"Correct. Some of the medication is related to the concussion, which you will not have to take much longer."

"But the other stuff and the insulin tomorrow."

"Why not you cross that bridge when you get to it?"

"I am not unhappy you are here, my mood notwithstanding."

"All part of the service."

"Lucky for me Orenstein is tied up with his religious duties."

"Funny how this worked out. Here I was wondering how I would spend these two days. I had some reading planned. I was going to study up on some Montreal artists."

"Like who?"

"An Israeli artist who has lived here for many years."

"Oh, him. Chaki. He lives around the corner. Some of his works appear in the galleries on Greene Avenue from time to time."

"There was a poster in the washroom last night dating from the Second World War."

"The VD one?"

"You know it?"

"Sure, Mayerovitch, who did it, also lived 'round here. He was a character for sure; very much a man about town: architect, painter, photographer, writer, *bon vivant*. He lived to a ripe old age and was active until the end."

"I was also going to research an item I heard on the radio concerning women participating in religious rituals."

"As long as they do not offend the community?"

"Is there anything you do not know?"

"How to look after myself, obviously."

"I have faith in you."

"Speaking of faith, what about yours?"

"Evolving."

"Evolving? I am surprised you have resorted to a cliché."

"Look, for many years I was that. Now I am this. I am not entirely sure what this is. I have no schedule. For the first time in thirty years, my time is not regulated by the calendar. I answer only to myself."

"Is that playing a role in your decision around Molly?"

"Yes. I have no doubt I can do it. But is it really what I want to do?"

"You know she cannot go back to her village. No good will come of that. Are you thinking of giving it a shot?"

"There is a part of me that wants the challenge. Another part of me does not want my life circumscribed by a young teenager."

"You realize that becoming a foster parent involves a vetting process, which could take many months. It is not automatic. They are going to check you out. You will need to attend information sessions where you will hear people give testimonials about their experiences. Do you have the patience for all that?"

"I guess the real question I have is what does Molly want? And am I the best alternative—not am I the best alternative of no other alternatives. Maybe she is homesick and wants to go back to her village, even though she could be assaulted again. I wonder what it is like to belong nowhere."

"Oh, my. You have raised a very stark issue. Ideally, she should have been dealt with locally. Except that someone is lurking around. I am actually surprised that this person has not been found out. But then, as you say, there is the issue of her disorder."

"I do not want to get into the mindset that it is only for a few years, until she is eighteen, for example. For me, it would be a forever thing."

"Are you having bonding issues?"

"What?"

"Look. You have spent your adult life alone. You went about your duties, and I am sure you did an admirable job. And I am sure you bonded with Jesus, and that bonding took different forms as time went on. But here you are faced with a different dilemma. Someone may physically be present in your life. Someone who will be dependent on your decisions, on your guidance.

"You have never had that before. You have never been in that position before."

"Yes, and would I do this just for the sake of a new experience, or would it make a meaningful difference in someone else's life? And am I at this stage capable of that kind of intimacy?"

"You have been thinking about this."

"Obsessively."

"I see where you have come to letting nature take its course."

"And yet there is a decision to be made, which I do not think will happen tonight."

"Never can tell."

"Time to wash up and try to get some sleep. Who is first in the washroom?"

"I am second."

CHAPTER TWENTY-ONE

We both slept through the night. The recliner was remarkably comfortable. I got up at five thirty. It was still dark. The paper had been delivered. I stood in the kitchen reading it, standing next to the sink where there was a separate light.

There was movement from the living room. Reg was sitting at the table taking his blood pressure.

"Not bad results. I'll take my before-food pills. Could you bring me some water?"

"How are you feeling?"

"Unnerved."

"You seemed calm overnight."

"I had a conversation with Betty!"

"And?"

"The talk was real. It was very much one-way. She wants me to look after myself. She thinks I should move into the Manoir. She looked peaceful and serene and lovely. The experience is still with me."

"And what do you think?"

"That she is right. What was I doing running around chasing after Molly?"

"It made sense then. Now, not so much."

"I guess."

"We should eat and get ready to leave."

He went to wash up and shave.

I stood next to the dining room table reading more of the paper. I mostly looked at the pictures; none of the words were making any sense. There was a picture of religious Jews walking to their synagogue.

"Your turn."

I went to shave. Staring in the mirror, I asked myself the question of the day, "What do I do with Molly?" No answer came.

"Is the diner open yet?"

"No, but the coffee bar across from the diner is."

"Can I get a bagel?"

"Yes, in addition to quite good coffee."

"You up for that?"

"Bring me something back. I still need to take my meds and I do not want to do it in public."

"Coffee?"

"Tea. I have some bags here. Don't bother with that."

First light in the eastern sky—it was really getting light later these days. The coffee bar had inviting light and the rich smell of freshly made coffee. I gave my order, paid, and was halfway out the door.

Coming in was Elyse. She was dressed in a very striking dark-blue sweatsuit ensemble with perfectly white sneakers. "My walking attire. I do it every day, Rosh Hashanah or not. How is Reverend Ferguson? I heard about him from Martha."

"Pretty well, considering. We are going to the clinic this morning. Boy, the jungle telegraph is well-oiled around here."

"Top-flight. Now if you will excuse me, I came in here to use the loo. Speak soon."

Returning to the apartment, I passed a few joggers. The traffic on Sherbrooke Street was picking up. It was virtually daylight and a tinge warmer.

Ferguson was sitting at the dining table, staring at his medications.

"Problem?"

"I misplaced my glasses, and I cannot read the labels. I cannot see well enough to find them."

I put down my package and went on a hunt. I looked in the bathroom, the kitchenette, and, finally, under the cushions on the sofa. " *Voilà!* Here they are. A little bent, but I can straighten them, I think. Here. Try that."

"Thank you, my good man. That's better. Now can you bring me those soggy crackers from the kitchen cupboard? I will get started here. And some of that juice."

"We should leave here around seven. Cab?"

"Yes, the bus is complicated. We would have to transfer. Not in the mood."

He took his meds. He was getting the hang of it. One of the many by-products of old age: more medications. My cell phone rang; it was Martha. "What time are you coming to see me today?"

"Afternoon, probably around two. Why?"

"Call first, please."

"Sure."

I had forgotten my phone charger, the power indicator notwithstanding. I took some sips of coffee and went to toast the bagels. There was some margarine in the fridge; the date was more or less current.

"No butter?"

"Hate the stuff."

I went to sit beside him at the table.

"No jam."

"Skip it."

"Do you have a number for a cab?"

"Don't need one."

"Is there a grocery store around here?"

"Two. I prefer the one on Victoria. I guess I should stock up."

"After your appointment, we will go there."

"Is that going to interfere with your afternoon plans?"

"Not too much. And besides, it has to be done."

While I washed the dishes, he got himself ready to leave.

I washed up and patted down my hair with damp hands.

Taking the paper, we made our way to the corner of Sherbrooke Street. A cab appeared immediately.

"Which entrance do you want?"

"Cedar."

"You do have your Medicare card?"

"And my hospital card."

We went up Mountain Avenue past some large homes. All were different and all interesting. Most were pre-Second World War, and some pre-First World War. Some were modern, but they were in the minority. The driver turned east at the top of the hill and continued past more elaborate mansions. We reached Cedar, and he turned right. There was a large sign advertising "luxury" condominiums for sale. There did not appear to be any building.

Ferguson saw me looking. "Through the trees, there is a building which was a college and now is being converted to apartments."

"Oh, yes, yes. The building was owned by the Congregation of Notre-Dame. It started as a women's college. It became coed when the junior college system was introduced."

"The building has been sold to developers. And the college moved elsewhere and is open to everyone. I hope they do not mess up that old structure."

We reached the front door of the hospital and were told to go to a room down the long corridor.

Ferguson registered at the desk. He was given a sheet and told to go across the hall to get a blood test. He would not have to wait long; his condition gave him priority. He lined up at the door. I waited in the hallway. Before he went into the testing room, I told him I would wait in the clinic.

A few minutes later, he came back with a patch on the inside of his elbow.

"I am surprised I have any blood left; I have given so much lately."

"You know we have to wait for the results; that could take a few hours."

"I fear you are right."

I gave him part of the newspaper. He tucked it under his arm and closed his eyes.

I looked at the headlines. There had been some police raids. Several characters had been arrested with links to organized crime. No names were mentioned.

A woman in a white coat came out from behind the receptionist area. "Mr. Ferguson."

I elbowed Reg. "Here."

We both got up and approached her.

"Which one of you is Ferguson?"

Reg raised his arm.

She smiled.

"His minder, Glasheen."

"Why don't you both come with me? I am the dietician, Claire."

We followed her into a small office that was plastered with pictures of food. On her desk, she had photos of two young children, presumably hers. She also had plastic dishes, *bas relief*, of meat and potatoes, green vegetables, and salad.

"Mr. Ferguson, you need to adjust your diet to better control your condition."

She gave him a sheet that contained a list of foods not to be eaten, or at least eaten in moderation.

"Overall, when you shop for groceries, read labels. Stay away from salt. Try not to eat in restaurants; and if you do, make sure that you avoid certain obvious foods. Commercial soups generally contain a lot of salt. Eat boiled or baked potatoes and small portions of beef. And try to get better-quality fish and chicken. Try to stay away from shellfish. You should eat more fish. If you open a tin of tuna, wash it in a strainer. Cured meats are filled with all kinds of things, so try to moderate eating bacon or ham. Eat salads, but be conscious of commercial dressings. And when it is all said and done, you should consider becoming vegetarian. Do you drink alcohol?"

"On occasion."

"Well, I would advise you to make it very occasional, if at all. Questions?"

Ferguson paused before he responded, "You know, my first response is to be very cynical about all this. I am being pumped full of medication. I hardly ever took a pill until now. I take my blood pressure. I have had the gismo for a few years; it stayed on top of the cupboard. And now, I have to be very conscious of my diet. And that is before I have been trained to take insulin."

She nodded, and broke into a smile. "What was your work?"

"I still am a pastor."

"Now you are going to have to get used to tending to yourself." She laughed at her little joke. "You are married?"

"I live alone."

Looking at me, she said, "Are you going to be around to give him a hand?"

"Not all the time; he has arranged for someone to come in for the next week or so."

"That's good. Here is my card if you have any questions. If you have access to the Internet, there is lots of reading you can do."

We went back out to the waiting area. A few minutes later, another white-coated woman came around looking for Ferguson. She stood in front of him and introduced herself. "I am Geneviève, the social worker. Why don't you come with me?"

I sat reading more of the paper. A few minutes later he came back.

"What was that all about?"

He sat down and looked at me, "She wanted to know if I still had my marbles."

"Do you?"

"I never could remember my postal code. I never write to myself."

"I wonder what is next on the agenda."

"You know, across the street from the Children's Hospital is a library which offers computer courses for adults. I guess it's about time I did that."

"Might be a good idea."

Another white coat appeared at the reception area. "Mr. Ferguson?"

We both got up and walked over. She was wearing a headscarf and leggings.

"My name is Dalia. Follow me please."

We went into an office, which was bare except for a box of medicine on a desk, an unopened box of crackers, another box of alcohol swabs, a yellow container with a flap lid, and a couple of chairs.

She stood in front of us. "Which one of you needs insulin?"

Ferguson started to laugh, "I would love to say my friend, here, but it's me."

"Well then let's get to it. This requires your complete concentration."

"I am all ears."

"I want you to go wash your hands. The washroom is down the hall on the left."

He did as he was told. She waited until he came back.

She opened the box and out came a pen, a vacuum package of cartridges, and a package of very small needles, also vacuum-packed.

She took a cartridge out of the package and held it up. "This is the insulin, which you will inject once a day in the evening." She gave him the cartridge. "Hold that in your hand. Get the feel of that as well."

She had a pen in her hand. "Now, I am going to review this again. So watch me—here."

She went over the parts of the thing and what their uses were.

She was very patient, and she had a very assured tone. There was lots of information to take in.

She explained the dosage and how to dial it up, how to install the cartridge, when to discard the cartridge, how to install the needle, and how to dispose of the needle properly.

She went over the last stuff, more slowly this time.

She sent him out to wash his hands again.

"Well, you are almost ready to inject yourself," she said brightly when he came back.

Ferguson was sweating. She handed him a wipe, and when he finished that, she handed him some crackers. "Eat these, please. And you should always carry something to eat just in case."

Finally, the pen was primed and ready to deliver the dosage required. Ferguson had dropped his pants so as to inject himself in the thigh. Very slowly, she instructed him on exactly what to do.

When he had finished, she told him to sit still for a moment. He pulled up his drawers and was told how to finish off the injection process.

"Give yourself a few minutes to collect yourself."

He did as he was told.

"Now can I leap tall buildings?"

"If you wish. You must remember to put the unused cartridges in the refrigerator. Not the freezer. And if anything does not look right, it probably isn't, so throw it out. If I am off duty, call the helpline if you are unsure of any part of the process or the equipment. I am going to give you a packet of information, including the written instructions on how to administer the insulin.

"Here is my card. For the next while, if you have any problems, call me. And I shall be calling you regularly to see how you are doing.

"Go wait in the waiting area. If you feel faint or anything like that, tell the receptionist immediately."

"Thank you," we both said together.

Ferguson went into the washroom, and when he came back, he sat heavily in the chair.

"Whew."

"Indeed. I was wondering why they did not go through this with you last week when you were here. I think I understand. You were in no condition to absorb all that information."

He grunted. He was sitting with his eyes closed. "That was tough. I am glad it is over."

The waiting room was filling up. I wondered how long we would have to wait to see the doctor. How long does it take to produce blood results?

"Mr. Ferguson?" A tall white-coated gentleman appeared. We had both dozed off.

He was holding Ferguson's file.

"I am Dr. Matthews."

Ferguson shook his hand. "This is my friend Glasheen, who has been instrumental in keeping me on the straight and narrow for the last couple of days."

Matthews smiled. "High praise. Now just follow me over here."

We went into a slightly larger office than the dietitian's. The desk was bare. No files piled up. Behind the desk was a credenza that contained a laptop computer.

We sat in the two chairs in front of the desk.

"Your blood results are pretty consistent. What that means is we are going to continue your medication as is. You had Insulin 101 this morning, correct?"

We both nodded.

"I strongly suggest that you read the instructions that come with the medication. And any questions you might have will be answered by Dalia. If she is not available, there is a hotline you can call. Of course, as a last resort, there is Emergency. How is your head?"

Ferguson responded by saying that his headaches were pretty much gone.

"Good. So as not to drag you back here, I want to send you to Neurology for them to take a look at you. They are expecting you; you will not have to wait long. You will come back here next week. Any questions?"

"Probably, but I will save them up for the next time. And thank you."

Ferguson, for the first time all morning, did not display any anxiety.

"Where is Neurology?"

"Third floor of Langston Hall."

"Thank you, again."

CHAPTER TWENTY-TWO

On the way to Neurology, we bought coffee from a kiosk in the main foyer, which by now was crowded with people. We walked down a long corridor past the chapel. Ferguson went in for a minute. I stood outside. He re-emerged. "I prefer the one at the Children's."

We continued our trek. Turning left at the end of the corridor, we found volunteers selling all kinds of knick-knacks. I spotted a package of diabetic socks. There was a sign above the table: "Cash Only." Ferguson reached into his pocket and paid the guy with a twenty. He got change.

To the left was a bank of elevators with people waiting. One of the four elevators was working.

"Want to take the stairs? It's three flights down."

"I will wait here." And wait we did.

Finally, a car came, and we found the department. Ferguson went to the receptionist to register. We sat down in a waiting area; luckily there were not many others around us.

A few minutes later, a young woman came out. "Mr. Ferguson." We went over to her. "Which one of you is Ferguson?"

"Guilty."

"And you?"

"Terry Glasheen, friend."

"I am Dr. Marinelli; please follow me."

We went into an examining room close by. Her badge said Carmen Marinelli, Resident. She asked Ferguson many, many questions. At this point, I knew his chart by heart and could have answered for him. I refrained. She had the recent blood results and read the brain scan report. Eventually, she said, "How do you feel?'

Ferguson paused a moment. He was deciding whether to be flip or serious. I was getting to know the drill.

"Well, I mostly want to go home for a nap."

She smiled. "You had the diabetic clinic earlier?"

"Yes, and then I was told to come here: like an assembly line."

"You need to give yourself permission to relax, to be a patient. For some people that is really difficult. You are still active?"

"It is difficult, and I am still active."

"Please wait here until I get back. I have to confer with my senior."

She came back in short order. "When are you next at the diabetic clinic?"

"Next week."

"Good, you will come see us at the same time. Speak to the receptionist before you leave."

Ferguson made the appointment for two hours after the diabetic clinic. I thought he was being safe with the timing.

Back up to the sixth floor. The sale was in full swing. I bought some gloves for winter.

We went out the door in front of us. We were left of the main entrance. And to our left was the shell of a building, incomplete. I was sure there was a story about that.

Ferguson took several deep breaths. "I just want to stand out here for a few minutes."

A cab came by. "Are you ready?"

"Just a few more minutes."

I shooed the cab away.

I continued to look at the construction site next to us. A fellow walked by, saw me looking, and began a dissertation about the structure. He ended with, "And they refused to allow the hospital to take it over to be used as a research facility." With that, he disappeared into the hospital.

"You know anything about that?" I asked Ferguson.

"What?"

"Using that building for research."

"Someone has to finish it first."

"Ah, there's the rub."

"*Oui.*"

Another cab appeared. "Ready now?"

We got in.

"Grocery store on the corner of Victoria and Sherbrooke, please," Ferguson announced.

"Are you sure?"

"Makes the most sense; another half-hour is not going to be a big difference." He expertly went through the aisles; he was familiar with the layout of the place.

And he did read labels, replacing many canned goods on the shelves. His focus was on fresh fish, canned fish, and some chicken. No red meat. There were fresh fruit and vegetables. He found lightly salted potato chips. "My one indulgence."

Several shoppers stopped to say hello. Some looked as if they would like to chat longer. He very nicely told them that he would be in touch. I went outside to phone Doris, who answered on the first ring. She would meet us at the apartment.

He came out with his basket and told the car order guy that we were waiting for a cab, which came immediately. We loaded the cab, and off we went.

A tall, thin Black woman was talking to Flo in front of the apartment building. Ferguson and I alighted from the cab, gathered the shopping bags, and were introduced to Doris.

Up to the apartment we went. I put away the groceries while Doris and Reg became acquainted. When I joined them in the living room, they were reviewing the instructions for the insulin.

"You know that in short order you will be giving yourself the dose without even thinking about it."

He looked at her over his glasses, "I do not share your optimism."

She burst out laughing. "Lighten up!"

We all started to laugh.

My cell phone rang; it was Martha.

"What's up over there?"

"Come on over and join the party."

"Wish I could; I am tied up. I cannot see you until at least four o'clock."

"Hmm."

"What does that mean?"

"That means I am thinking."

"Why don't you walk over here, take my car, go home, change your clothes, and then come back for four?"

"Nice offer. I think I will stay here, help Doris and Ferguson get to know each other, and see that his afternoon meds are taken care of."

"Suit yourself. See you later."

"Lunch, anyone?" Ferguson asked.

Doris and I went into the kitchen. We managed to perform a ballet in the small space to organize something to eat. Ferguson took his blood pressure. He did not share his results.

We sat around the table and ate ravenously. Doris got up to make tea. "Where are the tea bags? Never mind. Found them."

"Nap time," Reg announced as he went to the couch.

We cleared the table, and Doris did the dishes. I dried them and put them away. When she finished, she did an inventory of the cupboards to see where things were. She opened the fridge and moved some things around.

The phone rang. It was Dalia, the diabetes nurse, wanting to know if everything was all right. I assured her that everything was fine.

Doris and I sat at the table to drink tea together. "I am not usually a tea drinker," I said.

"Shame. It's good for you. Much more civilized than coffee."

From the couch, Ferguson spoke up, "But we all know how uncivilized Glasheen is."

I drank the tea. It was not bad, really. But it was not coffee.

She cleared the table, and I went to the chair beside the sofa. I looked through the paper at the want ads. I scanned houses for sale in my area. The prices were in my favour, but at the same time, I then had to buy something. Not a good trade.

Next, I looked at apartment rentals downtown, assuming I received a decent price for my place. At first blush, it seemed cheaper to do nothing.

Doris was sitting at the table doing word games in a book.

"How late are you going to stay tonight?"

She thought for a moment. "I will make him his supper and see that he is settled and then leave."

"And tomorrow?"

"I will come in before lunch and stay until after dinner and his shot. I will do some laundry and encourage him to go out for a walk."

"Maybe when I leave later, we can all go for a walk together, and I will continue on to the Hospital."

"Sounds good to me. He really needs to get some exercise."

"Agreed."

"He does not need to be encouraged to go for a walk. He needs to be encouraged to get some well-deserved rest. He has been rendered an invalid."

Doris looked over to where he was lying. "My friend the Governor General will send you a get-well card."

"The Queen will be good enough, thank you." Laughs all around.

I started to gather up my stuff. I was antsy to get going. I was missing my own space.

I also was beginning to think in earnest about what the meeting with Martha was going to produce.

"Well, let's get going, shall we?"

It took a few minutes for people to get organized. And then we were off.

CHAPTER TWENTY-THREE

We walked slowly down Greene Avenue. There were more people out this afternoon. The late September sun had warmed up the street. Ferguson stopped to chat with several passersby, all of whom did so with a smile. The man did not have an enemy in the world.

The shoe shop, which had been empty yesterday, was much busier today. The coffee shop likewise had more traffic. The unopened grocery store had signs in the window advertising jobs. "Look, Reg, your store might open soon."

"Too expensive; only come here as a last resort."

"Pardon me."

"Caters to the carriage trade. Not me."

One gentleman took particular delight in meeting Ferguson. He walked with a cane. We were introduced to Ted the Professor.

"Next week, I am giving a book review at the Atwater Library; please come. Wednesday at noon. And then we will do lunch. I will call to remind you."

Ferguson brightened up. "I think I would like that. What's the book?"

"A new book on Trudeau."

"A work of fiction?"

"Hardly, very critical. Please come." He smiled.

"Anybody need to go into the pharmacy?"

Doris piped up, "I do."

We waited outside. "Who's Ted?"

"He was in the Sociology Department at the college we passed this morning. Good man."

Doris rejoined us.

At Sainte-Catherine Street, Reg announced, "This will do. We will cross and go back up the other side."

"I will check in with you tomorrow after my appointments around here."

"Good luck with Martha, and thanks for your help."

"A friend in need . . ."

"Oh, cut it out."

"Doris, you have my phone numbers, just in case."

"I think we will be just fine."

I continued east on Sainte-Catherine Street to Atwater. I passed two Chinese restaurants. Each one advertised lunch specials, and both currently looked empty.

I reached Atwater and turned south toward the hospital. And here was the Atwater Library: a fine old building. But my focus was now on my meeting with Martha.

I went around the building to the René Lévesque entrance. A different receptionist took my name and told me that Martha was delayed and would be along shortly. I decided to go back outside to wait—enough sitting in waiting rooms for one day.

Martha came around shortly. "Greetings. Do you want to walk and talk or sit in my office, which today is sort of neat."

"Given the subject matter, I think in your office."

"Fine." She led the way.

To the receptionist, she said, "No calls. And when you leave, lock the door and put on the night line. I will do the rest."

Her office was remarkably more coherent this time. Her desk was almost devoid of files and memos. We could actually see each other.

"You want to talk about Molly."

"I do."

"And?"

"Ambivalent."

"Ambivalent because?"

"Part of me thinks it is a great idea. And part of me thinks it is nuts."

"It's nuts because . . ."

"I am a sixty-year-old ex-priest who has never parented anyone in his life. Let alone one who comes with a diagnosis."

"And it's a brilliant idea because. . ."

"Of the challenge."

"Of the challenge? Surely there's more to it."

"I know her. I think I have a better chance of making a difference in her life."

Martha nodded. "You realize that there is a vetting process involved. It is not automatic. I can make a recommendation to the Social Service Centre, and they take it from there. The Foster Care Programme is run by a sharp old biddy named Claire Thomas, who should have retired years ago. Your charm will not work on her."

"I would not want any special consideration. But there is more to it than that. I now live in a one-bedroom flat. She would sleep in the bedroom and I on the couch."

"Is there room in your world for her? Can you make space for her?"

"That is the challenge part of it. And does she want that as well? Does she have the capacity to accept the situation?"

"There is usually a trial period. She would come back here for a special school programme, at least initially. And her living situation with you would be evaluated on a weekly and then monthly basis. Assuming, of course, that you are acceptable to the programme."

"How is she doing?"

"She is progressing nicely here. She is getting comfortable. Perhaps too comfortable. One or two of the staff feel that they have created a relationship with her. So her ability to relate to adults is not entirely shot. I spoke to the principal of the school in the village, who assured me that, in his opinion, she should not return there, at least in the short term.

"We tried interviewing the family, but that produced less than positive results. She was close to her grandmother, who has since died. She does not know this."

"And her mutism?"

"She communicates. Just not orally. She has taken to the tablet. And she is very adept at it."

"How much longer does she have here?"

"A few weeks."

"And then?"

"We have our own group homes around the city."

"So the immediate issue for me is to decide whether to apply to become a foster parent. What guarantee is there that I will not be asked to take some other child and not Molly?"

"None. However, this is where I may become useful. I would write a strong recommendation that Molly should be your charge."

"Claire Thomas could refuse."

"Yes."

"On what grounds?"

"The obvious: 'What is a sixty-year-old man doing fostering an eleven-year-old girl?'"

"I will hire a wife."

"That is not funny."

"You realize, of course, that the potential roadblock to this has only added fuel to the challenge."

"Listen, the fact that you have had a prior relationship with her and the fact that you were her priest and the fact that you probably are the only one who may be able to communicate with her in a really meaningful way will play a large role in their decision."

"That is the part of this that makes me feel uncomfortable. All that you say is true. And it may be just as easy as that. But this is one of those things I do not want to rush into."

"You do not want to fail."

"Exactly."

"And neither do we."

"What is the next step?"

"You need to contact the Foster Care Department and arrange an appointment."

"I still need to decide if I want to go through with this."

"It might help if you take the appointment step first. You might even be interviewed by Ms. Thomas."

"You will want a transcript of the conversation?"

"Damn right."

"I am going home now. I miss the place."

"You miss dusting?"

"That and my gourmet cooking."

"What are you making tonight?"

"Arsenic."

"How tasty."

"Beats mac and cheese, which is where I think this is all heading."

"I would give you a lift, but I need to interview that young social worker we met at dinner the other night."

"You may have something for her?"

"Maybe."

"Thank you for your time."

"Is that all?"

"Meaning?"

"Skip it."

"You are impatient with me."

"I guess I am."

There was a knock at the door. I stood to open it. Standing there was the young woman from the other night. "Oh, excuse me."

"I was just leaving."

I turned to Martha. "I would like to continue this conversation another time."

"Hopefully sooner than later."

I nodded and went out the door. The young woman went in and closed the door behind her.

CHAPTER TWENTY-FOUR

I walked through the park across the street from the hospital. Many of the people from the last time I walked through were still sitting. Those picnic tables must have been reserved.

The sun was setting, and the temperature was dropping. I wanted to walk a few blocks to clear my head. Another intense conversation with Martha. She had a way of wedging herself into my thought process.

A guy stopped me to ask for a cigarette. "I do not smoke, my friend." He shuffled off. I just kept walking. I had stopped thinking. Before long, I found myself at Saint-Laurent Boulevard.

A bus was waiting at the corner. I gave it a pass. I started up toward Sherbrooke.

A young woman walked by to ask if I wanted to go out. She was wearing a leather jacket with a blouse, top buttons undone. "Not this evening, thank you." She quickly moved off.

I passed the electronic stores, which were still offering fabulous savings. Everything was "*En Vente.*"

At Sherbrooke, there was a small Mexican restaurant on the corner. I was hungry, but tonight was not a Mexican night. I kept going up past fancy-looking restaurants. Most of the people I passed were young or at least much younger than me. I was in a walking groove. I noticed everything and nothing at the same time. Again I passed the X-rated cinema; it was open for business. The stores next door also looked like they were open. The meeting with Lawyer Gold tomorrow no doubt was going to focus on Mike Green. Ironic that I was walking by here this evening. This was not my only route home.

I needed groceries. I turned back to the food store next to the movie theatre. The place was a jumble of food carts, produce, boxes, and people. It was the opposite of the store I had been in with Ferguson earlier in the day. But the prices were good. I bought a few necessities and got out of there as quickly as I could. Resuming my pace, I crossed Mont-Royal Avenue and looked up the mountain to see the cross; its lights would soon be coming on.

My street was still quiet. Rosh Hashanah was not quite over. Orenstein's place was dark. There was some mail in my mail slot, bills mostly. There was also a very slick booklet advertising properties for sale in the area. Bedtime reading.

I was hungry, and I had nothing ready. I made myself a cup of coffee, recharged my cell phone, and opened the computer. Maybe eggs and some toast?

But first, a shower.

Refreshed and dressed in sweats and a t-shirt, I went about preparing dinner. I ate ravenously. The artisanal French bread was worth the price. With coffee in hand, I went to the PC to check emails. Nothing of any great import. A few northern friends were impatient for snow. The news headlines, likewise, were not of much interest.

I went to lie down on my bed, leaving my cellphone on the kitchen counter. I must have dozed off; I dreamed that my phone was ringing in my ear. Stumbling into the kitchen, I had missed an unknown caller—no message. That was the third or fourth time in the last few days I had had one of those. Strange. A cell phone stalker.

Back to bed, this time, I had the cell with me. I turned on the bedside clock radio. The CBC had a documentary about something or other; I could not focus. I found a classical music station. That fit my mood. In French, the announcer came on to describe the next selection. He was hypnotic. A few minutes into the first piece, I relaxed into a nice sleep.

CHAPTER TWENTY-FIVE

I awoke with a start in the early dawn. There was a commotion on the back porch. A hissing cat fight was going on. One of the two combatants was the marmalade cat I gave milk to the other day. I could not see its foe. I decided to let nature take its course.

Another few minutes and hostilities ceased. Marmalade was not running off.

I stood at the back door and we stared at one another. It had a cute face. I went to fetch some milk; by now the half-pint was reeking. I put on slippers and a windbreaker to go to the *dépanneur* to get a newspaper and some milk. The cat would probably be gone by the time I returned.

When I arrived at the store, Raoul, the owner, was just opening. He ushered me in. He ran to turn off the alarm and turn the lights on. He then went back outside to round up the papers.

There was only one in English. I went looking for milk with the latest sell-by date.

While I was paying, Raoul launched into a discussion about how his newspaper sales had declined to virtually nothing. I assured him that I still preferred to read a newspaper in hand and not online.

The cat had followed me to the store. I introduced myself. Cats have this adorable twisting of the head movement that I have always interpreted as their way of taking in human communication. Or judging us.

I glanced at the papers on my way home. Front-page headlines announced that Levi Epstein, the owner of the apartment building on Pine, had been arrested on various charges, including money laundering. The police also found him in possession of several passports issued under different names and jurisdictions.

"Wow," I said to no one in particular. The cat jumped ahead of me. It came with me up the front steps. I opened the door to the flat. With that, it took off down the stairs. The light above Orenstein's door came on; he walked out in dark slacks, a white shirt, and slippers.

"Epstein has been arrested," I blurted out.

"Good morning. I want to leave here at eleven thirty for our Gold appointment."

"Did you hear what I said? Epstein, the suitor, has been arrested."

"I know."

"You involved in this?"

He shrugged his shoulders, turned, and walked back into his house. I stood on the landing staring at his closed door.

Just then, the cat came back around the front of the building. I went into my flat, opened the milk, put some in an aluminum pie plate, and placed it on the back porch.

From the kitchen, I could see through the door. Within seconds, the cat was lapping up the milk. It was not running off. I went out and filled the plate with more milk.

I scanned the front sections of the newspapers to see if there were any more details about Epstein's arrest. There were none. But lots of ink was spilled to say that. I went to see if there was information on the Internet. I found nothing more than had already been reported. This was exciting, real sleuthing.

I went onto one of the US news sites. Several trans-nationals had been arrested in New York, Chicago, and LA. I checked the CBC News site. One or two gents had been nabbed in Toronto as well. There had been a well-coordinated series of raids by many police forces.

I went onto another Toronto site, which confirmed the CBC story with no further details. I sat staring at the screen. Wow, again.

Coffee time. While it was brewing, I came back to go to the CBC radio site to listen to the news. Several items in the news spoke about the arrests. The operation was dubbed "Black September" and had been in the planning for over a year, involving police from North America, Europe, and the Middle East.

Orenstein knew more about this whole affair than he was letting on, as usual. He would make a great poker player.

I sipped coffee while listening to the end of the newscast. The local show came on and started off with the weather and sports. Then there was an interview with a local police spokesman about the arrest here in Montreal. They had been onto Epstein for some time. They had received information from elsewhere about him. He did not foresee any other arrests locally. Epstein was being held without bail. A court date had not yet been set, and he was undergoing questioning.

The interviewer asked, "Is he co-operating?"

"Not really. He only wants to be questioned in Hebrew. So we found someone who could do that. Then he said he wanted to speak only in Russian. So we found someone who spoke Hebrew and Russian."

"And did that work?"

"Let's just say he is sitting in a cell thinking about it."

That was more information than I had ever heard from one of these interviews.

It was too early to call to see how Ferguson was doing. I cut more of that bread and ate it with a light coating of margarine.

Time for a walk. I dressed for the occasion: windbreaker, ball cap, walkers, and a newer pair of sweatpants.

The day was cloudy, and the wind was coming from the east, a sure sign of rain. I would walk for an hour or until it started to rain. I headed south on Parc to Mont-Royal. Turning right, I decided to climb the mountain. I was sure there was a trail, but I could not find it. So I stuck to the road up the right side. Cars were whizzing by, but there was a walking and bike lane to ensure some margin of safety.

I was not puffing too much. On my right, I could look down into a cemetery.

Eventually I reached the lookout where Martha and I had parked after the party. I crossed the road and found the trail that would take me up to the cross. Looking out over the city, I saw the Olympic Tower and the Saint Lawrence River to the right, with ships traversing the water. I checked my watch. Time to go.

Back down to the parking lot, where a few cars were parked, and some people were looking at the sights. The tour buses would be by later.

I made my way back to Mont-Royal Avenue. A few drops of rain started to fall, then stopped.

Back in the flat, I looked out the back to see if Marmalade was around. It was not; the milk plate was empty. I took it in and washed it, putting it aside for the next time.

On the walk, I had decided to call the Foster Care Department at the Social Service Centre. It was time to see if I was fit to be a foster parent. It was much simpler up north.

I ate some more bread and had a bowl of yogurt with granola. Very satisfying. I went to shave and take another shower.

My cell phone rang; it was Ferguson.

"I was thinking about you."

"Good thing."

"How is that?"

"This Doris lady is very demanding. She is strict, too."

"Tough love."

"You bet. By the time she leaves here, I will be positively svelte. You will not recognize me."

"But how do you feel?"

"Much better, actually."

"Well, is that not good?"

"Yes, but such hard work. After supper last night, she made me go for another walk."

"For shame. How did the insulin go?"

"She was very helpful with that. I feel much more confident about administering it. By the way, how did your meeting go with Martha?"

"As you said, she laid out the parameters. I need to make a move on this. I am calling the Foster Parent place to find out what the next step is. Do you know the woman who runs the unit?"

"You mean Claire Thomas. You will have fun with her. She and I go way back. Ms. Thomas knows her stuff."

"After lunch with Sarah, I plan to drop in to see you."

"Your lady friends are multiplying like flies."

"Should I call before I come? You might be on a forced march."

"Not necessary."

We hung up.

I went back to the desktop. There was no additional news about the arrests.

To the meeting with the lawyer, I would wear slacks, a blue button-down shirt, and the blue blazer. I did not decide on the shoes. But likely the runners if it rained.

Umbrella, umbrella. I found it: very anaemic-looking. Not appropriate.

One of the big chain pharmacies on Saint-Laurent was open all the time. I decided to walk there to see if I could get a decent umbrella. Out the door I went. Mrs. Orenstein was sweeping the stairs.

"Good day," I said.

She nodded. "Do you have a cat?"

"No, but there has been one hanging around."

"Yossi, my son, is very allergic to cats."

"I will remember that."

"He has a lot of allergies. We have had a difficult time with him."

I was stunned. Not only at the news about her son, but at the length and breadth of the conversation.

"In the beginning, when he was young, I spent all my time at the Children's Hospital with him. Between the doctors and me, we have him more or less okay. They don't know as much as they think. A mother always knows best."

She banged her broom on the walk to accentuate her point, then went into the house and closed the door.

I walked down the street laughing to myself. What an interesting example of nesting. Now what would she think if a young Inuit girl came to live with me? If I got past Claire Thomas, I would still have Mrs. Orenstein to deal with . . . a double whammy.

The pharmacy was mostly empty. The stock of umbrellas was meagre, given the time of year. I did manage to find a big, sturdy one with a logo on it. I thought most of the price was to pay a royalty for the logo. Unfortunately, it was the only one that fit what I was looking for.

Walking to the cash, I noticed that Halloween decorations were up. Rushing the season, I thought. It wasn't for another month. Standing in line in front of me was someone who looked familiar. She turned to put down her purchases and said hello to me. I must have looked puzzled.

"Carolyn from the furniture store," she said.

"Oh yes, and I was going to get back to you. I have been busy with one thing after another."

"We are still there."

"Later this week, things are quieting down."

"Good day. Look forward to seeing you."

"Likewise." And off she went with a smile.

The cashier looked at me, "I think we can give you a senior discount."

"If you wish, but I am not sixty-five."

"You are over sixty?"

"Oh yes, over sixty."

I was sure that when I left the store, the alarm bells would go off, and I would need to explain myself to the manager. Nothing of the sort happened. My lucky day.

Rounding the corner into my street, Mrs. Goldberger, Joel's mother, was approaching. She had on a cloth coat and a kerchief covering her head. She was carrying an empty shopping bag. She did not notice me. I stopped to say hello and ask after Joel. She pretended not to hear. She barely looked up and said, "Go away and leave us alone." I stood staring at her back as she walked by.

What was that all about? I could not begin to interpret what just happened. Did it mean that we were getting too close, or what? Strange.

I returned home. And the rain had held off.

I waited till nine o'clock to call the Social Service Centre, whose number I looked up on the Internet.

I stared at the wall clock.

At five past nine, I dialed. I had to patch my way through to the receptionist, punching a bunch of numbers as I went. I waited in the queue for my call to be answered. The receptionist came on. "Foster Care."

"My name is Terry Glasheen, and I am interested in becoming a foster parent."

"Just one moment, please."

A few seconds later, I got an answering machine: Press one to leave a message in French. Press two to leave a message in English. I left my cell phone number and hung up.

I found some black bread in the freezer, which I toasted. The freshly made coffee was very good. The toast, not so much; it had that freezer-burn taste. I threw it out. I still had some of that artisanal bread from the other day, which I was saving for I do not know what. I toasted a few pieces of that. Much better, with a little marge and some jam.

I went through the freezer and took inventory. While I was at it, I went through the cupboards as well. I made notes. Some of the stuff I had on hand made no sense, like three cans of peas and a box of icing sugar.

My cell phone rang. "Am I speaking to Mr. Glasheen?"

"You are."

"This is Janice Leduc, foster care counsellor at the Social Service Centre. You are interested in becoming a foster parent?"

"Yes, I am."

"Your call is timely. We are having a group interview and information session tomorrow night. Are you available?"

"I am available."

"Plan to spend about two hours with us."

"Where and when?"

She gave the address, which was in Westmount, off Dorchester. The meeting was to begin at five.

"Any questions?"

"Is this Montreal time?"

There was a slight giggle over the line, "Let's just call the time-ish. Do you have access to email?"

"I do."

"I am going to send you a short information sheet and a form to be filled out requesting general information. The form can be filled out online and returned to me."

"Understood."

I gave her my email address and we hung up.

I phoned Martha, who answered after the first ring.

"Good day, sir."

"To what do I owe that salutation?"

"Too early for such big words. What is on your mind?"

"I phoned the Foster Care place and there is a group interview and information session tomorrow."

"Glad to hear it. If you get past that, they are going to give you a very lengthy questionnaire, which you need to fill out and return. Essentially, they want to know your entire life story, warts and all."

"Then what?"

"You will be called in for a personal interview, where all this information will be reviewed with you in person. You will be asked to give references. And they will be checked out. I would prefer that you not use me. I want to stay behind the scenes. I believe they ask for three. Do you have three people who can vouch for you?"

"I can probably dig up three."

"Well, you have gotten to this point; how do you feel?"

"Positive. This is a natural thing for me to be doing."

"Seems that way to me, too. How's Ferguson?"

"Complaining about Doris. She is very demanding. She makes him walk a few times a day.

"Seriously, she has been helpful with his insulin. He feels a lot more confident injecting himself."

"That's all to the good. We should talk more. Speak later."

"Bye."

The email had arrived from Janice. I started filling out the questionnaire, which wanted to know very general information like address, date of birth, marital status, profession, etc.

I fired that back within a few minutes. The information letter thanked me for my interest and told me what a noble thing I was doing for the community. I was joining a very select club of people in North America who open their hearts and homes to children who really need both.

The letter went on to talk about the history of foster care in Quebec and Montreal, the current number of kids who are being fostered, and the crying need for more foster parents. This was an impressively produced blurb.

I had received an acknowledgement email from the Centre, no reply necessary.

Time was marching on. I went out back to check on the garlic beds. There were a few shoots breaking through the mulch. I made a mental note to go to the large box hardware store to buy more mulch. Surely, the borough must have a supply of mulch somewhere. So I phoned. Sure enough, I could go and get as much mulch as I wanted from a municipal garage not too far from where I lived.

Shmully called. I looked at the time. It was ten past ten.

"I am at Number One Notre-Dame Street East. I would like you to pick me up. The van is in the alley. The key is in the usual place. I will be waiting outside. Should take you twenty minutes."

I got myself organized and left the apartment. Just before closing the door, I remembered the umbrella. I went back up to fetch it. When I came down a second time, Mrs. Orenstein was standing on the landing. "Here, give this to Inspector Clouseau." It was a small shopping list.

I found the van key and off I went. Number One Notre-Dame Street rang a bell . . . but what bell?

I drove right down Parc to old Montreal. Past Sherbrooke Street, the street changed its name to Bleury. Traffic was heavy but moving. Past Saint-Antoine, the road went up, and I could see part of Notre-Dame Cathedral. There were still tourist buses disgorging sightseers at this time of year.

Turning left on Notre-Dame, the road narrows, reflecting the fact that I had reached the oldest part of the city. The traffic crawled. I had to dodge a few delivery trucks. At the light at Saint-Laurent, I could see Orenstein standing outside Number One Notre-Dame Street—the courthouse.

As the light changed, I pulled over to the curb, and he got in.

"Take the Expressway and exit at Atwater. We are going to Greene Avenue."

"You involved in the Epstein arrest?"

There was no reply, and it appeared that he did not realize I had said anything.

A few seconds later, he asked, "How is your friend Ferguson?"

I could feel my stomach start to churn. "Look, I would like to know what is going on around here. This guy who threw me out of his massage parlour gets arrested and I do not know anything about this. And that woman Magda, you and she are in cahoots. Tell me, is anything she told me true? Is she Ukrainian? Is her name really Magda? And leaving her alone with no minder, are you nuts? If I am just the chauffeur, fine. If I am more than that, I would like to be included. I would like to be in the know. Would it kill you to share some information? Am I on some kind of probation? Well, I have passed the initiation. And Ferguson is fine."

I was totally oblivious of where I was driving. I was stopped at the light at the south side of the Bell Centre, where the Montreal Canadiens play. There were several people hanging around wearing hockey jerseys. I continued west to Greene Avenue.

Orenstein still had not responded.

"Gold is going to offer us a deal regarding Green. Magda is Ukrainian. And her name is not Magda. She prefers to work alone. And as you can attest, she is very effective."

"The fact that you allowed me to pick you up at Court, I guess, is a sign that I have passed some test, like getting a Boy Scout badge. You could have travelled to our meeting on your own. By the way, your wife gave me this to give to you." I handed him the note.

"Where do you want me to park?" I was now driving up Greene and under the expressway. "Is parking indoors an option?"

"There is two-hour parking on the side streets; we will find something."

Orenstein directed me to de Maisonneuve Avenue, where we found four-hour parking.

On Greene, Orenstein headed up the block to where there was a high-end fabric store. A short, skull-capped gentleman came out to greet Orenstein warmly. I was introduced to Mr. Mishkin. They chatted away in Yiddish. We were still early for the meeting, and I had left my umbrella in the van. I walked back to retrieve it. By the time I returned, Orenstein was just emerging from the store. It seemed he had purchased some material that he would pick up later.

Mishkin nodded in my direction.

"Nice meeting you," I said.

We continued down to Westmount Square. "What is Magda's real name?"

"Brocha."

"Her name is 'blessing'?"

He gave me that stare. "I suppose she has been a blessing."

We entered an office building through Greene Avenue, passing boutiques and a food court that was filling up for lunch. A medical clinic was located just past the food area, and the waiting room appeared to be filled. We veered to the right, passing a men's store, and farther down on the right a kitchen gadget store. Oh my, that was tempting. Orenstein looked up Gold's room number on a fancy keypad affair located near the elevators. We went to the eighteenth floor. Outside a law office was a roster of names, the most prominent being Gold's.

We entered. Orenstein put his hand to the mezuzah, which was high on the right door frame, on his way in. The gesture was so discreet that one would not even notice it.

On the left, a young pregnant woman was sitting behind a reception desk.

"Can I help you?"

"We are here to see Mr. Gold."

"And you are?"

"Glasheen and Orenstein."

Orenstein had adopted his Lorne Greene voice, the one that sounded like doom was upon us.

The door on the other side of the room opened, and another young woman came to usher us to Gold's office. We declined coffee.

Gold came to the door of his large corner office with a view of homes wedged on top of the Westmount side of Mount Royal. He greeted us in his well-tailored blazer, tartan vest, and dark grey slacks. Orenstein discreetly kissed the mezuzah on the way in. On the right was a small, round table with a single file on it. We were instructed to sit. How collegial.

Gold removed his jacket and hung it on a hanger on an antique clothes tree. He sat at the table.

Again, he wore cufflinks. This time they were small, round studs.

Orenstein looked up, staring straight at him. "And we are here because?"

Gold, who had been studying the file, looked up. "Mike Greengarten."

"And what does Mr. Green want from us?" I said, looking up at one of the homes that appeared to be teetering off the mountain.

"Who is in a tough spot, here, you, Green, or both of you? It was Green who was phoning you the other night every five minutes."

"I represent him for his business interests only. Someone else handled the divorce."

"And sometimes these issues overlap, correct?" Orenstein said very evenly.

The room became very still.

"You are no doubt aware that arson is suspected at the movie theatre."

We both nodded. The more this went on, the more haggard Gold looked.

"Well, Mr. Green has found a buyer for the property. And this suspicion of arson has put the whole deal in jeopardy."

Orenstein, who had been sitting with his hands in his lap, moved closer to the table and placed his palms down on the finish. "And you want us to do what exactly?"

"The arson charge is bogus. I do not know who floated this fabrication." Gold was virtually sneering.

The house had still not fallen off the mountain, and I looked right at the solicitor. "You still have not told us why we are here, so let me venture a guess. You want Orenstein here to intervene where you have failed. Green is blaming you for not being able to rescue him from himself . . . even though you have consistently and faithfully, over the years, been able to perform miracles on his behalf. Do I have that about right?"

Another poker player, never acknowledging whether I was anywhere near the truth of the matter.

I went on. "Is it possible that the purchasing party floated the arson story just to lower the price? Is it also possible that Green was going to turn around and pay off his wife? This transaction was going to cost him no money. Now he may have to pay some money out of his own pocket, which, at the moment, he does not have. I looked in the warehouse of 'Knitrite'; there was nothing there. And there was no one working. Maybe to avoid seizure, he has his inventory stashed elsewhere. But maybe not. Maybe there is no inventory. No one is willing to advance him credit. He has finally burnt his bridges. And to repeat, all of this is falling on your shoulders. How much money does he owe you?"

Silence.

Orenstein looked over at me; there was the hint of a nod.

Murray Gold took a deep breath, "Are you sure you were a priest?"

Orenstein looked at Gold, "And what do you want us to do? And what am I offered in return?" Orenstein said in his still-even manner.

"You know the answer to that," Gold whispered.

"Only if he voluntarily agrees to do what he should do," Orenstein said, bless him.

Gold looked as if he was about to burst into tears.

He recovered himself. "I will discuss your terms with my client and get back to you."

We both stood. The lawyer stayed seated at his table, not looking up at us. "You will leave your coordinates with my secretary, both of you?"

Orenstein replied, "I will leave my coordinates only. We need to simplify this."

"As you wish."

Gold's assistant met us at the door of his office and ushered us out to the corridor. Orenstein stopped to give her his card.

The elevator was empty. Orenstein said, "I need to make a phone call to the father and son who have made an offer for Green's building. I suspect that their story will be slightly different."

"Father and son?"

The elevator stopped, and two women got in. Further conversation ceased.

We got off the elevator on the concourse. There was an exit onto a large cement patio.

The space was largely empty. Orenstein continued, "Father is a developer, and the son is an architect. They do not play games, as Gold has intimated. They do not need to resort to that kind of behaviour. I am surprised that they are willing to do business with Mr. Greengarten. I will deal with them myself. I also did not want Gold to play us off against one another.

"What are you up to now?"

"I have a lunch appointment, and after that, I was going to visit Ferguson."

"Keep your cell phone on."

CHAPTER TWENTY-SIX

It started to rain. I walked back into the building and took the elevator down one floor. I wanted to go into the pots and pans store. My cell phone rang. "Sarah here; where are you? Are you finished your meeting?"

"I am in front of the kitchen gadget store in Westmount Square. The meeting is over."

"It's raining. So, what if we eat at the food court there?"

"Fine with me."

"Twenty minutes okay with you?"

"Twenty minutes."

I went into the store. This place was dangerous. I could spend a lot of money in a very short time. I could fancy an espresso machine, but five-thousand dollars was a bit too rich for my blood. I could use a boning knife. There were several varieties. I was sorely tempted. "*Et ne nos inducas . . .*"

Luckily, I was rescued by my appointment. I made my way to the food court area to wait for my date. The tables were emptying after the lunch hour. Sarah came along wearing a colourful cape and carrying an equally colourful umbrella.

"Greetings."

"Likewise."

"As you can see, there are several choices here. I fancy the Chinese food from over there. The mixed vegetables are quite acceptable."

I noticed a counter that offered Middle Eastern fare. "I am going to try the Middle Eastern place. Let's meet back here."

We separated. I decided on the vegetarian plate. It was piled high with goodies. I was offered hot sauce, which I thought was a great idea. I bought bottled water as well.

We met back in the corridor.

There were several tables in the middle separated from the walkway by a metal fence affair. We decided on a quiet-looking one. Sarah put two tables together to give us more space. One of the workers came over to clean both tables for our date.

Sarah removed her cape. She was wearing a university sweatshirt and red sweatpants.

S. John Diamond

"I was freezing this morning," she said as she saw me looking at her get-up. We sat side by side so as to talk easily.

We started to eat.

"Where were we?" she said, putting down her plastic cutlery.

"We were in the middle of several conversations, as I recall. I did take your advice and watched the film on Borenstein. In fact, I started to watch it a second time when I was interrupted by a sick friend. The film was really good and very informative. My sense is that he was a difficult man. His art leaps right off the canvas. He almost throws it at you."

"He does throw it at you. What sick friend?"

"I got that phone call—you know the one. The patient needs to be escorted home by a family member or friend. I was the friend. He is all right, by the way."

"Thank goodness for that. Tell me—I have been wondering, are you and Martha just friends?"

"Just friends."

"She and I go way back. And some of it has not been pleasant. They wanted to resurrect the art therapy programme at the Children's Hospital and they asked me to get involved. To be specific, Elyse thought it would be a good idea if I got involved. Martha and I clashed over the direction of the programme and who was in charge. To borrow a phrase, we were both full of piss and vinegar in those days. It became a turf war."

"Hmm."

"You have nothing to say on the matter other than 'hmm'?"

"Ain't my place."

She continued eating, as did I.

The eating space we were in was largely empty.

"You are teaching this afternoon?"

"I have a master class starting at three. It is the class that gives me the most pleasure week after week. There is no course material to deliver. The students just do art."

"Any stars this semester?"

"They are all good. Yet one is glaringly better than the rest."

"How do you judge that?"

"How she translates her vision onto the canvas."

"I am not sure I understand that."

"Look, they all see the same model or the same basket of flowers. When she reproduces it, she does it so simply and clearly. There is nothing omitted. She is able to reproduce the essence of the thing. You can see the model's personality; the model's uniqueness. And the same with the still life. It comes alive."

"She is able to get beyond herself."

"Yes, exactly."

We had finished eating. I got up to garbage the empty plates. People were walking through the concourse shaking umbrellas.

When I sat back down, Sarah asked, "When you were a priest, did you incorporate native customs in the service?"

"Over time I did. It fit perfectly. It added to the authenticity of the Mass."

"Do you miss it?"

"On balance, no. I am beginning to appreciate my life here. My one concern was that I would be idle. I knew I wanted to make a contribution somehow in some way. I was available, but I did not know for what. Orenstein took care of that. Martha, too. And look, I never could have predicted that I would be having lunch on a Wednesday afternoon with an art professor. And that we would have something to talk about, which did not involve me being a priest."

She looked at me. "You have had to transform your entire approach to people and yourself. You no longer have the collar to protect you."

"The collar doesn't protect. In fact, it makes you more vulnerable. And it has been much easier here in the big city where I am anonymous, invisible. I could not have done this in the north. And you, did you always want to be an artist?"

"I was a sickly kid, spending a lot of time on my own. Early on, one of the nurses at the Children's brought in some coloured pencils and blank paper. I was hooked. Another time, several of us worked on a mural on the wall: kids, nurses, volunteers, assistants. Everyone had a hand in it. The mural is still there. Others have added to it over the years. I came alive doing that and forgot why I was there."

"You are still passionate. The descriptions you gave the other night made all the paintings just come alive."

"Thank you, yes."

"Does Angela Green share your passion?"

154

She looked away. Then returned her gaze.

"I cannot really be objective when it comes to Angela." She stared off into the near distance, and her body tightened. "We were intimate." She looked at me again to gauge my reaction.

"You love her?"

"Yes."

"Are you still in touch?"

"A few years ago, I received her wedding picture in the mail. She and her partner were standing in a Vermont field, smiling into the camera."

"It hurts."

She looked at me directly. "Can you let someone into your life?"

"I am dealing with that right now."

"Martha?'

"No, Molly."

"Molly?"

"A young Inuit girl whom I may foster."

"You were intimate with the Church and I with my art. But when it comes to people, we have issues. I am a great teacher."

"And I was an effective priest: confidant social worker and hockey coach."

She took my hand and smiled into my face. "Birds of a feather. Speaking of which, I have to fly to my class. This was good. At least we did not talk about briskets."

"Next time."

We stood up and hugged. She walked toward the tunnel to the subway, and I walked to the Greene Avenue entrance.

CHAPTER TWENTY-SEVEN

The street was wet and filled with people using umbrellas. I pulled into a doorway to call Ferguson. Manipulating the phone and my umbrella was a chore, but I managed.

Doris answered. "He is entertaining. Come join the party."

"I will be along shortly. Need anything?"

"Nothing I can think of."

"Reverend Ferguson need anything?"

"Just come."

I moved slowly up the street, reviewing my morning. A brother and sister both experiencing pain for totally different reasons, but in pain, just the same.

Gold knew that Orenstein would know the potential purchasers of the property. But Gold would have known them as well. At least, I would have thought so. What is preventing him from bringing the two parties together? I could not figure that out. Maybe Orenstein would connect the dots.

And Sarah falling in love with one of her students. Not a great idea, but it happens. So now she throws herself into her work while at the same time grieving about a relationship lost.

Without realizing it, I was at Sherbrooke. The athletic clothing store to my left looked particularly empty today. Not a good time to buy jogging gear.

I crossed the street, headed west the one block to the apartment building. Flo was standing outside in a rain slicker under the doorway with a shovel. "The leaves clog the drain outside the garage. Someone has to clean them out."

"You look dressed for the chore, but what a job."

She grunted. "That's why they pay me the big bucks. Listen, you want to rent here? I have a great apartment for you: one bedroom facing the back, second floor, totally redone."

"I need two bedrooms."

She looked at me, opened her mouth to say something, and then stopped herself.

"You have a nice day; I am going upstairs."

She let me in and went into her office on the right.

I took the stairs to the third floor. I was not too out of breath when I reached my friend's door, which was slightly ajar. I heard laughter coming from inside. I wiped my shoes as best I could on the mat. I knocked and opened the door.

"Aw, look what the rain brought us. My guardian angel," Ferguson bellowed.

Sitting beside him on the couch, under the window, was a slim, grey-haired woman in a white blouse and black slacks. On her feet she wore knitted tartan slippers, which looked homemade.

Doris was fussing with something in the kitchen. "You want tea?"

"Coffee, if you have it."

"I think I could manage that."

In the end, I took off my shoes, found a hanger, and hung my raincoat in the bathroom. I left the umbrella by the door; it was too wet to carry through the house.

When I emerged from the washroom, Ferguson said, "Terry, I would like to introduce you to a dear friend of many years, Claire Thomas."

I went over to her and shook her hand. It was a sturdy handshake. "I am pleased to meet you."

"And I am pleased to meet you."

"You are the fellow who has kept my dear bridge partner here going."

"Bridge?"

"Oh, yes—for years, we used to play every Tuesday night, Betty, Reg, my sister, and I."

"Rain or shine," Ferguson added, and they both laughed.

Doris came out of the kitchen with a tray. "Tea time."

We all adjourned to the table.

Coffee, black, for me; tea with lemon for them. There were also some cookies, which Doris assured us were okay for diabetics. "This is what I went into the pharmacy to buy the other day when we were on our walk."

Ferguson looked pleased, giddy almost. He bit into a cookie, sat back to savour it. "Nectar."

"Oh, Reg, so dramatic," Claire said, laughing.

"Mr. Glasheen," Claire said, looking directly at me. "I understand you are interested in becoming a foster parent."

"Is there a conflict of interest here? I could leave and come back another day."

"Not at all—only to say that, as you must know, we need foster parents. Demand is high, resources low."

Doris left the table and went into the kitchen. She took a good deal of energy with her. There was a charged silence. She had her back to us. She wheeled around to come to the door of the kitchen. She was angry, looking straight at the social worker. "You people nearly killed me."

She paused. There was more, a lot more. "You took my two babies from me. I had everything arranged. The two older ones were going to live with my sister. But the two youngest gave you a real problem. You wanted to foster them. Anything I had arranged was not good enough. You had made up your mind. And foster them where? In the Eastern Townships! Very convenient."

I looked up right at her. "And your four children now?"

"Fine, upstanding citizens, thank you very much."

She took off her apron, went to the closet next to the door, put on her coat, and walked out.

The three of us sat there immobile.

After a few minutes, I decided to go looking for her. "I'll be back."

Some bloody retirement. Three anguished people in one day, *ça suffit.*

I walked east on Sherbrooke. There was a park across the street from a synagogue. Sitting on a park bench, her hands in her coat pockets, her legs stretched out, staring at the street, was Doris. She did not acknowledge I was there. I sat on the end of the bench.

I said nothing. She continued to stare out. "Are you the search party?"

"Seems to me you are not lost."

She turned to look at me. "What the hell does that mean?"

"Look at what you were able to do totally on your own."

"I still hate those bastards."

"You beat them. You know that. You proved them wrong. Leave it alone."

"You mean let sleeping dogs die."

158

I had moved closer to her. "Cannot deny it happened. It did." I drew a breath. "An uppity Black woman took on the system. And won."

With that, she turned to smile at me. I took her hand and held it up in the air. "The winner and still champ."

We rose together to return to the apartment.

Ferguson and Claire were sitting on the couch staring at us as we came in.

Doris was smiling. "Did not mean to be so contrary. But that whole issue has left deep scars."

Ferguson looked up at her. "Welcome back. Totally understood. And I mean totally understood."

Claire stood up, approached, and took Doris's hand. "I cannot take back what happened. I am privileged to know you."

Doris took off her coat. "Anybody want supper?"

I hung her coat up.

"Let's work on supper together," I said.

"Reverend Ferguson, time for your meds and pressure," Doris said.

I went to wash my hands. I stuck my head into the freezer. There was chicken and fish. I called, "Chicken or fish?"

Doris, finished with her charge, came into the kitchen and took out a package of hamburger meat from the fridge. "We are having pasta. Scram. I can handle this."

I walked back into the salon. Ferguson looked up from the sofa. "Anybody fancy a sherry?"

We all agreed that was a great idea. He got up and went into the den. He came out with a bottle. From a breakfront, he took four very dainty glasses and placed them on the table.

He then poured three decently full and one with just a touch. I went over to distribute three of the glasses. Doris initially refused, but I insisted.

Ferguson offered a toast to our good health. He left his glass on the table and went to sit down on the sofa. Doris came to the door of the kitchen to announce that supper would be served in ten minutes.

Claire, who was sitting beside Ferguson, took a large sip of sherry. Her face immediately reddened. "You know, Reg, if you and Betty had not fostered those two Native children, we probably would not have met."

"Well, perhaps. Though I think there were enough connections that we probably would have. Your sister and Beatrice had known each other for a long time."

"Anyway, the wolves are out. They want me to retire. And I think they are serious this time."

He looked at her. "Is it time?"

"I am sixty-nine years old. I have been doing this forever."

Looking down from his glasses, he said, "Is that dog years or cat years?"

She playfully slapped his wrist. He pantomimed being injured.

"Is it time? When is the right time? There is no fixed right time," I suggested.

Doris announced, "Dinner is served."

We sat around the table. Doris had found some serving bowls and sat down as well.

Reg rose to say grace; we all held hands. "For what we are about to receive, may the Lord make us truly thankful. Amen."

Claire looked at him. "You must be hungry."

"I am."

There was salad, garlic bread, pasta, and sauce. All superb. We ate hungrily with little table conversation. I complimented Reg on his restraint. He seemed to be keeping to his diet.

When we finished, Claire and Doris cleared the table.

Reg called to Doris, "Come sit next to me over here on the couch." As if on cue, Claire and I started to do the dishes; I washed, she dried.

"Why Molly? Why are you putting yourself through this?"

I stopped washing. "Because I know her. I have a relationship with her. And because I know, or I think I know, what I am getting myself into."

"You do not need the orientation, but you have to go through it. We are obliged to create a file. And we will need to check references. And at various times, we are going to have to check up on you."

"And Molly, too."

"Yes, and Molly, too."

Doris came into the kitchen. She had a tissue in her hand. "I am going to leave now. Tomorrow is another day."

I turned to her. "It certainly is. And it is going to be a great day."

"Thank you for all your help."

"You have a safe journey home."

She turned to go. I dried my hands and waited as she put on her coat and quietly went out the door.

Returning to the sink, I finished the last of the dishes and started putting them away. Claire was standing off to one side. "My sense is that Molly is one lucky young woman."

I looked at her. "I certainly hope so, for all our sakes."

Claire announced, "I am going home. It has been a very full evening. Thank you, Reg, for encouraging me to meet Mr. Glasheen here. Highly irregular, of course. But this is an unusual situation where someone is volunteering to take someone specific. In all my years, there may have been one other case like this."

"I have a question for you," I said, looking down at her. "You did not remember Doris?"

"Doris, no; the case, yes. And to be honest with you, I do not remember all the details. I am going to go home to check my private notes."

"Your diary?"

"Something like that."

I helped her on with her coat. She went over to kiss Ferguson on the forehead. He was sitting in his reserved seat. As she walked by, she shook my hand. "I will see myself out, and I will see you tomorrow evening."

"Pleasure meeting you."

After she closed the door, I turned to Ferguson. "What did you say to Doris?"

"How much I appreciated her company, and if any of her offspring got caught up like that again, she was to let me know."

"Are you planning to take your armour out of mothballs?"

"Never can tell when my knight duds will come in handy."

"I am going."

"You have cab fare?"

"I will take the bus and walk."

"Here. I have some cash. Take it."

"No thanks."

"Stubborn Irishman."

"You are feeling better, aren't you?"

"Last day or so, I am feeling almost back. Tomorrow, a longer walk is in order."

"Good show."

I put on my ball cap, turned to him, and said, "You know, you are looking better. I will call you tomorrow."

I let myself out and quietly closed the door behind me.

CHAPTER TWENTY-EIGHT

The bus was waiting at the light. I ran to catch it. The driver opened the door, and I thanked him for his gesture. I realized that I had left my new umbrella at the apartment. At least it was safe.

The bus was almost empty and headed east on Sherbrooke with little difficulty. I sat down, pulled my cap over my eyes, and tried to gear down. Someone else rang to be let off at the Main, which was lucky, because I would have missed the stop.

The 55 bus was just coming up the hill. It, too, was nearly empty. I got off at Fairmount and made my way back home.

The apartment and I were strangers. It was time to bond with it again. As I climbed the stairs to my front door, Orenstein came out to greet me.

"Evening. How is your friend?"

"Good and getting better."

"You look tired. Let's talk in the morning."

"Fine with me."

I trudged up the stairs, took off my jacket and cap, and lay on my bed.

I rolled over, opened my eyes, and stared at the clock radio, which read five twenty a.m. I had slept the entire night, fully clothed, and without waking once. I turned on the radio to hear the beginning of the morning show.

After a few seconds, I turned it off. I found the FM station; it had classical music, which suited my mood better. And, more importantly, there was no chatter.

I undressed, got into my robe, and took a long (for me) hot shower. Shaving was next. I took extra time to get it just right. In the kitchen, I made the special coffee I had been saving for an occasion. That was now. Somewhere my cell phone rang. I let it go. I had left the thing in the breast pocket of my blazer. I sat in one of the squat living room chairs, thinking about nothing and everything at the same time. I finished the coffee and went to make another. My cell phone rang again.

I went to fetch it. Two unknown calls with no messages. My stalker friend was on the job early.

After brushing my teeth, I put on sweats, a jacket over a t-shirt, and my black walkers to go to the corner store to get the paper. I was early, or he was late; either way, I simply continued walking. There was really no activity in our little conclave. Just me and the neighbourhood cats.

The fall air was crisp, and I was probably a sweater underdressed. As I picked up my pace, I began to warm up. I walked to Mount Royal, arriving just as the lights on the cross went out. This time, I continued straight up the road parallel to the mountain. On my right were several nice homes. On my left was a forest. There was no sidewalk on the left. I stayed on the road.

Eventually I came to a cemetery. In the first light I could make out tombstones that started at the side of the road and stretched up the side of a mountain. There was a main gate, which was locked. Above was a sign saying, "Shaar Hashomayim Cemetery." A little farther on, there was another sign which read, "Spanish and Portuguese Cemetery." There was the occasional jogger. Other than that, I was alone.

My mother's grave was on the other side of the mountain. I had not visited there since last Easter. I found it hard to visit. I believe there was a plot beside her reserved for me. She was nothing if not thorough. I wondered how she would react to my taking in Molly. I knew the answer to that: she would smother the child with affection.

The road dead-ended at another cemetery—Mount Royal. There was a gate open on one side; I turned and started walking back down toward home.

Traffic had picked up significantly. Today was going to be a chore day round the old homestead. I was going to try to focus on not running around town until later for the orientation meeting.

The sun was beginning to provide some warmth. I went back to my *dépanneur*, where my friend had kept the newspaper aside for me. Nice gesture. As I walked up the stairs to my flat, Mrs. Orenstein came out with her broom. She nodded.

"Good day, Mrs. Orenstein," I said brightly.

There was a grunt. "I will tell you at the end of the day if it has been a good day."

"Shmully in?"

"He will be back soon—at least that is what he told me. One never really knows. Don't set your clock."

Collecting the mail, I went up into the flat. I opened windows everywhere. The post was mostly flyers, which I deposited in the green bin.

Fresh air in the apartment was a welcome treat after the last couple of days in hospitals, high-rise offices, and Ferguson's apartment, where the windows were too old to open. I had kept my windbreaker on. I gathered up my laundry and got that going. I made more coffee. The cell phone rang. It was Martha. "Good morning, Sir Galahad."

"Saints preserve us. I cannot even pee without somebody knowing about it."

"Just after you left Ferguson's last night, I called and he filled me in on your evening activities.

"You wowed Claire Thomas, good job."

"What is up with you?"

"I am turning into a fan. What happened with your meeting with Gold?"

"I am not sure I want to discuss that yet. I am invoking privilege."

"Understood. I have been dealing with Mother, who has been feeling poorly lately."

"Mummy duty."

"Yeah. It is my time to go through the experience: driving her to medical appointments, helping her shop, all that stuff. It needs to be done. And I need to work it around my hospital duties."

"I have faith you can pull off this balancing act. Is there anything wrong with her?"

"They are doing tests. She still has a few to complete."

"Good luck."

"Thanks."

"I have no schedule today and I am going to keep it that way."

"Don't you have orientation at Foster Care?"

"Except for that."

"Speak later?"

"Yup. Have a good one."

She rang off. I looked out the back window and Orenstein was sitting in his chair in the yard. I took my coffee mug and went down to join him. He looked up. "Mike Green is a very self-destructive fellow. He had a deal in place and he scuttled it. He missed the signing."

"Do you think you can put it back on the rails?"

"If he behaves himself."

"Any indication he will do so?"

"I am counting on Gold to advise his client accordingly."

"Gold created that meeting because he assumed you knew the purchasers. He was taking quite a gamble. I guess he figured he had no choice.

"You need the van today? I need it for about an hour."

"Help yourself. You still want to sell?"

"I have a lot on my plate at the moment. I have been asked to take in a foster child."

Orenstein looked up directly at me. "Really. A member of your community in the north, someone you know, no doubt?"

I nodded. "She needs a home. She has had a very rough time."

"You feel obligated."

"I know her. I had a relationship with her. Seems like a natural thing to do."

"But?"

"I have no experience with this."

"When is she coming?"

"I do not know. There is red tape; I am going to a meeting tonight to start the process."

Orenstein continued to look at me. "I was an orphan after the War of Independence. I was taken into a family. Good. All was good."

"Thank you for your support. It has not happened yet. I will let you know what is going on."

I noticed for the first time that the frame for the *sukkah* had been erected on the back porch to the right of his back door. Orenstein noticed my gaze. "In the old days, I would go and cut the pine boughs myself. No longer. I tried coaxing my boys to join me. That proved to be too difficult. So I stopped doing that. I now count on some members of the community to provide me with what I need. After Yom Kippur, I will finish erecting it."

"I will bring the van back in an hour."

I went up to fetch the keys, wallet, and cell phone. I also took some large plastic bags to fill with mulch. The city depot was located off a small street near the train tracks. They had no mulch, and in fact, the city worker did not know what I was talking about. As a gesture to me, he made a phone call to find out that there was mulch to be had at a location in the east end. That was not practical, as I had only an hour, and there was no guarantee that that information was correct either. I thanked him for his trouble.

I went to the big box hardware store and paid for four bags of the stuff. My garlic had better be pleased. I pulled the van into the alley and threw the bags over the fence. I then went up to get the hand vacuum to clean out the rear of the truck. In the interim, my cell phone had rung with an unknown number and no message. Every day for the last week, this had been going on. I wondered if these calls were from the same person or just random misdials. I decided on the former, based on nothing but a gut feeling.

I spread the new mulch over the old, making sure that all the spaces were filled in.

There was another frost expected, and I had several unused bulbs I could still plant.

Again, eyes from the first floor were watching my activities. This crop had better come in, or my reputation as a master urban gardener would be in tatters.

Back in the apartment, I washed up and decided I was hungry. I ate some cold cereal and fruit mixed in a bowl of yogurt, and then toasted a bagel, but without cream cheese, it was a disappointment.

I phoned the furniture store and got the message machine. My need now was for a fold-out or a decent couch that could accommodate me adequately.

My phone rang. "Carolyn here, from the furniture store. Do you still want the two chairs?"

"My needs have changed," I told her.

"Well, come on by and let's see what we can do," she said brightly.

I went back to my PC. Epstein, or whatever his name was, was being held without bail. He was considered a flight risk. There was no other information available. Orenstein could supply a good deal more. I doubted he would, even if I asked him. My picking him up at the courthouse led me to believe that he was involved in the investigation. They wanted someone who spoke Russian and Hebrew. Between Magda and Shmully, that would have been taken care of. I wondered if they would use her or if she just disappeared for a while. And would she reappear when Epstein was brought to trial?

I checked the sports page. The home team's hockey season was going to start October second, the night after the Day of Atonement. Was that an omen for the coming season?

Just before noon, I left the apartment to go to the furniture store. Mrs. Orenstein was waiting for me on the front porch. "You are going to take in a little girl. What experience do you have to do this?"

I looked her right in the eye. "Mrs. Orenstein, when I am stuck, I am going to come to you, the professional, to ask for advice."

She did not take the bait. "You need your head examined. *Meshuga. Goyishe kop.*"

She went into her house and slammed the door.

I had received her opinion and it was not positive.

However, she was not entirely wrong. Perhaps I was *meshuga*, crazy.

And as for a *goyishe kop*, well, there was nothing I could do about that. For sixty years I have had a Catholic head.

I reached the furniture store just as the young couple was opening up. Jack ran inside to turn off the alarm. A few seconds later, he came to the door. "All clear."

Once inside, he suggested that we sit for a chat.

"You no longer need the two overstuffed chairs."

"My life is about to change. I am going to have someone living with me and I need a comfortable couch or a Hide-A-Bed."

"I have a great couch for you. We do not make Hide-A-Beds."

"Let's look at the couch."

"I do not have it here. I can show you a picture of it. And I can take you to the workshop to see it up close."

He took out his tablet to show me a picture of a long, sleek sofa with a couple of throw pillows.

The material was beige.

"I do not like beige."

With a couple of strokes of a finger he turned the colour to a shade of blue. I smiled. "That is much better."

"We will be finished in about a week or so and I can bring it in for you to sit and lie on."

"Price?"

"Around two thousand dollars."

I was wondering then how much a Hide-A-Bed was. But they were heavy and bulky and not usually comfortable to sleep on.

"I see."

"It's all labour and the material. I have several kinds of cloth in various shades of blue."

"I do not want to be difficult. Finish the sofa you are working on and I will test it out. It is either going to be a yes or no. What is its length?"

"This one is sixty inches. I may be able to stretch the design to seventy-two inches."

"Can you design something which is seventy-five inches?"

Carolyn, who had been busy in the back of the store doing something else, joined the conversation.

"You know, I have something in my laptop that we were playing around with some time ago; I will send it to you. It needs fine-tuning. Would tomorrow be okay?"

"Sure."

Smiles all around. I left them my email address and phone number.

On the way back to the apartment, I went into the fruit and vegetable store to stock up. Today was going to be a salad day. Too much heavy food lately.

Meanwhile, once outside the store, my cell phone vibrated. I put down my package to answer; again, there was no one there, and the number was unknown.

Shmully was standing on the landing when I arrived.

"Your wife does not approve."

"She is a woman of very strong opinions. Our friend Green received several recommendations from insurance to fix the wiring in the roof of his building. Of course, he did the minimum required, and at that, it was not to code. So arson was not the cause of the fire; Mr. Green's stubbornness is."

"What is with him? He really is very demanding and, quite frankly, infantile."

"We are going to do nothing with him until he does what he needs to do."

"What happens . . . if?"

"Stop. He has no choice."

"You are certain of that."

"I am certain that he is going to try to get a hold of you individually to put you up against me."

"Yes, I have been expecting that. And I have received several anonymous phone calls with no message. I have been wondering if it was him."

"You sure it was not one of your secret admirers?"

"I think not." It was my turn to give that stare.

"We still have one other major issue to resolve. And I was virtually hissed at the other day by Mrs. Goldberger. She walked by me, and when I tried to say hello, she admonished me to stay away and leave well enough alone."

Orenstein did not seem surprised, he simply nodded.

"Is she okay? Her reaction was very strange."

Orenstein looked at me. "You know this is not a community which is used to this sort of thing. And especially having outsiders poking around asking questions."

My turn to nod. "You notice that there have been no further incidents."

"Makes it harder for us to find the person. A random act, out of nowhere. No clues. No evidence. We have nothing to work on."

Orenstein was rubbing his beard. "You know that something will happen. It could be today or tomorrow, or next year. Some germ of a clue or a whiff of a conversation; it always happens. We must be alert for it."

"I guess I have come to that notion as well. In the meantime, how is the young man?"

"From what I hear, he is doing well. Better than before. He shows an aptitude for science."

"Strange, is it not, that we are left thinking there should be another attack to help us with the investigation."

"You mean like a human sacrifice?"

"Yes. Is that not awful to contemplate?"

He nodded, "You know the hospital destroyed evidence by cleaning up the room so quickly. I wonder who gave that order."

"It may have been simply protocol."

My cell phone rang, and I answered automatically.

"Is this Mr. Glasheen?"

"Yes, and who is this?"

"Mike Green."

I looked at Orenstein and pointed at the phone. He nodded.

"And what can I do for you on this fine day, Mr. Green?"

"I will get to the point. Could you convince your pigheaded friend to change his mind?"

"The short answer is no. He does not change his mind easily."

"Look, if this deal goes through, there will be money to compensate you both."

"Mr. Green, as far as I am concerned, this conversation is over. There is nothing to discuss. Mr. Orenstein has made his position very clear. Good day."

I looked at Shmully. "He will call back."

"Should you choose to take his next call, you might want to put on your charm."

"To what end? His mind is working overtime to save himself. The solution is right in front of his nose. He gives his wife the *get*; he grants himself all kinds of slack."

"Exactly my point."

"You play chess?"

He gave off a small laugh and shrugged.

Sure enough, the phone rang again.

I walked to the end of the porch. "Yes."

"I want you to listen to me."

"Stop! You need to listen to me. I need your undivided attention. And by the way, I could not care less what you do. You are a smart man acting foolishly. You need to think this thing through. We can both see that the thing that you need to do is the thing you do not want to do. You might, for about four seconds, put your hostility on hold."

I stopped. There was no response from the other end. I waited.

After what seemed an eternity: "I could go out and find some other buyers."

"All of the players in town would know why. You have any foreign money lined up? That takes time and more work. You have a deal in the bag; take it."

"For a priest, you're a tough bastard."

"The Lord works in mysterious ways."

Green slammed off.

Orenstein looked at me. "Is that your definition of charm?"

It was my turn to shrug. "Today it is."

"I expect Gold to call shortly. His client's mind is still too restless."

I was pacing. "I have probably done the opposite of what was needed. But boy, did it feel good."

"You bullied him. You kicked him when he was down. I expected more tact from you."

Sure enough, ten minutes later, Murray Gold called Orenstein. Shmully did not put the phone on speaker. He stood listening to the call, saying nothing. Finally, he wished Gold a good day and rang off.

"You insulted Green. Neither gentleman wishes to speak to you again. They will talk only to me. Green needs more time to sort out his affairs, and he is undergoing a round of medical tests. Could I be patient?"

"So this good-cop-bad-cop routine really works."

"Sometimes."

"What are you going to say to the potential buyers?"

"I will tell them the truth and wish them an easy fast."

"You have that much credibility with them?"

"So far."

"Are you suggesting that at some point they will pull the plug on the whole idea?"

"Yes. They may have some attachment to those buildings, but after a while they could simply decide not to do business with Green."

"I am surprised they are still interested and that they have patience for Green."

"The door is closing."

"Just one other thing still bothers me."

"And that is?"

"What were you doing at the courthouse?"

"I was not directly involved with the Epstein Affair except they needed someone who speaks Russian and Hebrew as well as French."

"You were able to provide the service. And it could not have been Magda, though she could have done the job?"

"They had a choice of three people. One was a woman, not Brocha."

"And there were two men, both of whom were employed. Epstein would switch from language to language."

172

"Another snake."

"That may be. But that has to be proven in a court of law."

"You think there is a chance he will not be found guilty?"

"Yes, of course. There is always a chance of that."

Orenstein put on his black fedora and headed to the alley to take the van somewhere. He did not tell me where he was going or what he was doing. He also did not say goodbye.

He could be brusque like that; his mind focused on the next thing, the next item in his life.

I needed another walk.

CHAPTER TWENTY-NINE

I went south on our street. At the corner, three frock-coated men were deep in conversation.

They were talking in Yiddish. I noticed for the first time that the black coats were buttoned from right to left. How come I never noticed that before? And what was the significance? Keeping the heart in its place? Balance. Another thing to check out.

I remembered Martha saying that her parents spoke Yiddish when they did not wish her to understand the conversation. In her mind, Yiddish was a taboo language, and therefore she never learned it. She had some regrets about that now.

My route brought me to Laurier. Turning right onto the avenue, I noticed that the stores were all unique. Many were housed in buildings that had once been residences. All looked like they had been individually designed. There was nothing haphazard.

My eye was caught by a kitchen utensil store. Looking in through the plate glass windows, I was getting palpitations. Beautiful fry pans hung on the left wall. On an island near the door, cookware shone in the morning sunlight. The store was not open yet, so I gave my habitual prayer of thanks. And added, "*et ne nos inducas in tentationem.*"

I crossed Parc and continued up the street. I passed a bridal store with very elaborate gowns in the window. An attractive, blonde-haired woman came out carrying a garment bag. She looked up; it was Green's girlfriend. When she focused her gaze on me, her body language stiffened with fury.

"You bastard. Get out of my way."

She went into the street to get into a waiting cab. As she got in, she let out a burst of profanity in a Slavic-sounding language I did not recognize. The cab sped off.

Who else could I annoy today? And I wondered what colour the woman's gown was?

The cell rang as I was still standing in front of the bridal shop.

"What is up?"

"This is your friend Martha sitting in the bowels of the General waiting for Mother to have a test."

"Is that the place where you drink a lot of water, change into those beautiful gowns, sit with ten strangers similarly attired, and attempt to look dignified?"

"You know what, you really can be a shit."

"Number four."

"Number four what?"

"You are the fourth person I have pissed off today."

"It is only ten o'clock. You are doing well."

"I am going for president of the class."

"More like president of the crass."

"Oh, I like that. That is rich."

I had continued walking up the street. I was now oblivious to my surroundings.

"I called to wish you well this evening."

"You did that already. You called now because you were bored and you thought I might relieve the boredom. How am I doing?"

"I would say moderately well."

"You are a tough audience. Ever been to Philadelphia?"

"What?"

"Vaudeville joke."

"Can I see it on YouTube?"

"Predates YouTube by several lifetimes."

"You know you are the repository of a fair amount of really useless information?"

"Those long winter nights in the north."

"Alone."

"Not really. I could choose to go to the hotel and chat with my neighbours."

"How exciting."

"Beats sitting in a waiting room."

"Things are going so well for you; who are you going to use to vouch for your good character?"

"Joseph Stalin, Benito Mussolini, and Idi Amin Dada."

"Just in case, you might want to throw in Papa Doc Duvalier."

"How long have you been sitting there?"

"About an hour."

I had reached Côte-Sainte-Catherine. I turned to walk back to Parc Avenue.

"Is the flirty guy still working the reception desk?"

"Every white-coated woman who walks by in the corridor is greeted—how should I put it—warmly."

"Observing him is at least worth a few minutes of your time."

"I have another call. Speak later."

I walked back to the apartment with my head down, determined not to offend anyone else this morning.

Carolyn had sent along her drawings for the sofa. I took out the tape measure to check that my idea would work. If I got rid of the two overstuffed chairs and moved the small dining table slightly, it would. She also included a picture of blue fabric. I was not sure about her choice.

I wrote back to tell her I would be in in the afternoon. She replied immediately that she looked forward to seeing me. There was an email from the Foster Care people reminding me of the meeting tonight; included was a map to the location.

No other stuff on the Internet interested me. I went to the *dépanneur* to buy the *Montreal Gazette*. He was sold out.

I had energy this morning that came from deep inside and was largely unfocused. I wanted to do something, but I didn't know what. Sitting at the computer was not satisfying. Going to work on the garlic bed would take five minutes. It was as if I was supposed to do something, but what? I decided to take a bath to see if that would calm me down and focus me.

Clad in a t-shirt and sweatpants, I sat at the desktop, staring at the screen. I decided to write a synopsis, in point form, of my current state of affairs. I started with all the activities I was involved in with Orenstein. I then went on to discuss my relationships with Ferguson, Martha, and Sarah.

I then outlined my current financial situation: cash in, cash out. I then discussed Molly and Foster Care. I reread the blurb from the Social Service Centre. I noticed for the first time that there was a financial consideration involved. There was no mention of how that worked.

I then added a section on my living situation. How much might I realize from selling the apartment?

If I did sell, was it realistic to live in Flo's building in Westmount? Would that not depend on where Molly was going to school, if she should be living with me? Next, I had a section titled "Five-Year Plan."

Where did I see myself in five years? I stared at that for a good long time. I was blank.

This was the confrontational issue. This was where my energy needed to be this morning.

I got up to make some coffee. I started to pace. I started to imagine the new couch where the two overstuffed chairs were. I sat back down and reread what I had written. It occurred to me that, starting from nothing, I had created quite a network of people and events in my life.

Back to the Five-Year Plan: Finish a Master's Degree in counselling; have an intimate relationship. I stared at the last item. I started to perspire. A cold shiver went through my body.

I went to put on a sweatshirt. This was the issue. I sat back in the chair to stare at what I had just written. My body relaxed. I had no idea how to do that. I knew how to take a course, any course.

I knew how to teach several courses. I knew how to fix a car. I had no idea how to engage in an intimate relationship. Maybe there was a course for that?

I saved what I had written. I went to my emails. Sarah wrote to invite me to a concert at the Museum Concert Hall. The programme was Klezmer Music. I begged off and thanked her for the invitation. I went out on the back veranda to stare at my garlic. That stuff might grow in spite of me. Since my conversation with Mrs. Orenstein, the stray cat had not made an appearance.

She had willed it away.

I could do laundry. I lightly watered the plants. In the fall sunlight, I decided to move two around to more advantageous positions. I took out the hand vacuum and went around the flat in search of things to clean. I moved the stuffed chairs to vacuum underneath. I took the cushions off to do likewise. To my surprise, when I cleaned out the machine, there was a fair amount of lint and dust.

I then went into the kitchen and cleaned all of the counters. I took the mop and did the floor. I was tempted to empty the cupboards to clean them as well.

Shmully rang. "Are you busy? I want to go look at a new car."

"For that, I am not busy. I will be downstairs in five minutes."

We drove up Parc Avenue in silence. At Beaubien, I turned left past some factory buildings.

At the dead end in front of us was a religious school, where I was instructed to pull into the parking lot. A few minutes later, a large black, spotless behemoth drove in and parked beside us. A large, white-shirted gentleman got out of the driver's side. He had a grey-white beard, side curls tucked behind his ears, and a very colourful skullcap. Shmully went over to shake his hand and exchange pleasantries in Hebrew. I walked around the monster vehicle. There was no rust that I could see. In fact, there were no blemishes of any kind on the outside. The key had been left inside; I turned on the ignition. The odometer read 35,672 kilometres. The fellow, who introduced himself as Tanzer, had come over to watch me inspect.

"You know about cars?" he asked in a booming voice.

"A little," I said, looking up at him. I was not usually dwarfed. This guy was huge.

"Are you going to say this thing was driven by a little old lady on weekends only in the summer?"

He boomed with laughter.

He looked over at Shmully. "Where did you get this guy?"

Orenstein shrugged.

"What year is this?"

"It's three years old. And it was mostly driven to and from the airport. It belonged to a large clothing company, which sadly closed its doors here." He mentioned the name of the concern; it meant nothing to me.

I started the motor: a small tune-up would be in order. No leaking of oil.

"It was parked in the company garage at all times. Never outside. Drive it around the block."

I did. Shmully stayed with Tanzer as collateral. It drove well. I was high up. The sight lines were good.

When I came back and hopped down, Tanzer informed me that he had snow tires for it, which he had not put in, but were included in the sale.

"Thirty-five thousand kilometres to drive from Chabanel to the airport seems a bit much."

"So maybe there was some driving around the city to go to meetings and things like that."

"You and Orenstein agree on a price?"

S. John Diamond

I looked under the hood. I checked the oil level. I took out the long stick to check the transmission fluid. There was an odour I did not like. I replaced the stick and started the car again.

With the motor still running, I removed the transmission stick once more.

Tanzer came over, "Something wrong?" His tone was not as jolly.

"These folks have trouble with the transmission?"

"Not that I was told."

"The stick gives off a burning odour. Like caramel."

"I have given Orenstein here a very good price."

Just then the school let out. And two very small boys came over and jumped in Tanzer's arms.

He put them in the second row of seats. There were, in fact two, bench seats in the back.

Shmully came over. "And the verdict is?"

I moved Orenstein off to the side. "I would really like to check out the transmission. I have my suspicions. To replace the tranny on that thing is expensive."

"Let me see what I can arrange."

Tanzer shrugged. The two boys were punching each other and making a ruckus.

Tanzer turned and bellowed into the back of the truck. The noise subsided.

We convoyed south on Parc to Van Horne. Both of us made an illegal left turn onto Van Horne going east. On the left-hand side of the street was a large garage that advertised all things mechanical, including transmissions.

In we went. Tanzer got out of the truck and was met by a fellow in blue overalls who was wiping grease from his hands. The name "Elio" was stitched on his breast pocket.

He opened the hood, took out the transmission stick, smelled it, and put it back. He instructed Tanzer to start the motor. He took out the stick again, smelled it, and put it back.

"These damn trucks drive hot. Transmission okay."

Elio had done all this without even being asked.

I pulled Shmully aside. "Tell Tanzer you will speak to him after Yom Kippur. I would feel more comfortable doing more research."

179

Shmully went over to Tanzer, shook his hand, and thanked him for his time.

Tanzer eyed me with some hostility.

Orenstein said, "You will have something after Yom Kippur, no?"

Tanzer brightened up. "Mr. Orenstein, you can count on me."

I backed out of the garage and onto Van Horne, with Elio directing traffic. Driving up one of the side streets, parallel to Parc, we made it home in about ten minutes.

"Don't bother doing any more work on that model of car. I had read that the transmission was suspect before we went to see it," said Orenstein matter-of-factly.

"Thanks, bud; I almost got my head lopped off."

"You know your stuff."

For a moment, my mind drifted up north to many pleasant evenings in municipal and private garages with some very knowledgeable members of my flock.

"Your acknowledgement almost came a little late."

"Next time, he will treat us more seriously."

"I would not give him a next time."

Orenstein looked up at me. "I will."

And that was the end of that topic, for now.

We moved around to the front of the building from the alley. Mrs. Orenstein was on the front porch. "Ah, the odd couple."

"Good day, Mrs. Orenstein."

"Are you still adopting that child?"

Orenstein looked up at his wife. "*B'Seder*—enough."

She looked at him and went into the house. She did not exactly slam the door.

What an interesting exchange. Orenstein slowly walked up the stairs. I followed just as slowly.

When we got to the landing, he turned to shake my hand. "You know, at some point, if you bring the child in, adopting is something you may have to deal with."

"Shmully, I am not even sure if I am going to go ahead with this. And besides, I have not been accepted yet."

"You will be. And the decision will be yours. Have you seen the girl since she has been here?"

"Not formally. Only in the dark movie theatre when she was on the lam from the hospital. Would you give me a recommendation? I will need to fill out a lengthy application form."

"You write it and I will sign it."

With that, he went into his house and closed the door. I was left outside the door to my apartment with more issues running around my head than I thought was healthy.

CHAPTER THIRTY

I immediately sat at the computer to write Shmully's character reference for me.

After a few sentences, I erased the whole thing. It was reading like an obituary.

I started again. This time I highlighted the various tasks I performed in a "forthright" and "timely" fashion. Being a "self-starter" in our line of work was valued. What exactly was our work?

I had to work around that one. Essentially, I was a highly-regarded "volunteer" who could be "counted on" to perform his assigned tasks "diligently, no matter where or when."

"Unusually pleasant" no matter how "mundane" the activity. When I finished, I thought an ad agency should hire me. I would ask Ferguson to be the second reference. And as for the third, I drew a blank.

Should I add the bishop's name to the list? This meant I would have to ask his permission, which I was loath to do. His secretary and I were okay. I looked around in my desk for their coordinates. I found the card and stared at it for a few minutes. I really did not want to do this.

A sixty-year-old man providing character references for the first time in his life. In the meantime, I printed what I had written for Orenstein to sign. I drew a breath and wrote the secretary.

Within minutes, he wrote back. He would write a letter which he would encourage the bishop to sign. Was it a general letter of recommendation or specific?

I wrote back that I would forward the particulars tomorrow and thanked him for his help.

The sofa lady called, "We were expecting you at noon today."

"Yikes. I totally got wrapped up in other matters. Really sorry. Today is too late—I have another appointment. Tomorrow at noon, okay?"

It was. Some retirement.

Somehow it had gotten to be four o'clock in the afternoon. I had a quick shower. How does one dress for an interview to be a parent—a foster parent? Slacks, button-down blue striped shirt, black runners, windbreaker, and black baseball cap. Off I went to Parc Avenue to take the bus to Sherbrooke Street. I waited for the 24 bus for a few minutes and took it west to Atwater. It was now a quarter to five. Fifteen minutes to make my way down Atwater to Dorchester. On my left, ironically, was the Children's Hospital. Turning right onto Dorchester, I took the first left into a leafy dead-end street. On my left was the address of the office building where the orientation was to take place.

I went in. There were people milling about in the vestibule. We were herded into a meeting room to the left of the entrance. There looked to be about twenty of us squeezed into the space. A young man stood at a dais to welcome us. There was going to be a sheet passed around for us to sign. I found my name and signed beside it. There were not enough seats for everyone. I stood against the back wall.

He asked in both languages if anyone would prefer to have their meeting in French. Nobody put up their hand. So he continued in English, welcoming us. His name was Jean-Luc, and he was the assistant director of Foster Care. This presentation was going to last an hour, after which we would be given an application form. He could not send it beforehand without going over it first.

He thanked us for our interest and talked about what a great contribution we were making to the community. He then introduced a couple who had been foster parents for about fifteen years. In turn, they talked about what a rewarding experience it had been, how their lives had been enriched.

Someone asked how many children they had fostered. They differed by one number. Some child had been with them twice. It was pleasant banter. They got into it because she was drawn to a newspaper article that talked about how difficult it was to find parents. Their kids were grown, and though they still lived at home, there was room for more. They finished to kind and sincere applause.

A young assistant came in with a box of envelopes. Using a laptop, Jean-Luc opened the application and enlarged it onto a screen behind him so we could all see the form clearly.

The usual stuff at the beginning: Name, address, phone numbers, citizenship, etc. Owned or rented home?

Has anyone had previous experience as a foster parent? If so, where and when?

Level of education and where studies were completed?

Has anyone applied and been declined? If so, when, where, and why?

Complete employment history. If a couple, both were required to fill that out, including dates.

If retired, say so, and from what. If you were an executive, of what. Your own business, or did you work for someone else?

Does either partner travel extensively? Where and for how long?

Any criminal convictions?

Alcohol use? Medications prescribed?

Any non-prescribed drugs?

My eyes roamed the room looking to see if there was another single. There did not appear to be.

Two males were standing to my left. And two females were sitting together near the front. The rest seemed to be heterosexual couples.

Why do you want to be a foster parent? If necessary, attach extra information to the back of the application.

Provide three character references. It is suggested that you ask these people first.

No minors and no relatives. If you work in a family business, look around for others to vouch for you: parish priest, lawyer, accountant, bank manager.

That prompted a barrage of questions.

Patiently, Jean-Luc answered all the concerns.

He continued, "We are required to call these people on your behalf, so make sure to indicate when is the best time to call. And yes, we need their complete address and phone number.

"After you complete the application, keep a photocopy and mail the original to the address provided. No PDF and no Fax.

"We will call you for a personal interview, at which time we will discuss the compensation involved. That is a private matter and depends on many factors.

"Any more questions?

"My card is enclosed in the packet, should you think of something to ask.

"One final thing: thank you for coming this evening. Thank you for showing interest in being foster parents. And if you know anyone else who would like to be here, let us know."

The envelopes were distributed. One couple left theirs on the table and quickly left.

S. John Diamond

On my way out, someone called my name; I turned. It was Claire Thomas.

"I hear you are going to give us some interesting character references. Benito Mussolini, indeed."

I looked down at her. "You know, you guys have nothing on the RCMP."

She ignored my gibe. "When you leave here, are you going to see Ferguson?"

"I was planning on it, yes."

"You know this is Doris's last day."

"I know. Are you concerned?"

"Yes, I am. Maybe he should get someone else for the next little while. He has a contact at the CLSC, but there is a waiting list. You should put him on it. Just do it. If he does not need anybody, then postpone the service. At least he is on the list."

"You are right; we should have done that immediately."

"I am tied up tonight with a board meeting. Tomorrow I will come around to keep him company. You have never heard him give a sermon. What a joy. He was a great teacher. I am concerned that he is not reading as much as he used to."

"He does have a concussion. Maybe this week we will see him reading more."

"I have to run. I hope you have begun to line up your referees. Joseph Stalin, really!"

I left the building with my hefty envelope and turned left on Dorchester to walk to Greene. I passed large old homes, some of which had been in the same families for three and four generations. Others had been sold and carved up into small apartments. At Greene I turned right, past the RCMP Building, and crossed Ste Catherine. I doubled back to go to the bagel place and bought a half-dozen white seed bagels. I munched one as I walked up to Ferguson's. At the corner of Sherbrooke, I put the envelope and bagels down on a bench and called his apartment. Doris answered. "Reverend Ferguson's residence."

"Excuse me. I was looking for Reg."

"He is here in all his glory and was just asking where you were."

"I will be along very soon. I am across the street."

"He wants to know if you are bringing food."

"None of his business."

185

I rang off and crossed the street.

It was the end of September, and it was about six thirty and dark. The good news was the hockey season was about to start—six months of minutely following the team's every move. In addition, the heaviest burden fell to the general population, who were busy coaching the team. They twisted themselves into exhaustion until spring. The entire fate of the hockey club rested on their shoulders and their shoulders alone. None of them ever got fired. Labour of love.

The door to Ferguson's apartment was partially open by the time I arrived. I ceremoniously put the bag of bagels on the dining room table. Reg was sitting in his reserved seat on the couch.

"Bless you. I could eat all that is in there."

"How biblical."

Doris appeared from the kitchen. "Staying for supper? I am going to make an omelet, and we can use the fresh bagels to round out the meal."

"Sounds good to me. How are you?"

"You know, this is my last day. I am going to miss you guys. The Rev and I were devising a plan, which, until he moves into the Manor, could see me here one late afternoon a week."

I looked at Ferguson. "You are going to follow through on that?"

He nodded. "I think the time is good for that while I still have all, or most of, my marbles. I called my friend, the executive director. Would you believe I have to fill out an application? I have only been the chaplain there for twenty-five years."

"Speaking of applications, I have a lengthy one here to fill out in order to be a foster parent. Would you act as a character reference?"

He looked up. "Do I have to? Write something and I will sign it."

"I had to do the same thing for Orenstein. I started to write the thing and it read like an obituary."

"I trust you changed the wording to reflect your current state of life? This side of the turf?"

Doris came out of the kitchenette. "Soup's on."

Ferguson went to wash his hands. I was next.

We sat at what seemed like our assigned places at the table: me with my back to the door, Ferguson with his back to the window, and Doris in the middle with her back to the kitchen.

Ferguson stood and mouthed grace. After the silent prayer, he stayed standing for a moment, looked at Doris, and reached for her hand. "You know, you have been a great help in easing me into the next chapter of my life. I truly thank you."

She looked down. "Thank you, Reverend, and thank you, Glasheen."

There was complete silence.

Doris broke the silence. "Does anyone want ketchup with their eggs?"

We both looked up, horrified. "No. No!"

She started to laugh. "I guess I did not really know the crowd I was playing to."

We all had a good laugh.

The omelette was perfect: a little cheese, some broccoli, and some onion. She served the bagels as is; they were still slightly warm. We all drank water that had been cooled in the fridge.

Doris and I cleared the dishes. She then shooed me out of the kitchen so she could wash up.

I sat beside Ferguson on the couch.

"I took my medication, if that was going to be your question."

"And your blood pressure?"

"I have one."

"Better than the alternative."

"How was the meeting?"

"No surprises. I ran into Claire as I was leaving. She was concerned about your lack of reading."

He looked at me. "Another *yenta*. Did you explain that I concussed myself?"

"I did."

"Case closed."

I noticed that the tiny tea table beside where he was sitting was piled with books. The one on top was open in the middle.

"What are you reading?"

"I am loving Martha's gift. I am reading it very slowly."

"Doris and I went to the Westmount Library the other day. I wanted to borrow the new biography of Trudeau. I am on the waiting list. I managed to borrow some others."

187

"I did not get back to reading the information about women in the synagogue."

"Are you sure that is where your mind is?"

"I guess not as much as before. The Church will have to get along without my input."

"You have other priorities now."

"I tried my best. It's time for others to take up the torch."

"Taking in Molly is not taking up a torch?"

"Different torch."

"Still a torch."

Doris came into the room. "I am going to leave now."

We both rose. She went to the closet to the left of the door to get her coat. I went to help her into it.

"That will not be necessary; thank you anyway."

I shook her hand. "Thank you for all your help."

"No, thank you for all yours. I will be here next Thursday."

Ferguson put his hand on her arm and escorted her to the elevator. When he came back, he looked pleased.

"You know, I thought the whole idea of having a minder was ridiculous. I was wrong, especially in this case. Doris was perfect. It could not have been anyone else."

"She is not entirely leaving you."

"I really must thank Flo."

"I am going to go soon, as well. I need to write another letter of reference."

"Lay it on thick," he said with a chuckle.

"Will do. I will be by later in the week."

"You know where to find me. I am either here, at the clinic, or at the drugstore."

"And your exercise regime, do not neglect that."

"I am going to give myself another week and then slowly get back into my chaplain routine."

"You are missing it?"

"Sitting around here may be necessary for now, but not forever. I am not the shut-in type."

I got off the sofa, shook his hand, wished him well, and gathered up my stuff.

"I will be by later in the week. I have to go and complete this application. I have not applied for anything in years."

"Welcome to the real world."

"I guess. This was not something I had planned on."

"I did not plan to develop diabetes or get a concussion."

"So, planning is for the birds."

"Sometimes planning gets in the way of seeing what's next to do."

"It is too late for this stuff. I really do need to go."

"Soon, then."

CHAPTER THIRTY-ONE

The 24 bus driver welcomed me warmly; he had few passengers.

I sat in the front. There was a radio playing. It was tuned to a sports talk show station. There was one topic of conversation: the local hockey team.

After a few minutes, I tuned out and looked out the window of the bus to see Sherbrooke Street passing by at night. There were few people on the street and very little traffic. Next, I took the Parc Avenue bus to Fairmount and walked to my apartment. Just me and the parked cars. There was no one else out.

Back in the apartment, there was a message from Orenstein. There was another car to view at eleven a.m. And he still had not heard from Green or Gold.

I put the large envelope down on the kitchen counter to deal with first thing in the morning.

Checking emails, I saw that I still had not gone to the furniture store, as Carolyn reminded me. I wrote back that tomorrow for sure, around one or one thirty, I would be there.

There was a message from Martha. Distilled down from the ramble was that she was missing Ferguson and me. I wrote her that we could have supper together tonight, or whenever she was free. I was sure Ferguson would be okay with that.

I checked the news headlines. There was nothing that grabbed my attention. As for the sports, the Canadiens were ready to start the season. The one rookie who had caught my attention in preseason had made the cut and was going to start in the first game next Tuesday. There was a CFL game on the sports channel. I watched for a few minutes. It did not grab my interest. I would watch the highlights later.

I undressed, washed, and got into bed. I found the French music station with the hypnotic announcer. His playlist was eclectic. He played jazz, blues, and then he would throw in Jacques Brel. Sandwiched in between were random thoughts about life and love.

I imagined him sitting alone in a darkened studio with one lit candle and herbal tea laced with a little honey.

It worked. I fell into a deep sleep. Turning over, I looked at the clock, which now read four fifty-five. No dreams to report. I turned the radio off just as the news came on. I was not ready for that yet.

I showered, shaved, got into my sweatpants and ratty T-shirt, and opened the foster care envelope. I sat looking at the pile of paper without really focusing on it.

I made coffee, came back, and decided that as much as I concentrated, the form was not going to fill itself out. I found my fountain pen and started to fill out the application. I wrote as neatly as I could. The open-ended questions I left blank. My gut reaction to them was: "Because."

Why did I want to become a foster parent? This question was asked three different ways.

I went back to the computer and wrote the bishop's secretary to give him the address of the Foster Care Office where the letter was to be sent and to whose attention.

He wrote back moments later saying he would attend to it today. The bishop would be signing correspondence later this morning. My letter would be in the pile.

I thanked him and wished him well for all his help. He returned the thanks and told me I was doing a "noble act of charity."

I wrote the letter for Ferguson to sign and chose to keep it to the point: "Mr. Glasheen would make an excellent Foster Parent."

I printed it, found an envelope, folded it, and put it in my blazer pocket. I needed to get a stamp.

I went back to the application and wrote a bunch of answers to the three questions.

I did not think through what I was writing. I used the secretary's words as a springboard to my thoughts. Actually, the word "noble" figured prominently in my answers. I went over the application one more time, making sure that my references' addresses and phone numbers were correct.

I left the application on the table, put on a sweater, a windbreaker, and my Canadiens ball cap, and went out to get some morning air.

Shmully and three of his four sons were leaving to go for morning prayers. The boys went on ahead. Shmully lagged behind to speak to me. "Are you free at eleven?"

"What is Tanzer going to bring you this time?"

"Town and Country."

"What year?"

"Three years old."

"Driven by a little old lady to the grocery store and back?"

"He will come by here."

"I will be outside waiting."

Off he went to fulfill his morning obligations.

I went down to the Main and started walking south.

As if drawn to a beacon, I reached Duluth. The movie theatre reconstruction looked complete, at least from the outside. Gone was the scaffolding. There were posters advertising the latest double feature. A new sign offering couples a discount Mondays and Tuesdays was hanging to the left of the entrance. *Plus ça change!*

A few doors farther down was a diner offering breakfast. Deciding I was hungry, I went in. I had my choice of tables, so I sat in front near the window. The waitress brought coffee and a menu.

There was a newspaper lying on an adjacent table; I reached over and got it.

The menu had the usual breakfast fare. Since I had eggs last night, I chose lox, bagel, and cream cheese. The waitress came back with my order and the English paper. Nice touch.

The dish was piled high with cream cheese and two strips of the smoked fish. I ordered a second bagel. The first paper had a lot of police blotter stuff: arrests, trials, raids, and the like. There was an extensive sports section devoted solely to the Canadiens and the upcoming season. Pictures of the players without their helmets showed how young they really were.

The English paper was more concerned about other issues. In neither paper was there mention of Epstein. I was focused on my reading, so I did not notice that someone had slipped into the chair opposite me. I looked up with a start. It was Green.

I put down the paper. The waitress approached with her coffee carafe. When she saw us staring at one another, she took a detour.

"Listen, priest: I want you and the Rabbi to get out of my life."

I stared at him. "I believe you know how to accomplish that."

"I don't need you, and I don't need him to tell me what to do."

"You want your building sold. You want to marry your lady friend. You want your ex-wife out of your life. You want a lot for nothing."

My voice had risen. The restaurant had gone silent.

He got up from the table. As he was leaving, he turned. "You bastards will not blackmail me." Out the door he went.

The young man who had been at the cash came over. "You all right?"

"I am fine. Sorry for the disturbance." I followed him to pay up and leave. I left the waitress a large tip. "Stuff happens."

"He comes in here from time to time with a blonde lady. He eats; she drinks tea and complains."

"I am sure it will not happen again."

"Life is too short, eh?"

I nodded and thanked him for his understanding. I put on my ball cap and left.

Passing Green's theatre, I noticed that there was a ten a.m. show. Great way to start the day.

At the apartment, Orenstein was coming back with two of his boys. His eldest went to Yeshiva in the Snowdon area and travelled there directly after services.

Where the youngest son was, I had no idea. Maybe his asthma was acting up.

"I ran into Green."

Shmully nodded. "And I have a call from Gold which I have not answered."

"We had a scene in the diner down the street from his theatre. He is, ah, not fond of us."

"Did you research the Town and Country yet?"

"Just about to. And what are you going to do with Gold?"

"Nothing. The ball is in their court, as you might say. Father and son are still willing to deal with Green. They have conditions as well."

"Mr. Greengarten wants everything his way."

Orenstein nodded. "You know that this will have an ending."

"You know something I do not?"

"I think it is time to have a meeting with Mr. Green's ex-wife."

"What, about the *get*?"

"That becomes part of the conversation." With that, he went into his house, leaving me on the landing with my mouth open.

CHAPTER THIRTY-TWO

By the time I reached the top stair and opened the door to my apartment, I realized how good a strategy it was to meet with Mrs. Green. And how blind we had been to the obvious. Focusing on Green was a mistake. For all his bluster, he was incapable of acting in his best interest. He was too stuck on proving everyone else wrong.

I smiled to myself. With coffee in hand, I looked up the van on the Internet. Unless Tanzer brought us the "A" model, none of the reviews turned me on. I thought we should go at this the other way around. I would look up possibilities and ask Tanzer if he could find it for us.

In the meantime, I reread my application for the Foster Care folks. I changed nothing. I took the envelope, put on my windbreaker, and left the apartment to walk to the post office in the back of the pharmacy on the Main. I had about twenty minutes before the van appointment. The woman behind the counter took the envelope, weighed it on the scale, and charged me accordingly.

I hurried back home to await our eleven o'clock appointment. I went online to read the news headlines. The doorbell rang. It was five past eleven. I hurried downstairs, where Tanzer and Orenstein were waiting for me by the curb. Double-parked on the street was a large, black Japanese van.

Tanzer had brought a large Japanese behemoth.

I was invited to drive. Tanzer sat in the passenger seat and Orenstein sat in the back. Tanzer looked pleased with himself. He lounged back in his seat. The car drove well. The odometer showed forty-thousand kilometres.

"Well, Mr. Glasheen? What do you think of this car? By the way, it was driven around town and to a chalet near Sainte-Agathe. It is three years young." He laughed at his own joke.

I drove up the Main and went under the tunnel at Van Horne. Emerging from the tunnel, I went into the parking lot of the hardware store on the right. We all got out. The tires had good tread.

"I do not have the snows; you will have to buy them yourself."

There were no dents, but there were some small scratches here and there. Nothing I could not handle myself. Opening the hood, I poked around. Everything was in order. I got onto my knees and peered into the undersides, checking the rods, brake lines, and muffler. I noticed a hitch, properly installed. Good signs.

Next the transmission. I found the dipstick easily. There was no odour, and the fluid was perfectly clean. I started the van and rechecked the transmission. All was in order.

I looked at Orenstein. "You like it, buy it. It drives well."

I went into the hardware store to buy some tea towels. When I came back, Tanzer and Orenstein were shaking hands.

"Now, Mr. Glasheen, can I get you a car?"

"Not yet. I know how to get hold of you."

Orenstein showed no particular emotion, even though he had just bought a very expensive truck.

"I can come by tomorrow and we can go to the licence bureau. I will dispose of your old van."

We all got back in, and Tanzer drove us back home; he looked very pleased with himself.

Orenstein would need the morning to organize the finances. Then he and Tanzer would go to the licence bureau. We all shook hands, and Tanzer drove away.

"What happened to the other car he was going to bring?"

"You read the same stuff I did. I told Gideon Tanzer not to waste our time."

I nodded. "We will see if we are both right about this."

I stood on the street and called the furniture store.

Carolyn answered and would be happy to see me now.

As I was walking toward the Main, my cell phone rang. "Martha here. Remember me?"

"Vaguely."

"What are you up to these days? Did you complete the application?"

"Yes, and I mailed it off. How is your mother?"

"No easy answer to that one. I went with her to the notary to make sure her will is in order. We did the same thing a year ago. Medically, we are going to meet with the doctor tomorrow morning."

"And her mood?"

"Stoically dignified."

"Oh, my. In my mind's eye, stoic and your mother do not fit together."

"Correct. Oh, yes. Almost forgot. We are going to move Molly to a halfway house."

"Halfway to where?"

"You and only you know the answer to that."

"Look, I am where I need to be at the moment. Speak later."

Carolyn was standing in the doorway talking on the phone. She quit the call when she saw me.

I walked in the open door, and we shook hands.

"We have been waiting for you. We have designed a couch which we hope you will like. You will need to choose the material to cover it. We got a hold of some extra swatches for you to take a look at."

"And the other issue, it just occurred to me, is getting it into my upstairs flat."

"First things first. Let's choose the covering."

I stood at her desk and thumbed through a book of samples. One or two I held up to the light. None seemed right. She showed me some individual samples she had picked up from somewhere. These were getting closer to what I thought I wanted. Out came another set of swatches. This material was richer looking.

"My picture, I think now, is a cloth that makes a bold statement. Like a tartan."

"Let's go to the computer and look up tartans."

"Irish Tartan, if you please."

She found a website that featured various tartans. "Oh, they have them organized by county and family."

She passed by a beautiful red, beige, and blue cloth covering a pillow.

"That's it. That's it, exactly."

"County Cork."

"No matter. Close enough. But that is the look I want."

Just then, Jack came upstairs and looked at the screen as well.

"Wow, that is special. And expensive. I would need about six metres to be safe. Maybe seven."

"Can you get it here, or do you have to order it directly?"

"We will ask around and let you know. There is a place in Toronto that imports this kind of material."

Carolyn looked up from the screen. "Mr. Glasheen is worried about getting the sofa into his apartment."

Jack did not look fazed. "We deal with that sort of thing all the time. We will manage. You have a back entrance which goes straight into the house?"

"Yes, I do, and I guess you figured that the front inside staircase curves."

"That was a given. We will be okay. From the moment I get the material, it will take me about three weeks to build your couch. Have you seen the final design?"

"Not yet."

He took out his tablet and showed me a design from several angles. It was perfect.

"What are you going to use for the inside?"

"My bias is to use the good stuff; not that fiberfill."

"Should I ask about price?"

Jack pondered for a moment. "I do not want to scare you off. But we are looking at thirty-eight hundred dollars."

"You know what, let us go for it." I had figured about four thousand, so it was not far off.

We shook hands all around. They would call or email if there was anything to discuss. I left a deposit and walked out into the fall sunshine.

By the time I got home, I was second-guessing my decision. I squelched my urge to cancel the whole deal.

I sat at the computer to write the letter for Ferguson to sign. It looked sort of bare. I printed it, folded it, and put it in an envelope.

While I was continuing to muse about my sofa, Orenstein called. "We have a meeting with Mrs. Green at one p.m."

"What about Tanzer and the car?"

"It will wait."

"Do we have a game plan?"

"You know better than that."

He rang off.

I decided to go to the fruit and vegetable store on Parc. While I was there, my cell rang. In the hubbub, I could not hear a thing. I left my basket and went outside to take the call. It was Martha.

"Guess what?"

"Molly went AWOL from the halfway house."

"You know, you are a pain in the ass."

"So what is the deal now?"

"She has one more chance, and then we have to do something else."

"A more secure facility, perhaps."

"Something like that. You didn't get your application in a minute too soon."

"Keep me informed."

"What are you doing tonight?"

"Probably going to Ferguson's so he can sign his letter of recommendation, which I wrote for him."

"There is no end to your talents. And after that?"

"I have no plans at the moment."

"Call me."

I rang off and went back into the store; my cart had disappeared. The place was too busy, so I left empty-handed.

As I was walking back to the apartment, I noticed that Orenstein was in the alley beside the shiny new truck with a prayer book in hand. I stood behind and waited for him to finish. I think I said a few words, too. Mostly hoping I would not have to change a cable by flashlight.

"I would like to leave for the appointment soon."

He gave me a set of keys for the car. I held them up in my hand. "Did I get another promotion?"

He grunted, walked down the alley, turned the corner, and presumably, went into his house.

I stood still, admiring the car. It really was an improvement over its predecessor.

I looked inside the back. There were four snow tires in white bags. Nice touch. I hoped they were in good shape; new tires for this thing were going to be expensive.

I went into the apartment and looked at emails. There was nothing. I went onto the Internet and looked up Ladino, the language which Orenstein used to speak with Constable Elbaz.

Essentially, it was a mixture of Arabic, Hebrew, Aramaic, Spanish, and probably a few other things.

It was spoken by North African Jews like Yiddish was spoken by European Jews. I was more curious as to why Ms. Elbaz admonished Orenstein for speaking to her using Ladino.

Perhaps she did not want him to become too familiar. She was with us on "official" business, after all.

My mind wandered ahead to the meeting this afternoon. I wondered if Mrs. Green would be alone or with a family member, or maybe her lawyer?

Our job, it seemed to me, was simple. However, nothing about this Green affair had been easy.

I then started to write out some thoughts about Joel's abuse. The case had started us off but somehow had receded into the shadows. I wrote out what I remembered. I included all the players involved. I reviewed the meeting with the family and the talk with the child on the street.

I stared at what I wrote. Nothing jumped out at me. I made coffee. I came back to the screen. The one conclusion I came to was that the phantom cellphone calls were linked to the attack on Joel. Who was it? And why me?

I continued staring. I had reached a dead end.

Typing in "Rabbi Shinder, Montreal," there were two references. The first was for Rabbi Joshua Shinder. Born in Ukraine, he arrived in Montreal in the 1930s from New York. He was a major player in the Jewish Community in the 1940s, 1950s, and 1960s. He was involved in many community endeavours, including the dietary laws committee, the Jewish General Hospital, Jewish day schools, and the establishment of a synagogue.

The next Shinder entry was for the current Rabbi Shinder, Ariyeh, who more or less took over from his father. Shinder attended a Yeshiva in New York. Separately, I had to look up "Yeshiva," which to my Catholic eyes was a seminary for Rabbinic training. There was no mention that he graduated.

There was noise coming from outside in the back.

Orenstein and his oldest son were working on the back veranda stabilizing the tent-like structure for the Sukkah Festival. They were draping canvas around the sides of the structure, leaving the roof open to be covered by cedar boughs. The custom was to eat in the structure during the holiday. Some even slept there as well, though around here at this time of year, I hardly thought so. All these holidays reached far back into the past but served to bind the community and families together now. The structure commemorated the Israelites' forty years of travelling in the desert.

My cell rang again. "Martha here. I wanted to let you know Molly was found. She was tending a cat which had been run over and was still alive. Anyway, they took the cat and Molly and one of the childcare workers to the SPCA. They had to euthanize the cat. Molly was involved in the whole process. Interesting child you have got there."

"That is the thing. She is really special."

"She appears to have come through this in great shape. The vet was sensitive enough to explain why she was putting the cat down. Molly was given all kinds of strokes for aiding the animal. The SPCA gave her a badge of achievement. I really do not know what your problem is. You are the one, the only one who should look after her."

"Thanks for the vote of confidence."

"Skip the bullshit, it does not become you."

"Do you mind if I ease into the next phase of my life at my own speed?"

"Why do I get so impatient with you?"

"Yes, why do you?"

There was a pause. "I don't know. Listen, there is someone at my door."

"We will continue this conversation later."

She rang off very abruptly.

CHAPTER THIRTY-THREE

I had a message from the Foster Care Department. They wanted me to come in the following Monday at four thirty. If I could not make it, there was a number to call. I saw no reason to call back.

I went downstairs to get Orenstein to sign the letter of recommendation. He came to the door in a rumpled white shirt, black slacks, runners, and a dark blue skullcap. I gave him a pen and held the letter on the open door for him to sign. As he was signing, he read through it.

"Very flattering," he said as he turned to give me the pen back. I thanked him for his effort.

"It was nothing." He went back into his house and was about to close his door. "Ten minutes." I went up to dress for the occasion.

My cellphone rang; it was resting on the kitchen counter. I removed my shoes, and by the time I got there, I had missed the call. It was from my phantom friend.

I went downstairs to wait for Orenstein. He appeared a minute later.

"We are going to de Maisonneuve Boulevard west of Greene."

"I really have spent my entire week in that part of town. Maybe I should move there."

The rest of the drive was completed in silence. Orenstein sat staring straight ahead. Whether he was praying or meditating, I could not tell.

There was a semicircular driveway with one empty parking spot for guests. We were met at the sliding front door by a gentleman in uniform who asked us how long we would be. An hour satisfied him, and he walked us to a desk to sign in. He called upstairs and then instructed us that we were expected in apartment 702.

At the seventh floor, we got off the elevator and found Mrs. Green's apartment. Orenstein was wearing his black hat. I took off my ball cap.

The door was opened by a tall woman with short brown hair. She wore black slacks and a blue blouse. She had clogs on, and as we moved into the place, it was obvious that someone had just moved in.

"Gentlemen, I am Sheila Green."

We introduced ourselves. She was the woman I saw leaving Rabbi Shinder's office when we had our first meeting with him.

There were no rugs on the floor. And paintings were stacked against a far wall. There was a small sofa on one wall, and in the middle of the room opposite were two chairs.

"As you can see, I just moved in here. The rugs are coming tomorrow."

She was not what I expected. She did not look like the downtrodden victim of a bad marriage. And she would be three-fourths of an inch taller than her husband.

"I would offer you gentlemen something, but I have nothing but orange juice. We are waiting for Marie-France, my lawyer, to arrive; she has been delayed."

We were still standing in the middle of the room. There was a southern view of the city that included a stretch of the Saint Lawrence River. Sometimes I forgot that Montreal was on an Island.

Mrs. Green sat on the sofa, and Shmully sat on the chair closer to the window. I took the other.

There was a knock on the door. Mrs. Green got up and let in a young blonde woman dressed in a black pantsuit with a white blouse. She came right over to me and shook my hand. Shmully stood, did not offer his hand, and gave her a nod.

"I am Marie-France L'Ecuyer. I have been representing Sheila, Mrs. Green, for some time now. I am sorry to be late. Why are you gentlemen here?"

I looked over at Orenstein, whom, I could tell, wanted to slow the proceedings down.

"Well, we are here for a number of reasons." He was using his radio voice, the one in the lower register. "Mrs. Green wants a religious divorce from her husband."

"Yes. I am aware of that," Marie-France acknowledged.

"To date, Mr. Green has chosen not to grant her that wish."

"You gentlemen are to intervene on Mrs. Green's behalf, yes?"

"Yes, and we have not been successful, so far."

"What are you proposing? That is why you are here, *oui*?"

"The property on the Main."

"Which Mr. Green conveniently has not sold."

Orenstein paused. "You sell it."

"I wanted Mrs. Green and her family to buy the fifty percent they do not own, but Sheila objects to owning an X-rated cinema. Are there serious purchasers whom Mike Green has not yet annoyed?"

Orenstein nodded.

L'Ecuyer asked, "You know them?"

Orenstein nodded.

"Not riff-raff. You know them personally?"

Again, Orenstein nodded.

Her lawyer went on. "Mike Greengarten is impossible to do business with. For all his bluster, he is a bad businessman. He took Sheila's father's knitting company, how do I say, down the tubes in a matter of years. He cannot be trusted to make the right decision. He needs money to support his lifestyle."

In his quiet way, Orenstein suggested, "You should buy the building and roll it over to the other party. And eventually you will pay Green—if and when he grants Sheila her wish. If that party backs out, Sheila owns a hundred per cent of the property. If Green agrees to the *get*, he gets his share of the sale price."

L'Ecuyer turned to her client. "Sheila, you have to agree to this, even if it is a pornographic theatre. You own the building; you can show art films."

The lawyer's phone rang. She went into the kitchen to take the call.

Mrs. Green looked at both of us. "I really do not want to do business with my former husband."

Orenstein looked at her. "You may have no choice under the circumstances."

"I do not trust him. I would like to be finished with him."

I wondered out loud: "How come this property was not settled during the divorce proceedings?"

"I got the house to do with what I wanted. He was to sell the property, and we were to split the sale price. Since he has a history of not doing what he is supposed to do, well, that is why we are sitting here. I am tired of him and his nonsense. You know he interviewed all of the likely divorce lawyers, so none of them could represent me because of a conflict of interest. I had to search to find Marie-France. I could go on. About his girlfriends . . . there was always an attractive receptionist around. But mostly, I resent him for abandoning his children. He has never had any time for them." She stopped. We both said nothing.

Marie-France came back into the room. "*Je m'excuse.*"

Orenstein nodded in her direction. "Mrs. Green is loath to do business with her ex-husband."

I interjected, "Dragging him back into court is not an option?"

The lawyer looked at me. "He would love that, you know. It would give him yet another opportunity to drag this whole affair out. And, of course, cost Sheila even more money."

Mrs. Green, who had been sitting in the corner of the couch with her arms folded, looked at both of us. "The buyers, they are solid citizens? They are serious?"

Orenstein nodded and then added, "Yes, they are solid citizens, and they are still interested in the property. They would likewise prefer not to do business with Green."

"Why did he not show up at the signing; does anyone know?" I asked.

"According to the father and son purchasers, he was tied up at the hospital with tests," Orenstein continued. "This was on a Friday. So it was agreed that they would meet the following Sunday morning at lawyer Gold's office. He was a no-show then as well, and Gold could not explain Green's absence or account for his whereabouts."

Privately, I decided that this was not the way to go. Like an alcoholic, Green had not quite bottomed out. He was close; but he needed to fall a bit farther. His behaviour had inconvenienced everyone but one person. The question was how best to get at her.

In the meantime, I wanted to know where we stood with these two people. "What would you like us to do?"

They looked at one another. The lawyer opened her mouth to say something, but Mrs. Green said, "I want to get out from under my former husband. I want him out of my life. I also want a *get*."

"Do you want us to stay involved?"

The lawyer looked at Orenstein. "You know the buyers. We do not know them. For the moment, we are stuck. I think you should continue." She looked at her client. Sheila nodded her head.

"Mrs. Green, you are in agreement?" I asked.

"I want you both to continue."

Orenstein said, "This whole messy affair could get even messier."

"How much will this cost?" the lawyer asked.

Orenstein looked at her. "I am paid by the community."

Mrs. Green sat forward on the couch, looking at Orenstein, thn me. "This means a lot to me. I want my life back. I made a mistake years ago marrying a charming salesman who worked for my father. He could play tennis, and I fell in love. You know most of the rest."

I stood. "I think we have our work cut out for us."

Orenstein stood as well. "We will keep you informed of our progress."

Marie-France stood and gave us both business cards. I shook the lawyer's hand.

Mrs. Green slowly stood; I shook her hand with both of mine.

Orenstein had put on his big black hat. We bid our farewells and left the apartment.

Nothing was said in the elevator. We signed out at the main desk and went out in still-bright sunshine. Orenstein looked at me. "I hear your brain working. I am late. Are you coming?"

"No, I have some things to take care of around here. Speak tomorrow night?"

"Sunday morning will be fine."

"One question."

He turned to look as he was getting into his very clean SUV.

"You have faith that any of this will work?"

"Yes, I have faith."

He backed out of the parking space and drove off at a great clip.

What a nice car.

CHAPTER THIRTY-FOUR

I walked over to Greene Avenue and went into the office building. In the elevator, I pressed "18".

Without knocking or ringing the bell, I went into an office. I walked past the receptionist, who opened then closed her mouth. I went into the corner office.

Gold was sitting behind his big desk with his back to the pen sketches on the wall of English barristers performing in court.

He looked up.

"I am here to tell you that your client is a royal pain in the ass. But you already knew that. I would like you to know that we can help poor Mrs. Green rid him from her life and probably yours as well." I waited.

He thought for a moment. "You sure you were a priest? You come across more as a bulldog."

"Woof. Let us get to cases. If the father and son do not buy the property, then Mrs. Green is prepared to do so and sell it or not as she sees fit. She will pay Green his share of the proceeds on condition he gives her a *get*. Otherwise, he can chase her for the money. And since he does not have any, that would be extremely stupid.

"He may even be able to pay you with what is left over. By the way, how much does he owe you? Have you added it all up? Or do you have a round figure in your head?

"But if Green, as I suspect, will not do business with his ex-wife, will he drag the poor woman through further hell? So perhaps you can engineer this client of yours to see the light of day?"

Gold stood. "Green and I have not talked for a week—not since he did not turn up last Sunday with no explanation."

"Are you saying you have been fired?"

"I think I fired him."

"Finally! You do not have to say anything further. Do you know how I can get a hold of Green's lady friend?"

He picked up his hand-held to scroll through his list of people. "I have a phone number, that is all. No address, nothing."

He turned the device so I could see it, and I took down the number.

I looked at him and thanked him.

"Why are you thanking me?"

"Because we are going to close this file once and for all."

And with that, I turned and walked out of his office.

Thankfully, when I got to the lower concourse, the kitchen store was closed "due to illness."

I went out on the street and called Martha. There was no answer, so I left a message. I walked over to the bagel place and bought one bagel that I had demolished by the time I reached the sidewalk. I was going to go in for another when Martha called. "Where are you?"

"And hello to you, too."

"Greetings. I will be free in about thirty minutes. Where are you?"

"In the Greene Avenue area of the world, around the corner from you."

"Can you kill thirty minutes?"

"I will manage something."

She rang off.

I would have gone to a bookstore, but there were none around that I knew. It was time to take a look at tablets. I wandered down Sainte-Catherine to the to the office supply store, which, according to some minimal research (I looked at their window), sold tablets. I went in and found the tablet section of the store. I was lost.

To me, all these things looked about the same. And the brief descriptions beside the various models were mumbo jumbo in either language.

"Can I assist you?" The man speaking was young, wore glasses, and seemed eager to help.

"I want to buy a tablet for one purpose and one purpose only."

"And that would be?"

"To communicate with a young woman who has difficulty expressing herself."

I now had a secondary goal: to prevent this young man from becoming patronizing.

"You are looking for a machine which will run a certain application."

"Correct."

"You're not interested in games, videos, or music?"

"I am not: but my young friend will be, probably."

I had my hand on one that was much less expensive than the rest.

"That model does not have built-in Wi-Fi. All of the others here do."

"And are more expensive?" He nodded.

I was looking at twelve-hundred dollars for two.

There was a demo that I could open. The thing was light, and the picture quality was good.

"If you were going to buy one of these for your mother, which one would you buy?"

"If you had asked about my father, this one, here. It is a bit bigger, heavier, and has more power. As for Mother, I would go to the place further downtown," he said with a wink.

It took me a second to pick up on his recommendation to go to Apple.

Martha called. "I am finished. I can pick you up."

"I am at the office supply place on Sainte-Catherine."

"Walk west and meet me on the corner of Greene and Sainte-Catherine."

"Aye, aye."

We arrived simultaneously. I got in the passenger side.

"Where to, Magoo?"

"I am famished."

"Me, too."

We both said Chinese. That was a good sign. I do not think I could take any more discord.

"There are two right here—unless you want to go further afield?"

"Let us get out of this part of town."

"You know there is one near you on the Main. I have not been there in a long time. It's very good, and, more importantly, it's not crazy loud."

"Perfect."

She drove east to Atwater. Left on Atwater past the Forum where Ferguson had fallen or fainted in the theatre, and Molly bolted. Then right on Sherbrooke Street, east to Saint-Laurent Boulevard.

She was focused on driving, and I started to nod off. I was going to be great company.

"What kind of day did you have?" Martha asked without taking her eyes from the road.

S. John Diamond

"Well, it was a lot tougher and longer than I had hoped. I could not find Ferguson, so I called around. Eventually we connected, and I suggested he get a cellphone. He refused. Orenstein and I had a meeting which resulted in our becoming more involved in a sticky situation. I had hoped to walk away after having suggested the perfect solution. And you?"

"The usual hospital stuff. Plus, I have Mother to concern myself with. We have a meeting with the doctor next Monday morning. There is a fair amount of anxiety about that. The only thing I notice about her is she feels chronically fatigued. That is not my mother. So there is cause for concern."

We had gone north on Saint-Laurent to Fairmount. "From memory, we're getting warm. I am going to park, and we will walk to find this place."

We both put money in the meter for a couple of hours of time. We passed a very neat, clean storefront that turned out to be our destination. Subtle—you had to know it existed. There was a small, elegant sign etched in the glass of one of the front windows.

We walked in and were met by a very trim, tiny woman with menus in hand.

"Sit anywhere you like." We chose a table against the far wall. She did not mind that the table was for four.

The place was spotless. The walls were down to the brick. The kitchen was in full view in the rear. There was one cook and the woman who met us at the door.

A young woman appeared to fill our water glasses. Neither one of us wanted either beer or wine, although a beer was tempting. I closed the menu and looked at Martha. "Whatever you order is fine."

"Big responsibility. We will share stuff, okay?"

"Sure."

The young woman came back with a notepad. Martha ordered two dishes, some soup, and spring rolls, all of which sounded good to me.

The cook got busy, and a few minutes later, the soups came, followed by the spring rolls.

I ate half my soup and waited for Martha to do the same with hers.

"This is really good. I want the whole thing."

I agreed and went about finishing mine.

The spring rolls were perfect. Martha had one; I had three.

209

There was a pause before the rest came. "I have an appointment on Monday at four thirty with the Foster Care folks."

"I know," she said. "In the meantime, Molly has settled into the halfway home and has become a model citizen. She is behind in school, but has extra tutoring and is slowly catching up. She should continue in that program. It would be a shame to disrupt something that is working, at least for this year."

"Where is the program?"

"Across the street from the hospital."

"I cannot seem to get away from that part of town."

"She will learn to take the bus and subway. And initially, you can arrange school bus transport."

"Or I can move to Ferguson's apartment building when Flo has an opening."

"You would sell Mother's?"

"Yes."

"You have thought about that?"

I nodded. "I have been there long enough. The flat has been good to both Mother and me."

"Interesting that both of us are still dealing with our mothers in one way or another."

The main courses had been placed on the table and remained untouched.

"You think we should start eating, or is there something else on your mind?"

"You had lunch with Sarah the other day? Did the subject of me and her come up?"

"It did. Something about an art therapy program."

"Neither one of us would give ground to the other. And we lost focus on what the goal was, which was to serve the children."

"That was Sarah's explanation as well."

"The same thing would not happen today. We are both older and more mature, I should hope." She stopped and took some steamed rice, followed by a spoonful of stir-fried vegetables. She was distracted—something was on her mind. I sat with my hands in prayer position, waiting for the next shoe to drop. She looked up. "You know, I am jealous of Molly." I waited. "I am very possessive of you. I want to protect you from the big, bad, tempting city. We could not ever have an

S. John Diamond

intimate relationship because you would pretend to let me be in charge, but I would not be. I would never really know where your mind was."

"You are jealous of Molly?"

"She is going to have you all to yourself."

"You were the one who planted that idea in the first place."

"That was then. This is now. The idea is going to become a reality. It is the right thing— everyone knows that. In my mind, there is not enough room for both."

I looked at her. As she spoke, she was looking down at her plate.

"You know, it seems to me that you have issues with intimacy. You have made assumptions which may or may not be true. The net effect is that you have negated a relationship. Did you ever ask me whether I was interested?"

"You are right, of course. I have a crush on you like some fourteen-year-old adolescent. And I am tongue-tied and full of fantasies."

She picked at the remains of the vegetables on her plate.

I had eaten nothing of the main dishes.

"Where do we go from here?" I asked the top of her head.

She looked up. "I have absolutely no idea."

"Neither do I. This is new for me, too. I think not knowing will help prevent expectations."

"Yes. Leaving expectations out of this is a good idea."

The air lightened. The young woman came over to replenish the water. "Do you want me to warm your dishes?"

"Yes, lightly warmed. I am ready to eat now," I said, handing her two of the platters.

She brought a new bowl of steamed rice, and I helped myself. Plain rice never tasted so good. We finished off with tea and a sweet something-or-other courtesy of the house.

Once outside, Martha looked at me. "You know, you have this ability to abide me."

"Do I get a prize?"

She punched me in the shoulder.

I was to drive. I turned left on Saint-Viateur Street and then left again on Saint-Urbain Street.

"Where are we going?"

"Laurier. I want to check out a dress store."

"More sleuthing?"

211

"Indeed."

"Which case?"

"The divorce case. No more questions."

I was hoping the store was still open. It was. We found parking easily. "I would like you to come in with me."

"You buying me a dress?"

"You have never worn a dress in your life."

Before she could respond, I opened the door to the store, and we went in.

A quick look around told me that I would have to forgo the new couch in order to buy a dress. Martha busied herself looking through the rack near the front of the store. There was a small, discreet sign which said "*En Vente*"—on sale. They did not sell only wedding dresses, which were in the rear of the place. I had only a vague notion of how I was going to go about this.

A very attractive young salesperson went to attend Martha. I went to the cash, where an older, well-coiffed, grey-haired woman was doing some paperwork.

In French, she asked if she could help me. Before I could answer, there was a voice from somewhere in the rear asking her to come take a look. She put some pins in her mouth and went to the back of the store. The young saleslady, as if on cue, came to replace her.

"Do you have a wedding registry?" I asked in my most perfect French.

"Not really. Do you want to buy the bride something?"

"Yes, but I do not know her. I do business with her fiancé."

"Does she shop here?"

"Yes, I believe she does."

"What is your friend's name?"

At that point, Martha came to my side and put her arm through my elbow. The happy couple.

"His name is Green."

She looked at the computer. The older woman came back to rehang some very attractive black dresses.

"I have no Green here."

I turned to look at Martha. Her face told me she was enjoying this charade.

"How about Greengarten?"

"Yes."

"And the address?"

She gave me the warehouse address in Ville Saint-Laurent.

Just then the older woman entered the conversation. She looked suspicious.

Martha, acting the perfect lady, said that we had been invited to the wedding and she had left the invitation at home. The older woman warmed slightly. "You want to buy a gift certificate or some such?"

"Yes, exactly. I do not want to send it to the factory in Ville Saint-Laurent."

In the meantime, the woman who had been in the changing room appeared. The young sales lady went to the side, and a blue envelope was handed over. There were kisses and thank-yous all around. The cash, for I assume that is what it was, was placed in the till uncounted. She left, thanking the women for rescuing her.

Martha could never buy here or work here. She would not meet the height requirement.

"You would not have a second address for Mr. Greengarten's account?" Martha asked innocently.

"There is a cross-reference, yes. But we cannot give you that information."

"Okay," I said.

"You can send a gift certificate online to your friends."

Martha and I both said, "Perfect" at once.

We thanked the women profusely, and we left the store arm-in-arm.

Back on Laurier, we hurried to the car; it had started to rain, and the temperature had dropped. I opened the passenger side for Martha to get in. Once in the driver's seat, I held the ignition key in my hand.

"Back to the drawing board."

"You can be one smooth dude."

"Thanks. But I was not successful."

"What's the deal with that store?"

"Last week, I was walking by the place just when you called, and Green's lady friend came out with a frock in a garment bag. She stared daggers at me and, while entering a cab, launched into a Slavic rant."

"You want to get to her, because . . .?"

"I want her to get Green to come to his senses."

"I thought we made a lovely couple."

"Thank you for your help."

"You know I could never buy anything there, let alone work there."

"How is that?"

"Did you see how tall all those people were? Even you almost had to look up. I have to admit they were an attractive lot. By the way, the younger woman was the owner."

"Oh, my."

I started the car and drove slowly toward my place. For a Friday night, the streets were quite empty.

"How is your mother?"

"She has made up her mind that no matter what happens at the meeting on Monday, she will refuse any medical treatment. She fears the worst, and she has family history on her side."

"At the end, so did Mother. Too bad they never met; they would have gotten along like a house on fire."

"Skipped a generation."

I parked a block away from my flat.

We kissed.

She leaned her head into my chest. "I would like to see you tomorrow."

"I am going to spend some time with Ferguson. And then I am all yours."

"I hope you mean that."

CHAPTER THIRTY-FIVE

There was a note in my mailbox from Orenstein telling me to make myself available after the Sabbath.

This was going to cut into my social life. There had been a phone call, with no message, from a number I did not recognize. I reached into my pocket to find the number that I had been given for Green's girlfriend. It was not the same.

I wondered if Green could be charged for abusing his ex-wife in not granting her a *get*.

I was having one of those moments when I felt I was being torn in several directions at once. I tried bed. My mind was still working overtime. Next, I went into the shower to see if that would help. The hot water was relaxing and served to slow down the brain, but that was all.

I made oatmeal, but I did not have brown sugar or milk. I did have enough maple syrup to make the bowl somewhat interesting. I looked in the freezer to discover a frozen bagel, which I toasted. Not bad with a little unsalted butter. I wished I had another. I could have walked to the bagel place, but I decided that wasn't necessary.

I was avoiding thinking about the "M"s in my life: Molly and Martha.

I went to the desktop to see if I could work any of that out. I sat staring at a blank page for a very long time. I gave myself an agenda for the weekend: Ferguson, Martha, Molly, Green, Gold, Green's girlfriend, and Orenstein. I was sure I was missing something—like rest and relaxation.

I left the screen on and tried bed again. Turning on the radio with the sound very low, I lay on my back staring at the ceiling. The room needed to be repainted; I did not think I was going to start now.

I slept more or less soundly until six thirty. It was still dark, and it was raining. My morning walk could wait. I went back to the PC and looked at my list. I added: "Paint the bedroom." That was the only item I felt I had control over. I looked up a local paint store. It opened at seven thirty.

After making coffee, I started moving knick-knacks out. I stripped the bedding, found an old sheet to cover the bed, and put old newspapers on the dresser. There was a small ladder in the back shed next to the rear veranda. With the ladder, I could reach the ceiling to take down the light. The empty room had an echo. I had a half hour to kill before the store opened.

I perused the news headlines. There was some scary stuff about cutbacks in the medical system. Perfect, just when I might need it. The sports page had extensive stuff about the upcoming hockey season, with predictions for the Stanley Cup. No one picked the Habs, though at least there was consensus they would make the playoffs. Something to look forward to.

I found my fancy umbrella and started walking to the paint store on Rachel; it was still dark. The streets were empty, and the cloud cover made it even darker. The lights from the store acted as a beacon. Three gentlemen greeted me like a long-lost friend.

The ceiling colour was easy. The walls took a debate lasting several minutes. There were four different opinions; a pale yellow won out. Some brushes, two rollers, a pan for the roller, and some tape completed the purchase.

They called me a cab, and home I went. The ride turned out to be a lecture from the driver on the evils of capitalism and an interesting summary of the issues in the Middle East. This all in the time it took to drive six blocks. I paid him and thanked him for his insights.

Unloading took two trips, first to the landing and then up the stairs into the flat.

I had forgotten about the cupboard. Next week. I put the radio and the phones in the hall just outside the door to the room. I taped the walls below the ceiling. And then I applied the off-white colour in about twenty minutes.

I cleaned out the roller pan. There was a small ledge that went around the wall. I started there with a small brush. Next, I took the second roller to do the walls above the ledge. Then I did below the ledge. I included the sliding cupboard doors. I took a bigger brush to fill in where needed. I stood back and admired my handiwork. There were a couple of touch-ups needed.

I stood back to inspect again. I found a magnifying glass for going around to make sure I had full coverage. Not bad.

I made more coffee and went back in to inspect again. What an improvement.

I washed the brushes and cleaned the floor where some paint had splattered. A small fan would help. I opened all the windows. I went into the bathroom and decided I had to do that as well. I filled a carton with the contents from the medicine cabinet. Most of the stuff should have been turfed out. I did not need two boxes of Band-Aids.

I went back to the paint store. By now, we were on a first-name basis. There were other customers, so I had to wait my turn. This paint had to withstand dampness, so another debate ensued. They had the perfect thing, I was informed. Ceiling paint first. Then the colour for the walls had to be chosen. Should be a bold colour, they told me. I chose an interesting blue shade that was a compromise between bold and pale. Another bag of rollers and some new brushes, smaller this time to work around the nooks and crannies, rounded out my purchases.

I offered to become a partner in their enterprise. Big joke. I walked home this time. I had had my lecture for the day. The Orenstein women had just left their flat and were walking down the block in the opposite direction.

I went into the bedroom with a flashlight to inspect. It was much cleaner-looking. I took the ladder to remove the overhead light in the bathroom. I took the sheet from the bed and put it on the floor. I removed the light bulbs from beside the medicine cabinet. I covered the rest with newspaper. Manoeuvring around in the limited space was more difficult.

More tape between the walls and ceiling. I started with the brush around the light fixture, then carefully moved to the roller. I had to leave the paint pan in the hall. There was a small window high up behind the commode, which I was sure had not been opened in this century. I managed to crack it open and decided it had to be replaced entirely. Not today.

Another brush to work around the lights on either side of the sink. I had also taped the area between the wall and the floor, which had about two inches of bathroom tile. I needed to use a different brush for that. Then, carefully, I was able to use the roller to do most of the walls.

I finished with the brush. I took the flashlight to look around. I had missed some spots behind the toilet. I cleaned up and left the rollers and brushes on the back gallery. I had a deep feeling of accomplishment in painting the walls—my walls. There was the sense that this apartment was now mine and no longer a memorial to my mother's memory.

I rigged up a way of shaving, which involved using the kitchen sink. Since I had taken down the shower curtain, a shower would wait. A stand-up bath would do for now.

Still dressed in my painting clothes, I went out to get some air. Very apologetically, the fellow at the *dépanneur* had sold the *Montreal Gazette* to another. Just as well. I would read Ferguson's.

I needed to do one thing before I dropped in there.

I went back home and put together an outfit without disturbing the drying paint.

I took buses to Greene Avenue and walked down to the office building. I went in through the food court, which looked mostly empty. The elevator arrived quickly and took me to the eighteenth floor. I walked to Gold's office and turned the handle on the door. It was open.

He was sitting at his desk going through a file, which he closed when I came in. The sleeves of his white shirt were rolled up; there was no vest today. His suit jacket was hung neatly on the fancy clothes stand in the corner. His desk was clear except for the file he had been reading.

"Well, have you spoken to Green?"

He was sitting with his hands in prayer in front of him.

"No. Did you get to Green's girlfriend?"

"Not yet, I tried last night, but it did not work."

"Sophia can be even more difficult than Green."

"Is Green being hounded by the revenue people?"

"Would you believe he is current with both the Federal and the Provincial?"

"You are sure about that?"

"You know, I went to Shul this morning. I enjoyed the service. The Rabbi gave a wonderfully uplifting sermon. I left to go home and checked my cell phone. There was a message, so I came in here to deal with it. And you wander in here to discuss the one issue in my professional life which causes me to stay up nights. Over the last several months, I have spent countless hours attempting to advise Moishe Greengarten what to do, including allowing Sheila to buy the shares of the property. Then the fire, which highlighted the fact that the building had not been properly maintained. Now you and Orenstein come along with exactly the same strategy.

"I was hoping that he would sell to the father and son; he could not allow himself to complete the transaction. I am surprised they are still interested at all. I am not surprised that they would prefer not to deal with Green. So where is this all leading?

"Oh, and I forgot, when you came to dinner the other night and told me you were working with Orenstein, well, I figured he would know the prospective buyers. Everything is lined up except for one thing: Green will not budge. You have a plan, Mr. Glasheen?"

"Sort of."

"Is it sort of legal?"

"Perhaps."

"I think I will ask you no further questions."

"Wise move."

I looked down at my hand, which still had some paint under one of the fingernails. I put it behind my back. I went to shake hands with Gold. His grip was a little stronger than the last time.

"My sense is that this whole thing will eventually work out."

"I look forward to sharing your optimism."

I turned and left the large, empty office.

CHAPTER THIRTY-SIX

I returned to the ground floor and went into the washroom to the left of the elevator to clean my hands properly. Immediately across was that kitchen store again. This time, I wandered in.

With much willpower, I turned to walk out. But my, how tempting. Really . . . two-hundred dollars for a fry pan. I could never bring myself to justify that.

I phoned Ferguson. There was no answer. I wandered up Greene and realized I was starving. I went into the diner near the corner of Sherbrooke, and there was Reg sitting in a booth by himself. He had the Saturday paper spread out before him. I sat opposite him.

"You know, I read all the movie reviews avidly and never see any of them. Likewise, I read all the restaurant reviews and never eat at any of them."

"You lead a vicarious life."

"You want to start with coffee?" Our server stood over us with a fresh pot in hand. She also wore a very old Canadiens Cap and a badge that read "Trina."

"Please, and I would like a menu and some water. That hat lucky for you?"

"You betcha. I cannot wait until Wednesday night."

"Me either."

She went to replenish Ferguson's cup. He held his hand over it. "I have had enough."

"What restraint."

He looked up over his glasses for the first time. "My sense is you have several things on your mind. Your beautiful full head of white hair is mussed. Your hair is never mussed."

The menu arrived. I thought I wanted everything on it. "Could you bring me some pancakes with fruit?"

Trina disappeared to the kitchen in the rear and came back with a carafe of water.

I went to the washroom to neaten my hair and wash my hands. When I returned, Ferguson had folded the paper neatly and left it in front of me.

I moved it to my right.

My back was to the door, so I could not see who was coming in.

A young man and a blonde woman passed and were seated in a booth on the left in the rear. The young man was not Green: but the woman was Sophia, Green's girlfriend. She sat facing us.

She did not notice me. She put on glasses to look at the menu.

Ferguson saw me looking to the rear. "Someone you know come in?"

"Yes. One of the things on my mind."

"Small world."

"So they say."

My order came. The plate was a work of art, with fresh fruit piled high over three large perfectly circular pancakes. I started with the fruit, which tasted as good as it looked.

There was a shadow to our left. Sophia was standing there. "I need to talk to you."

"Right now? Here?"

She gave me a card with some numbers on it. On the back, she wrote another number. "Call me later at this number. At four thirty."

She went back to her booth. She sat and leaned across the table, speaking to the young man she came in with. Her son, maybe?

Ferguson looked amused. "For somebody who has had no connection to this city in a very long time, you have managed to create quite a network very quickly."

I had resumed eating. "You know what I did this morning? I painted my bedroom and the bathroom."

"How ambitious. One could also interpret that as nesting."

"Looks like I am here for the long haul. I also ordered a sofa, which is in the process of being made as we speak. I could live anywhere, but I feel a tie, a connection to the apartment and the neighbourhood. I have never lived in a place I could call my own."

Ferguson's eyes were closed, but I knew he was listening intently. "One of the reasons I want to move to the Manoir now is that I can do so with my faculties intact. I can still minister to the residents. I can still feel like I am making a contribution.

"I do not want to leave my cozy apartment in my cozy building and my lovely friend Flo. I really should not live alone anymore; that is the reality."

"And what about your library?"

"I will donate the bulk of it to the Divinity School. Some may have value on the market, but I could not sell them. I will leave that for someone else to do with as they wish. Please go through what I have in the apartment and take anything you want. The locker downstairs has several more boxes, which I have not looked at in years."

Sophia and the young man walked to the front to pay at the cash. She did not look at us. The man did, but I could not read his gaze. He looked away immediately.

"Attractive woman. She involved in one of your 'cases'?"

"I invoke the statute of limitations or confidentiality or whatever."

"Or any of those things which would prevent you from disclosing how you come to know an attractive lady of uncertain age."

Trina came to clear the table. "You want your bills, or do you want more coffee, or do you want me to go away?"

"We are fine, thank you. And how are they going to do this year?"

"All depends on the goalie. He's okay, we're okay. If better than okay, we win it all."

"Very true. Saves me from watching and listening to that stuff on radio and TV." She turned triumphantly and marched to the kitchen with our dishes.

I looked at Reg. "Need a nap?"

"Probably."

He took the bills and went to the cash. I left a tip on the table.

As we were leaving, Trina yelled out, "Go, Habs, go! And thanks."

Walking up to the light on Sherbrooke, I admonished Ferguson for paying. "You did not need to do that."

"Oh, yes, I did."

"My turn next time."

"Not likely."

Flo was outside sweeping the walk in front of the apartment building.

"Gentlemen. You both look like you need a nap."

"Our brunch was very demanding," Ferguson said with a perfectly straight face.

"You working today? How is that?" I asked.

"I have an apartment for rent; someone is coming to look at it and they are late. Mr. Glasheen, it is not for you; there is only one bedroom."

"You are determined to seduce me into your building."

"Not seduce, convince."

"Happy renting," I said over my shoulder as we went inside.

Ferguson took his place on the couch, and I on the recliner beside. I took the sports section of the newspaper; halfway through the statistical page, I felt my eyes drooping. The next thing I knew, Reg was gently urging me to wake up. I opened my eyes.

"It's four forty-five. Don't you need to make a phone call?"

I went into the bathroom to wash the nap from my face. I was groggy. I had just had the best sleep I had had in about a week. I was still not entirely refreshed.

I made some coffee and boiled water so Reg could have tea.

I took the phone into the small den off the living room to dial Sophia's number.

She answered on the second ring. We were to meet in Lower Westmount on Academy Road in an apartment next to the new arena. I said I would be there as soon as possible.

Reg gave me directions; he estimated it would take me fifteen minutes to walk there.

After finishing my coffee and making tea with lemon for Ferguson, I left with the promise I might be back in an hour or so.

I walked west on Sherbrooke Street to Westmount Park, left on Melville, and continued south toward Sainte-Catherine Street. In front of Westmount Park School, I headed right through the end of the park to Academy Road, where several apartment buildings were lined up one after the other. I found the one I was looking for and made sure my hair was neat.

I rang the bell and, within seconds, was buzzed in. The first door on the right was open. I knocked and was met by Sophia, still dressed as she was earlier and still wearing her glasses.

I followed her down a narrow corridor to a front parlour, where she sat on a small sofa and encouraged me to sit on a chair beside a small table against the far wall.

"This apartment belongs to my son, who is out with his girlfriend. I know you were trying to find me last night. Why?"

I waited for a minute before answering. "You know, you strike me as a survivor."

She looked at me and then looked down. She really was an attractive woman, though there were signs of strain on her face.

"I must leave here at six to pick up Mike. He will be finished with his appointment. How blunt do you want me to be? You want me to get poor Mike to make some decisions—to make the right decisions."

"I know this is something for a man who has always been in control. You strike me as capable of the job."

She did not say anything, and then, "I am not used to him being like this. His health has declined."

"He needs to sell the building, and he needs to give his ex-wife a religious divorce."

"He is scared. He has never been ill."

"We both know that. Does he know that?"

She looked at me. "I think his sense of himself has been dimmed."

"Can I assume you know a lot about his affairs?"

"I, ah, know some things."

I was slowly taking in the dimly lit room we were in. It was sparsely furnished. There was a bookshelf in the far corner with what looked like engineering books on one shelf. At the bottom were piled editions of a running magazine. There were some posters on the wall of soccer players. There was a picture of mother and son on an end table next to where Sophia was sitting.

She sat up on the couch with her arms bent over knees.

I looked at her. "You know most everything."

"The reason he missed the meeting with Gold and the father and son was because he felt so awful. And he did not let me call to explain his situation."

She went on, "I am tired. I have fought for everything I have. I fought to get here. I fought to stay here. I have learned how to speak English and French. I have a son who is about to get a degree in engineering and wants to get married. I brought him up alone; no one helped me."

She now looked haggard. She looked up at me for the first time in a few minutes. She raised herself off her elbows and continued looking at me. "I have been running his business for the last few years. The divorce and health issues took his mind off all that. I have been doing it all. Time is running out. What do you want me to do? Please tell me."

"You really are a survivor. We both know he does not like to be told what to do, especially now. I do not say this is going to be easy. I do repeat what I said earlier. You are the one to determine the way ahead."

"My son's wedding is next week, and when I saw you outside the dress store, all that came to a boil in my head. I know what I need to do. And I know I am the one who must take charge here. I have been working myself up to it."

"Is it a little like taking the car keys away from a loved one who should no longer drive?"

She gave a little smile. "Yes, exactly."

I stood. "Do you think you can arrange for you and Green to meet with Gold at his office tomorrow? Orenstein and I will be there with the prospective buyers, assuming they are still interested. And if they are not, you are aware that Mike's wife has the right to buy him out?"

"You know, I have never met her. Green blames her for the way the children turned out. I was organizing his papers one night, and I found the agreement. I could not believe it."

"So do we have an arrangement?"

"I will call you tonight or early tomorrow." She stood. "I must leave. He gets agitated if I am not on time."

I got up and nodded in her direction. "Tomorrow, then?"

CHAPTER THIRTY-SEVEN

I walked out into the autumn darkness. The wind had picked up, and there was a hint of rain in the air. I walked east along de Maisonneuve, my hands in my pockets. I passed the church on the corner of Clarke. Some parishioners were coming out from Saturday afternoon mass. I started to visualize my celebrating the mass. How many times had I done that over the years? I felt a tingle of delight. All those places. All those faces.

I continued up Clarke to the corner of Sherbrooke. Another church stood there, too. Parishioners, mostly older, were coming out.

Crossing Sherbrooke, I went east to Ferguson's building.

I rang myself in. His door was open. He was sitting in the chair to the right of the sofa reading. "And how did that go?"

"Not sure. Let me put it this way: the money is not in the bank yet."

He looked up over his glasses. "Did you shut off your phone? Martha called here looking for you. She's at her mother's in Côte-Saint-Luc."

I took the thing out. I had two messages, one from Martha and one from a number I did not recognize. I phoned the second. The message was from Jack; he wanted me to come by and look at the sofa. He was nearly finished.

I dialed the number Martha left. She answered on the third ring. "Tonight is turning out to be probably a no." She lowered her voice. "I am with Mother, and I do not know when or if I can leave. She is being difficult, and I think she should not be alone. And you?"

"I could come around to spread my Irish cheer; but driving out to Côte-Saint-Luc is not going to work. I do not have a car."

"You know, she would love you. You would be a perfect antidote."

"I am waiting to speak to Orenstein; he will be free around eight thirty this evening."

"Call me later, please."

"Will do."

Ferguson had put down his book. "I do have a car parked in the garage. I never use the thing. If you need it, borrow it."

"Does it work? Is it licensed?"

S. John Diamond

"All up-to-date. Flo starts it every few days. I can never be bothered. My world here is all within walking distance."

"Do you have any food?"

"Doris was here the other day. Help yourself."

There were containers neatly stacked in the freezer. In the fridge there was some stew in a jar. I emptied the contents into a saucepan. There was some crusty bread.

Looking back out into the salon, I saw Reg sitting at the table, taking his blood pressure.

I waited for him to finish. He jotted down the results. "Okay if I finish the stew?"

"Fine with me. I am going out to dinner with Claire Thomas."

I left him to finish his medical routine. I ate over the sink, right from the pot. The bread cleaned the saucepan of the very tasty sauce. I really wanted a beer; I took cold water from a jug in the fridge instead. I took a second glass and drained half of that.

I rejoined Ferguson, who was back sitting in his favourite corner of the sofa.

"You giving a sermon tomorrow?"

"I am going to the Manoir to spend some time with my friends there. And I will go over to the Children's Hospital after that. Not in a sermon mood. I will lead the old folks in hymn-singing.

"There is an old piano which two old dears can play, one of whom is deaf. They bicker but eventually they get organized and share the playing. Everyone has a rollicking good time. You should join us."

"How long would it take me to drive to meet Mrs. Lang?"

"Twenty minutes."

"Martha thinks I can cheer up her mother."

"Martha is right. Just go. There is one good deed left in you today."

I phoned Martha to tell her I was coming. Her voice picked up as she gave me directions.

He gave me the car keys, described the car, and told me where in the garage it was parked. And, more importantly, how to open and close the garage door. "Bring it back at your convenience. The registration is in the glove compartment."

"Thank you, this is very kind. Enjoy your dinner with Claire."

I found the car, a ten-year-old grey Japanese model with 32,000 kilometres on the odometer. Into the night I went. I drove up Clarke to

227

the Boulevard and then west to where it became Côte Saint-Luc Road. I passed the street where the Golds lived. At the top of the hill, I could see the western sky and the city lights below. Down to Décarie and west again to Cavendish, where there was a gas station on the corner.

On my way back, I would stop to fill the tank. The car drove well. Somebody, probably Flo, kept it clean.

I had to turn right off Côte Saint-Luc Road. The apartment building was on the left. I found parking. I was buzzed in immediately. The elevator eventually arrived, and a young couple came out bickering in Russian about something. I was going to the ninth floor. At the fifth floor, a small, grey-haired woman in a housecoat got in, looked at me, and said, "I am going up to visit my sister. She is not well. Do you know her? Her name is Silver, Goldie Silver. She lives on the eighth floor."

I answered that I did not have that pleasure.

On the eighth floor, the woman slowly got out.

At my knock, Martha opened the door, her greeting interrupted by a voice from the interior of the apartment.

"Who is that?" a voice called.

Martha answered, "A friend, Mother."

"A friend. I was not expecting any friend."

I went in and walked right up to her. She was sitting on a chair with a blanket wrapped around her.

"My name is Terence Joseph Glasheen. It is a pleasure to meet you."

She looked up at me. "Whose friend are you?"

"I am your daughter's friend."

She inspected me up and down.

"Martha, where did you find this guy? He looks alive, unlike some of the others I have met.

"You will excuse my appearance. I was not expecting company. What do you do?"

"I am retired."

"From what? Do you have a good pension? I have a crappy pension."

Martha said, "Mr. Glasheen is a volunteer at the hospital, and he is thinking of fostering a young Native girl."

"You are a tall one. And you have a full head of hair." I felt like a prize horse. "Martha, offer the gentleman something."

"I am fine, thank you."

My cell phone rang. It was Orenstein. I excused myself and went out into the corridor.

"The new car was vandalized. There is lots of broken glass in the alley. The alarm made a racket and scared off the vandals. The police are coming to take a report. Tanzer is coming to get it fixed. Luckily, I do not need it for a few days."

"I have the use of a car for the weekend, so we are okay for now. We may have a meeting with the lawyer Gold tomorrow. I had a meeting with Green's girlfriend, Sophia. She has taken charge of his affairs for the moment. Can you reach out to the father and son to see if they are still interested? Sophia is supposed to call me to let me know if the meeting is on."

"I will not call the father until I know something for sure. I will see him first thing tomorrow morning anyway."

"That is all for tonight from my side."

"You were busy this morning. I saw paintbrushes on the back gallery."

"I got tired of looking at drab walls."

"That was not the interpretation I came up with."

"Speak later."

He rang off.

I walked back into the apartment.

"We are having tea and a little nosh. Please join us," Martha said.

"Thank you. I will pass on tea."

"Instant coffee?" Martha asked.

"Not necessary."

"By the way, I have not been formally introduced." Mrs. Lang extended her hand. "My name is Rhoda, Rhoda Lang."

I shook her hand. "Pleased to make your acquaintance." Her handshake was a lot sturdier than I would have thought.

I sat beside Martha at the table. There was a croissant with chocolate in it.

"Do you want half a croissant?"

"You know I do. If you have some cold water, that would be great."

Martha went into the small kitchen. I looked over at Mrs. Lang. "So how are you feeling?"

"Like shit. Can we change the subject?" She had put a little rouge on, and around her shoulders was a colourful shawl. The blanket had disappeared. "Where do you come from?"

"From here."

"Glasheen, what kind of name is that?"

Martha returned to the table with a small plate and the water.

"Irish."

She was sitting with her chin in her hands, studying me.

"You are a bit of an iceberg, aren't you?"

"Mother."

"Well, he is. Only says exactly what is necessary. Not a syllable more or less."

The old lady might be right. I was warming to her.

"You did not answer my question from before. What are you retired from?"

"The priesthood."

Without missing a beat, she said, "That accounts for your reticence."

I started to laugh.

"Rhoda, you promised not to interrogate this man."

"A mother's prerogative. A tall, white-haired gentleman comes calling on my daughter,

I am allowed."

"And what are *you* retired from?"

"Hospital administration. They could not get rid of me. And then they appointed this complete nincompoop as executive director. That was it. After a few months of his bumbling and harassment, I walked into his office, told him he was incompetent, and walked out."

"Mother, you forgot the part where he called security to have you escorted out."

"The little creep was afraid of a little ninety-five-pound old lady."

"You also forgot the part where you started calling him names."

"Well, I did get an ovation from the office staff as I was escorted out. And I got the attention of the board."

She was getting warmed up. She sat straighter in her chair. Her eyes had come alive. Natural colour had returned to her cheeks. She was obviously enjoying her show.

"Six months to the day later, they got rid of him. Charges are pending. Seems some monies could not be accounted for. That's why the harassment. We were on to him." She sat back in triumph, looking very pleased with herself.

"I eventually received a letter thanking me for my years of service. I filed it."

"Well, ladies, I have had a long day. I think it is time to go. And I have a full day tomorrow."

As I was standing, Rhoda looked up. "You still have Church duties?"

"Not exactly. I help out a fellow who . . . Martha, help me out, here."

Martha interrupted, "Glasheen here is a professional volunteer. He drives this older man around to various appointments. That is how we met."

"You have told me nothing. Am I going to see you again? I like the mystery about you."

"I look forward to seeing you again as well. Thank you for the hospitality."

Martha escorted me to the elevator. When the car came, I held the door open. Martha pulled me down to give me a kiss.

"You really are tall. I never really noticed. Thank you for visiting. You made a difference."

"Too bad the two women never met, Mother and Rhoda. I would have paid admission."

I got in the elevator. Just before the door closed, Martha said, "Please call."

CHAPTER THIRTY-EIGHT

I slowly drove home. I was tired, and it was late. I found some jazz on the radio, which was soothing to my overloaded brain.

Over the mountain, past Mother's plot. And mine as well. The mountain really got in the way of east-west travel, beautiful as it is.

I found parking within walking distance of the flat. I suppose I could have parked in Orenstein's spot in the alley. I inspected for broken glass. Someone had done a sort of a job cleaning it up. In the morning, I would do more.

As I was walking upstairs to the apartment, I remembered that I had not put the place back together after painting earlier. I went to bed fully clothed with just a sheet covering me.

I instantly fell asleep.

I awoke with a start. I went to the computer. It was six fifty-five a.m. Sunrise would be in ten minutes. As I waited for coffee to brew, I did a survey of what I needed to do to spruce up the flat. I decided that the paint job was passable. There were a couple of omissions, but nothing glaring. Only I would notice.

I started in the bathroom, replacing the light fixtures, restocking the medicine cabinet, and putting up the shower curtain. The bedroom took longer to organize. But once I did, I was pleased with the results.

What a difference a coat of paint makes.

Of course, I now thought of the front room and the kitchen, both of which needed sprucing up as well. Not today.

My cell phone, which had been charging, rang. I hurried to the kitchen to answer it. The caller was displayed as unknown.

"Mr. Glasheen, this is Sophia. What time should we be at Gold's? He has agreed to at least that."

"Can I call you back at this number later?"

"Yes."

I quickly emailed Gold. Within minutes, he responded, "Thanks for screwing up my golf game. Eleven a.m. is fine."

Sophia answered on the first ring. "Eleven is fine. At Gold's office. We will be there. I really would like to bring this to a conclusion, if only to make Mike's life a bit less stressful. He is really difficult to be around when he is like this."

I doubted that he would ever be able to turn it down a notch or two. "Well, let's hope this helps ease both of your lives."

We rang off.

I went outside with a broom to sweep the area of the remaining shards of broken glass. Orenstein joined me. We started on either side and met in the middle. He had brought a small pail and a shovel. When we had finished, we stood in the middle of the alley. "Are we meeting?"

"Yes, at eleven at Gold's office."

"I will speak to the father soon. You will be here later?"

"I may take a walk; but I will have my cell."

He left with the pail, broom, and shovel. I stood admiring our work.

A few seconds later, he and his sons were walking by the alley to go to morning services. They would be back in an hour.

I put my broom inside my door at the bottom of the stairs and went for a short walk around the neighbourhood. I needed to restock the larder; I had not had a chance. I walked up to the vegetable store on Parc, which was bustling with activity. I picked up just a few items and walked back to the apartment.

I went on the computer. Carolyn had written another message about the sofa. I wrote her saying Jack had already contacted me and asking if later today was convenient. She wrote back that they would be open until five. I thanked her and promised either to be there or to phone her to make it another time.

Typing "Rabbi Shinder" into the search engine again, I was informed that there were two Rabbi Shinders, father and son. This from another site. The first, Beryl, arrived in Montreal from New York in 1936. He had studied at a yeshiva, a rabbinical school, in Europe and had come from a long line of scholars. There was a picture of a severe looking man with a well-trimmed beard. The biography included his list of communal accomplishments. There was also a description of his scholarly writings on subjects that were lost on me.

The second Rabbi Shinder, son of Beryl, took over from his father. He had attended a seminary in New York. I looked up the place, which still existed today. The history included side references to more current events, mostly newspaper articles about alleged abuse some of the students may or may not have inflicted on children they taught in high school and grammar school. The older students, as part of their program, were expected to give several hours a week to the Jewish Day Schools.

Suggestive, but nothing conclusive. And I did not know and could not tell if the current Rabbi Shinder's time coincided with these alleged abuses. There was something rather vague about the whole thing. A cover-up in plain sight? All too familiar.

Surely Orenstein would be aware of all this. And, of course, he would have kept it to himself until I mentioned it to him. Who was the real iceberg, Mrs. Lang?

I showered and shaved. I wolfed down a quick breakfast. I decided to dress formally for the big event: blue blazer, blue shirt, grey slacks.

Orenstein called. I demanded to know if we had a back-up plan.

"Let's let nature take its course. I am open to being there all day if necessary. We will leave at ten thirty."

"Make it a bit earlier."

I went back to inspect my wardrobe. Perhaps I would wear a tie.

Martha called. "Well, my mother badgered me with questions about you for an hour."

"And a good morning to you."

"Listen, do you have plans today? I thought maybe brunch."

"Rain check. Orenstein and I have an important meeting later."

"You sleuths never rest."

"Darn tootin'."

"Call me when you are free."

"Later, then."

I sat at the PC and stared at the screen. I picked up the landline and dialed a number from one of my pieces of paper. She answered after two rings. "Sheila Green."

"Terry Glasheen here."

"I am meeting Elyse in a few minutes to go for a walk. Otherwise, I am available."

"I hope it will not be necessary. But you never know. We are meeting, ironically, at Elyse's husband's office at eleven. You are two blocks away, and I really hope I do not have to call you."

"Whatever, good luck. Let me know how this turns out."

"Have a good walk. And regards to Elyse."

Today of all days, I wanted to read the *Sunday Times*, not online, but the actual paper. I could walk down to the Main and buy it at the corner of Rachel. I started to laugh. The store was across the street from this prize piece of real estate that had occupied our lives for the past few weeks.

I put on a baseball cap, the old Expos one I found when I was cleaning out the bedroom, and off I went. The weather was cool. Clouds were forming, and the wind was coming from the east. In Montreal, that means rain.

I walked down the Main at a good clip. When I got to Rachel, I stood staring at the buildings across the street. I may have made a private incantation. So much fuss over an X-rated cinema, and not because of any of the films. The fight was over bricks and mortar and ego, lots of ego. That sometimes was where the real pornography lay.

I walked back with the paper, which seemed to get costlier by the month. Its weight was still hefty. Over the next few days, I would slowly work my way through it.

Orenstein called. "Where are you?"

"Nearby."

"I will be in the back."

I quickened my pace. I went up through the apartment and down into the garden. The used paint brushes were still on the back gallery.

Orenstein was standing staring at my garlic patch. I stood beside him. "You called Mrs. Green?"

"As a matter of fact, I did. She is ready to join us if necessary."

"The father and son are very leery of doing business with Mr. Green."

"Will they show at Gold's?"

"I am to call them before we leave for the meeting."

"We have about half an hour."

"Shmully, I, ah, did some research on Rabbi Shinder."

He turned to look at me. "You found some interesting information in New York, didn't you?"

"A coincidence? And can I assume the information about that is scant? And that even you cannot access it?"

He nodded. "We are in a delicate area. I am hoping that everyone here is subpoenaed if only to force the matter." He went back into his house. I stood staring at my plot, really not taking anything in.

I went back upstairs, made another cup of coffee, and read the front page of the *Times*. I put on a tie and the new shoes. I checked to make sure that everything was in order. I looked like a lawyer, or a public servant, or a retired priest. Oh, well. I took the coffee with me in a travel mug and went downstairs to wait for Orenstein.

He came out dressed in his black suit with a white shirt, no tie. He had his black fedora on. We walked up the block to Ferguson's car.

"So?"

After we got in, Orenstein said, "They will be there. They do not want to meet with Green. We will use shuttle diplomacy: back and forth between meeting rooms."

"Have you done this before?"

"Sometimes it is necessary."

"You have to admit it is a weird way of doing business."

He sat back in the seat and pulled his fedora down over his eyes.

I parked on Greene Avenue. No money was required for the meter: a bonus for meeting on Sunday. It was ten forty-five.

The building seemed particularly empty this morning.

We made our way to the elevator and rode up to the eighteenth floor.

I knocked on Gold's door. His assistant opened it.

"Good morning. Overtime?"

"Gentlemen, you will go into the boardroom."

Gold was sitting at the head of the table. There were several small cold bottles of water in the middle of the table, along with sparkling clean glasses.

"Morning, gentlemen. Sophia called. They are on their way." He looked at Orenstein. "And your two?"

"They will be here; they do not wish to be in the room with Green."

"Of course, they will be in my office. Are they bringing a third?"

"The father will act for them."

"He was a year or so ahead of me in law school. I think he won the gold medal when he graduated."

Gold had a file and a legal pad in front of him. Beside it on the table were several sharp pencils.

Green and Sophia were escorted in by the assistant. He was wearing a baseball cap and a windbreaker. His colour was worse than I remembered. He said nothing and sat at the end of the table facing Gold. He removed neither the hat nor the jacket. Sophia sat beside him, to his right, and by comparison was looking positively upbeat this morning. She had on a beige jacket over a white blouse. No jewellery.

A minute later, the assistant came to the door to announce that the other party had arrived. They were to be ushered into Gold's office. Orenstein went with them. The assistant then returned to sit in the back of the room against the wall to take notes.

Gold started, "I would like to begin by welcoming everyone here."

Green was about to say something, and Sophia took his hand and gently squeezed it. Green sat glowering but said nothing.

Gold continued, "We have an offer to purchase properties owned by Moishe Greengarten, a.k.a. Mike Green, and Sheila Green et al located etc."

I focused on Green. Sophia started taking notes.

Gold was impressive. He was very relaxed and very much the master of ceremonies. The gist of what the lawyer said was that if Mike could not or would not sell the property, Sheila Green could sell it or buy him out at the price previously agreed to in the divorce settlement. Mike Green could do the same in reverse. This assuming the offer to buy was legitimate and above-board. Gold added that, to the best of his knowledge, the offer was genuine.

Why Green did not sell when he had the chance in the first place may have been accounted for by his condition, but I was not convinced. This way, he lost control of the transaction. It was the control that he needed, for whatever reason.

"I object to that gentleman being here," Green blurted out. He was looking at me.

Gold, very calmly, as if talking to a belligerent adolescent, responded, "Mr. Glasheen has been asked to represent the interests of Sheila Green. In the interest of time, I have no objection."

Sophia looked up from her notes. "Mr. Glasheen is here as what, exactly?"

Gold said quietly, "An observer. He has no decision-making authority. Under the agreement, Mrs. Green can appoint anyone she likes to act on her behalf. In this case, Mr. Glasheen has been appointed in a limited capacity."

Green glowered even more and pushed his chair farther back from the table. Sophia, losing none of her poise, asked if Mike had the same right.

"Yes, Sophia. And are you acting in that capacity for Mr. Green?" Gold asked evenly.

Brilliant.

"I believe then that I have limited authority, like Mr. Glasheen."

Gold looked at Green. "Are you okay with that?"

Green did not immediately respond. Finally, he nodded. "Limited, yes."

Gold opened the file in front of him and read out the offer. When he finished, he looked up, removed his glasses, put them on the table, and said, "Does anyone object to this?"

Green: "I do."

"And your objection is?" Gold said, putting his glasses back on and looking at Green.

"I object to being railroaded. The offer is too low."

"Are you prepared to make a counter-offer?"

Sophia: "I would like to confer privately with Mike. Is there another office we could use?"

Gold looked at the assistant. "Escort Mike and Sophia to the small room next to the entrance."

I stood to give my back a break. I went over to the window, which looked out over Greene Avenue.

A minute or so later, the assistant and the couple came back into the room. They all resumed their seats. Green's face was red.

Sophia spoke. "We would like to submit a new offer for consideration."

Gold: "As long as it is not frivolous, I have no objection."

Sophia looked directly at Gold. "I will summarize what we want. Is that okay?"

"Go ahead."

She looked down at her notes and read aloud. There were some alterations. Green wanted more money up front. When she finished, Gold looked at me. "Do you have anything you wish to say?"

"On the substance of the offer, I do not think there is anything there which Mrs. Green would object to."

Gold asked the assistant to move to the table as he dictated the new offer, which she recorded digitally. She then played it back for us all to hear. She was then instructed to type and print the offer for Green to sign. We waited while she did so, returned, and placed the documents before Green to sign. She then took the signed offers to Gold's office.

Twenty minutes later, she came back with a new offer from the father and son. Orenstein trailed her. He sat down in a chair in the middle of the table opposite Sophia. Green was on his right. He looked across at me. I excused myself to go sit in Gold's office with the prospective buyers.

The two gentlemen were seated at the round table with the view of the mountain. The houses had not fallen off. I introduced myself as Orenstein's assistant. Neither gentleman stood. Both were wearing identical black skullcaps. The son was working on a tablet. The father, who looked to be about seventy, was sitting with his hands flat on the table, staring straight ahead.

He had a trim white beard, a cashmere herringbone blazer, and a light blue tie over a light pink shirt.

The son, who looked about forty, wore a leather jacket over an open-necked, black sports shirt.

Gold's assistant came into the room with a document that she gave to the father. He read it quickly and handed it to his son. Orenstein appeared at the door.

The father said something to Orenstein in Yiddish. Orenstein nodded and shrugged.

The son threw the paper down on the table, turned to Orenstein, and said, "This is garbage. We are wasting our time."

His father looked up at Orenstein and shrugged.

Orenstein looked directly at the older man. "Then leave."

The two men stood up and, in turn, shook Orenstein's hand and walked out.

Orenstein looked at me. "You might want to call Mrs. Green."

There was something so right about that. The issue belonged to the Greens and the Greens only.

I called her. She answered immediately. "Glasheen here. I am sorry to say you need to come to Martin Gold's office. The prospective buyers walked out."

"Oh, my. I guess I am not surprised. I will be there in twenty minutes."

Orenstein nodded and headed to the boardroom. I followed.

Orenstein went back to his seat. I sat against the back wall beside the assistant.

Gold looked at Orenstein. "Did you call Sheila?"

Orenstein nodded. "She will be here shortly."

Green was about to say something. Sophia intervened. "I need to use the washroom, and Mike should get up to walk around."

Gold told her where the washroom was. The assistant followed with a key. As Green was about to leave the room, he turned to look at the three of us. "You have orchestrated a conspiracy against me."

Orenstein said severely, "You have done this to yourself."

Green turned and left the room.

Several minutes went by. The front doorbell rang. The assistant got up and ushered Mrs. Green into the room. We stood. She had on a beige raincoat, which she declined to remove. We greeted her warmly. She sat to Gold's right and beside Orenstein.

A minute or so later, Green and Sophia came back into the room. Green did not acknowledge his ex-wife. Sophia eyed Sheila as if examining a piece of art. Sheila did not return the favour.

Sheila said nothing. Green sat in the same chair at the end of the table and immediately moved it back against the wall. He sat with his arms wrapped around his chest.

Gold started, "Under the terms of the divorce agreement, Sheila Green will buy back her shares at the previously agreed price."

Green burst out, "And if I refuse?"

"You could refuse, of course. We have been down this road before. But then Sheila can seize your share of the property, and you get nothing."

Sheila Green looked at her ex-husband and blurted out, "You stupid, petulant child."

Sophia: "Now, is that necessary?"

Mrs. Green continued, "Today it is Sophia and tomorrow Melanie, or Lise, or Estella."

Gold, attempting to bring the meeting back into some semblance of order, said, "May I remind everybody that we are here to resolve an issue of the utmost importance? Mike, you need to accept the offer."

Green moved his chair back to the table and put his hands flat on the edge, as if holding on. "So I have no choice. Can we get this over with?"

Orenstein interjected, "So this part is resolved. There is one more issue. Mrs. Green can arrange with Mr. Gold how best to proceed at this point."

Gold looked at Sheila. "He is right. We can conclude very quickly."

Looking at Gold, Sophia asked, "And then what?"

"After deducting some expenses, Mike's numbered company will be issued a cheque," Gold responded.

She wanted to know how long this would take. She said, "There will be a delay until Mike agrees to give Mrs. Green her *get*, right?"

Orenstein very slowly and calmly explained that Green had to agree to give Sheila a *get* voluntarily.

Sophia looked at everyone around the room. "This was really what this meeting was all about."

No one said anything.

She looked at Orenstein, and she turned to look at me. "You two have been relentless on this point. Neither one of you could care less about the real estate transaction. You knew it was important to us. For you it was always about the *get*."

She looked at Orenstein. "I assume you could arrange this in a very short time."

Orenstein nodded.

Green exploded. "Over my dead body. I volunteer for nothing."

She looked at Green and she looked at the rest of us around the room. "Now I feel, how to say, railroaded."

She got up from the table. She took a few steps toward the door, then she turned to face us. "You people are a bunch of thugs. Gold, here, has been Mike's lawyer for years. And look what that has done for us: nothing. These two characters invade our place to badger us about some strange medieval nonsense. And the poor, maligned ex-wife gets treated like a queen. This after she sells her home for a tidy sum. Some justice."

Orenstein looked up at her. "You know that you have our respect. To repeat what we have been saying, you want to be rid of us? This how it can be done."

I had been studying Green. There was something about the way he looked that had been nagging at me the entire time. He was sitting with his jacket on in a room that was not cold. He kept scratching his forearm. And his colour was off.

And the insistence from Sophia that she must pick him up at exactly six o'clock the previous evening.

I looked directly at Green. "You are on dialysis, aren't you?"

Without looking at Sophia, Green reddened. "Sophia, what did you tell this man?"

Sophia looked at me. "How dare you. What gives you the right to antagonize us like that?"

She returned to her chair; some of that spark had been dimmed.

There was silence in the room.

"And how much would it cost to get a kidney transplant in the States? Half a million, give or take?"

They both looked down. Sophia reached over and put her hand on top of Green's. He looked up at me. "So what if you are right, smart guy?"

"I guess that explains a few things. And it also brings up a few more questions."

Gold cleared his throat. "Might I suggest a recess in the meeting so that we can gather our thoughts? I would like to confer with Mike privately."

That was a cue for us to leave the room. Sheila, Orenstein, and I went into the hallway outside the office. Sheila excused herself to go to the loo.

I looked at Orenstein. "You, of course, knew he had started dialysis."

Orenstein looked up at me. "Where did you complete your medical studies?"

"There were two dialysis chairs up north. I was the champion bingo caller."

I looked at my watch; it was two thirty in the afternoon.

"Think we can conclude this soon?"

Sheila came back to join us. She had been crying. "I do not want them to see me like this. I cannot go back in there yet."

I offered to take her downstairs so she could get some air. She agreed.

We took the elevator to the concourse and exited onto Wood Avenue. The sun was blocked by the tall black buildings.

S. John Diamond

"I would love a cigarette; but I stopped smoking twenty years ago. Still get the urge at times like this."

I looked at her. "You have a lot of feelings running through you at the moment?"

She looked down and nodded. "I want him out of my life, yet he hangs around refusing to leave. Now this. He couldn't wait in line like everyone else around here. His majesty needs to spend a bundle to have a transplant done now. On my dime."

I opened my mouth, but she continued. "I am weary of him. My father bought those properties, and Mike managed them. And eventually my father made him part owner. I have an attachment to them because of my dad."

"So selling them severs two elements out of your life. Your dad on the one hand and your ex-husband on the other. A mixed blessing."

She nodded. "I guess there is a time for everything. I am not inclined to offer him any more money."

"Understood."

Orenstein came to the door and held it open. "Time to resume."

Sheila and I climbed the stairs to go back into the building.

Once in the elevator, she looked at Orenstein. "How did you know where to find us?"

"I assumed you were not going to be standing on Greene Avenue. Too many people might walk by and ask questions. And Glasheen hates standing in the sun, so Sainte-Catherine Street was out. So you had to be on Wood."

She started to smile. "You sure there is not more to your relationship than meets the eye?"

The elevator reached the eighteenth floor, and we went down the empty hall to Gold's office. Back in the meeting room, we assumed our seats.

Gold stood. "Mike Greengarten has agreed to offer Sheila a *get*."

Orenstein excused himself and went into the darkened office out of earshot of the rest of us. He came back a few minutes later. "It can be arranged for five o'clock this afternoon. I will need some information from both parties. There is a document that needs to be prepared. And there is a fee for this."

Gold said he would pay for it out of his trust account and bill the parties accordingly.

Orenstein made another call and then came to report that, under the circumstances, that would be acceptable.

He met first with Green, Sophia, and Gold.

He then asked Sheila to come out of the room and meet with him in the office area.

When they came back, Orenstein gave everyone the address of where we were to meet.

Green and Sophia left first. They neither said anything nor acknowledged the rest of us in any way.

I looked at Sheila. "We could give you a lift there."

"Yes, thank you. I will go home to ready myself for this. Dumb question: What does one wear to a *get?*"

"I have faith you will come up with something," I said, almost laughing.

"I will be ready by four thirty."

She got up to leave. "He *will* show up, won't he?"

Orenstein stood and looked at her and said, "We will pick you up at four thirty."

Gold's assistant was excused from the room. She had been in attendance throughout. We all thanked her for her efforts.

Gold was sitting at the end of the table looking at both of us. I asked him what had happened.

"A number of things helped. But I guess this kidney thing really has taken a lot out of him. You two helped. And Glasheen meeting with Sophia yesterday placed her in the middle of the action. It gave her the impetus to at least get Green here."

"Your relationship with him helped as well. I mean, notwithstanding what she said about you, you stuck by him all these years."

"And from my perspective, and more importantly, if we'd failed, I would have to go home tonight to face Elyse."

Orenstein and I left the building together. Once on Greene, he looked up at me. "I will meet you back at the car at four twenty-five."

"And what will you do until then? It's ten after three."

"I will go visit a friend who lives in the area. His wife makes great tea."

"I think I will go up the street to get something to eat. He *will* show, won't he?"

"We will uphold our part of the bargain."

We went our separate ways.

Entering the diner up the street, I had a second of light blindness. When my eyes adjusted, I noticed that the place was largely empty. I took a booth on the right-hand side facing the street.

"Coffee?"

"Please."

"Something to eat?"

"Bring me a menu, please."

Just then, a menu appeared, as did Sarah, who slid into the booth opposite.

The waitress looked at her. "More tea?"

"Please."

She came back with the coffee carafe and poured me a cup. "And you'll have?"

"An egg salad sandwich on whole wheat."

"Sure thing."

She disappeared into the kitchen.

I looked at Sarah. She was looking directly at me. "What brings you to our part of the world on a Sunday?"

"A meeting . . . in fact, a meeting with your brother."

"Anything resolved? I know it's none of my business."

"Not sure about that. Anyway, what are you up to?"

"Just getting some air. I was correcting papers. I suppose I could figure out who was involved."

"Let us just say that a long, sad chapter may have come to an end."

She smiled a little. "You are far more effective than you let on."

The server brought my food and placed it before me.

"More coffee? And more tea for you?"

"I am fine with the tea."

"More coffee for me."

I ate very deliberately, not wolfing down the very tasty sandwich. I looked at her. "You know, in the last little while, I have met more interesting characters than I have ever met before."

"Present company included?"

"Yes."

"I rather think that you were open to it, that you wanted to experience life in a new way."

"Perhaps. My life has never moved so quickly."

"Speaks to your flexibility, your adaptability."

"I do have to leave here for another appointment shortly. This was good."

"To me, you are still a man of mystery."

"I was called an iceberg yesterday."

"Oh, I can see that. Nothing more than is necessary. I, on the other hand, can blabber away about anything."

I finished the meal and sat back from the table to look at her. "You know that I was offered an apartment in these parts. Actually, let me rephrase that. I was encouraged by a local landlady to rent one of her rather overpriced units near here. And when I inquired, she had none for rent."

"We would become neighbours. I live in a coach house up the street above the garage belonging to a rather large mansion. It is a loft. It has high ceilings and a skylight so I can paint. You should come up to visit sometime."

"I should come up to see your etchings, you mean."

She smiled. "I did not mean it that way, you letch."

"That is the first time I have seen you smile."

"Being around my sister-in-law and talking about a former love affair gone wrong are not exactly knee-slapping experiences."

"I suppose."

"To you, maybe, but not to me."

"I really must go. So nice to see you again."

"You have plans tonight? We could do dinner. I could cook us something."

"Tempting. I will call you later."

Once out on Greene Avenue, I was happy to focus on the task at hand.

Orenstein called on the cell. "There will be a delay until seven tonight. The scribe has not finished the document. And he is not used to being rushed like this. I have alerted Sheila. Could you call Sophia to tell her? You will pick me up at the synagogue west of Greene off Sherbrooke."

"I will get Sheila first, then."

"If there is a problem with Mrs. Green, let me know."

Standing on the street corner, I phoned Sophia and ended up leaving a message.

I then phoned Ferguson. He answered immediately. "Are you dropping in? I have a great story to tell you."

Around the corner to Reg's I went. His apartment door was open. He was entertaining a neighbour's cat.

I went in. "Greetings. I see you have company."

"This is Cleo, who is a wonderful fellow. Very friendly, and if you stop petting him, he shoves his nose into you to remind you to keep going."

Cleo looked at me and wandered out into the hallway to make his way back home.

"I have this wonderful effect on cats. They immediately leave wherever I am."

"Not popular with the feline population, are you?"

"My circle may be getting smaller all the time."

"Not a good omen."

"What is the story you wanted to tell me?"

"I was at the Manoir this morning, and, as usual, I was making my rounds to visit those who could not or would not join the group for chapel service. Well, I opened the door to a certain woman's room, and she was, ah, how to put this delicately, busy with one of the other residents."

"You mean busy as in BUSY."

He nodded and started to chuckle. I started to laugh as well.

"I excused myself, closed the door, left, and told no one but you."

"What kind of den of iniquity are you moving into? Sodom and Gomorrah?"

"Exactly. The woman happens to be a favourite of mine. She is full of gusto. The man, I must admit, I really did not recognize. He may be new."

My cell vibrated. It was Sophia. "We were starting out for the meeting; what is wrong?"

"Delayed until seven. We have no choice. The document must be handwritten, and the scribe is working at it. Is that okay?"

"I will take him out to dinner, then. He is on this stupid diet. He cannot eat anything good. Bland, bland, bland. Anyway, we will be there."

I think I exhaled after I rang off.

"I need to take my meds and have a little something. Want to join me?"

"No, thanks, I just ate."

He went into the kitchen to prepare his snack. He came back to the dining table to sit facing the window. I sat under the window and started looking through yesterday's paper.

Ferguson organized his medication. It was quite the production. Plastic jars filled with pills to be loaded into a plastic box with coded lids for each day of the week, four containers per day. Finally, he took his blood pressure. He wrote down the result. He kept the cuff on his arm and sat very still with his eyes closed. The second result pleased him more, and he wrote that down.

He returned to his station at the end of the couch.

Martha called. "What is up with you? How did your meeting go?"

"Fine and fine. And you?"

"Are you finished with your day?"

"Not quite. We have the last act later this afternoon."

"And after that?"

"So far, I have no plans. And at the moment, I am not sure I want any."

"I was hoping we could spend some time together. Mother appears to be content today. I am going to stay with her tonight and then go with her to the hospital tomorrow. I thought we could catch a bite together before I go there."

"I do not know when I will be free. I could call you."

"Give it a shot and good luck."

"Speak later."

I rang off and looked over at Ferguson. "That was the second dinner invitation I have received for this evening."

He looked at me over his glasses. "Martha is a friend of mine, a close friend of mine. Perhaps I feel a little protective toward her."

"What are you saying?"

"I do not want you guys to get hurt."

"I think we are at the level of mild flirting. Though I did meet her mother last night. She is quite the enjoyable character."

"You know, in a very short time, you have managed to create quite an active life around here."

"Yes, I was thinking about that the other day. I have a very busy life for someone who is retired."

"Must be your charm."

The land phone rang. Ferguson answered it. "Ferguson here." He broke into a grin. "You know I cannot think of a better reason to miss one of my chapel services."

He listened some more, then said, "I do not think you should do a thing. On second thought, maybe make them a cake." He waited some more. "I *am* being serious. I might call the Psychology Department at McGill University to do a research study on geriatric sexuality." He began to laugh. "There have been several anecdotal articles about this stuff. I will send you a few. I am being serious." He listened some more. "Yes, I will attend a meeting tomorrow."

He hung up. "What nonsense. A tempest in a teapot. Someone must have bragged."

We both had a good laugh.

It was almost six in the evening. "I need to leave soon. Tomorrow I have a meeting with the Foster Care Department ."

"Are you concerned?"

"Not really. Whatever happens, happens. I assume they are going to review my application and some other details like the financial arrangements."

"I assume you are not in it for the money."

I excused myself to go into the washroom to freshen up.

"I hope you do not mind if I keep your car until tomorrow?"

"You need it more than me. And tomorrow is fine."

I took some cold water out of the fridge, found a large glass, and drank thirstily.

I headed toward the door. "Do you want the door left open?"

"Please."

"Keep me informed."

"Will do."

I left to walk to where I had left the car so many hours ago. Luckily, it was Sunday, so there were no parking restrictions. On the way, I called Sheila, who promised to be downstairs waiting.

I drove over to her building. She was standing outside talking to another woman just to the left of the main door.

She got in the front seat, and her friend eyed me with some curiosity. This was going to be fodder for discussion in the laundry room.

"Do you think this is actually going to happen?"

I was at a stop sign, so I was able to look at her. "I do not know. We shall see what influence Sophia has been able to exert on him."

"She reminds me of Kate Parr, Henry VIII's last wife. She outlasted the bastard." Sheila chuckled quietly at her own joke.

"Nice to see you are able to inject some humour into this."

"At this point, I just want it to be over. I am not particularly religious. I am doing this for my kids, for my late father, and perhaps for me. Though I cannot foresee ever marrying again."

"You are doing it for principle?"

"Something like that, but more than that. It's hard to explain."

"It is the right thing to do."

"Yes, it is the right thing to do."

Shmully was standing outside the synagogue talking to someone. It seemed that Orenstein could not go anywhere without meeting someone he knew. He shook the chap's hand and got into the back seat of the car.

"Where to, sir?"

He gave me the address and sketched a general route of how to get there. The drive was silent. We reached our destination at five to seven.

The building, a synagogue, was on a street corner where one had a view of people driving by from several directions.

A few minutes later, Sophia and Mike Green arrived. Orenstein greeted them warmly. He escorted Sheila and Green into a side door of the building.

Sophia and I stood on the sidewalk in the dark.

"Do you want to sit in my car to warm up?"

"No, I mostly want a cigarette."

"Cannot help you there."

"Good. I really have stopped."

"Took a lot of work to get Green here."

"I needed to coddle him like a child. He is very vulnerable at the moment. He has lost his, how do I say?"

"Bravado."

"Yes." And then she mimicked someone strutting.

"And you, how are you holding up?"

"I am looking forward to my son's wedding. He has chosen the right girl. She is very *sympathique*. They will be good together."

"I am very happy to hear you say that, Sophia. You, above all, deserve that."

She nodded. "By the way, how did you know Mike was on dialysis? Did someone tell you? You have spies at the hospital? I know I did not tell you."

"Let us just say a lucky guess."

"No one told you, then."

"No, no one told me. At least not directly."

Just then, the side door opened, and Green walked out, put his arm around Sophia, and headed back to where his car was parked. No eye contact, no acknowledgement of any kind.

Sheila and Orenstein came out a few seconds later. She came over to me, put her head on my shoulder, and started to cry.

She lifted her head up and pulled a tissue from her pocket. "What I really want now is a stiff drink."

"How about a sigh of relief instead?"

"Thank you both. Thank you both very much."

We slowly walked to the car. Sheila got in the front seat, and Orenstein in the back, as before.

I drove slowly back to her apartment in Westmount, deciding not to take the hurly-burly of the expressway. The car was silent, but it was a good, contented silence.

Sheila got out of the car as I hurried to open the door for her. She shook my hand. Orenstein had gotten out as well and nodded in her direction. If he was pleased, he did not show it.

"Thank you both again. I never thought this ordeal would ever come to an end. I will go upstairs, call my kids, and then take a hot bath."

"Be well," Orenstein and I said together.

She turned and went through the sliding electric doors. We got back in Ferguson's car to head back to the Plateau. At least we had finished something.

CHAPTER THIRTY-NINE

I found parking one block over from where we lived. I did not want to park in the alley.

We slowly walked back to our flats. When we reached the landing, Orenstein turned to me. "Not a bad day, really, all things considered."

"You were not concerned? You were not concerned in the least?"

"Things fell into place. I knew eventually they would."

"Any delay in organizing the *get* was going to be deadly. How did you manage that?"

He turned to open his door, then turned back to look at me. "We may have more work to do." With that, he went in, closed the door, and turned off the outside light.

I was left standing outside my door in the dark. The only thing I could think of was, if Martha's mother thought I was an iceberg, what would she think of Orenstein?

Upstairs in my flat, I had one message on my landline and two on the cell, which I had turned off.

Two messages from Martha and one from Sarah. I had one hang up on the cell.

I dialed Sarah's number and left a message. I called Martha's cell and also got a message. They would not be talking to each other.

What I really wanted to do was take a walk, if only to get some air. I opened the fridge door to see if there was any snacking material. Nothing. And what was in there should have been thrown out.

I looked in the small pantry to see if there were any crackers. I put what there was in a plastic bag to feed the birds in the park. The cell rang; it was the sofa guy, Jack. "We finished your couch. Could you come by first thing to see it, pay us, and arrange for delivery?"

"How early is early?"

"Nine tomorrow."

"I will be there."

I took my stale cookies with me and walked over to a small park around the corner. I broke up the crackers and spread them around the back of the area under some bushes.

After putting the plastic bag back in my pocket, I started a fairly vigorous walk up the Main as far as Fairmount. Turning left, I passed the bagel place, turned around, and went in to buy six.

I left empty-handed; I had no cash.

At Parc, there was a bank. I got some cash from the ATM. I turned north and walked the long block to Saint-Viateur, looked at the "Y" again, and promised to check out their program online. The bagel place on Saint-Viateur gladly accepted cash. I left with six.

I came home with four.

Martha called. "You spent all this time sleuthing?"

"Is saying a simple hello an unnatural act?"

"My, my. Do I hear a sense of triumph in your voice?"

"You hear fatigue and a need on my part to reconnect with my apartment."

"Does that mean we are not going out for a late-ish repast tonight?"

"That means I had not considered it."

"Do."

"I need to take a shower and all that. Really, can we put this off until tomorrow? I could show you my new acquisition."

"Tomorrow is Mother duty. She has her big medical meeting. Also, I am laying low; it is Yom Kippur."

"I thought you did not buy into any of that stuff."

"I observe in my own private way."

"How private?"

"Usually in nature."

"Is there room for one more in this rite?"

"Sure. I have no itinerary at the moment."

"Whatever you come up with is fine with me."

"We will speak tomorrow. Have a good night."

And with that, she rang off.

I went to see if my passport was up to date. It was still good for a few more months. Martha had talked about liking to spend time in Vermont. I wondered if going there was a possibility for Wednesday.

I checked the news on the Internet. I bounced from article to article, not really absorbing anything.

Then to the sports site to check on football scores. There was a game still in progress. I chose not to watch it. I tried bed. I found the French radio station with the fellow with the hypnotic voice and the eclectic music. I dozed for an hour or so, and woke when the program went off air. I started thinking about Green and decided that my involvement with him was not complete. He had been railroaded into doing something he did not want to do.

One could argue that he had brought the whole thing on by making—or not making—certain decisions. And yes, he had certain contractual obligations. Still, there was something that needed to be said to him. In the end, he came through.

Coffee time was seven a.m. I dressed in my walking uniform and, looking out, saw there had been an overnight rain. The weather site informed me that the day would clear and the temperature would be an unseasonal fifteen degrees Centigrade.

I started out by passing by Ferguson's car, which I had parked a block away. Everything appeared to be in order. I would have to move it by ten thirty this morning as per the contradictory hieroglyphs on the parking signs.

I kept going north to Bernard. Taking a left turn, I crossed Parc and passed the butcher shop on the corner, which appeared to be open even at this early hour. Across the street, the bakery had things piled in the window. I went across to inspect. There were several varieties of sweet roll to choose from. I went in to choose three. I overheard someone say that the store would be closing at noon to prepare for the holiday.

I continued up Bernard and passed a sign that told me I was entering Outremont. Again, there were stores and restaurants at street level, under older apartment buildings. I was munching on one of the pastries. I fought off demolishing the remaining two. The deli was opening. I could start the day with a smoked meat omelet. Not today, and maybe not ever.

I crossed the street and passed the movie theatre, which had been transformed into a performance space. There were ads posted announcing upcoming events. I made a note to check out their schedule.

I passed the grocery store with the same name as the one in Westmount. I went to the sliding door, which did not slide. There was a fellow on the other side who indicated with his arms that they were closed.

I decided not to go into the butcher. I still had meat in the freezer from my previous trip here.

Back in the apartment, I had left the cell charging on the kitchen counter. There had been a call from my secret admirer. I was sure one of these days, this person would come forward. In the meantime, the mystery continued.

More coffee, and the remaining sweet rolls finished off breakfast.

I needed to think about the rest of my day. I knew that I would be returning Ferguson's car. Was that going to be after or before the interview at the Social Service Centre?

I would no doubt hear from Martha about her mother. And now I needed to prepare to go look at my new sofa.

At eight thirty, I walked down to the Main and wandered over to the furniture store. They were still closed. I kept walking south for a few blocks and then turned to walk back, reminding myself that I needed another haircut. By the time I returned, both Jack and Carolyn were there.

The new couch was displayed prominently in the front of the store. They had put paper down so I could sit on it. More paper was placed so I could lie on it. A pillow was fashioned from some material lying around. It was a comfortable experience all around. The material worked perfectly. Jack stood admiring his handiwork as if showing me his first-born. He was chuffed.

"I can deliver this later today. When would be convenient?"

"How about eleven?"

"Sounds good. And I know there is no place to park. We are used to that around here."

"You will remove the two overstuffed chairs that this is going to replace?"

"Yes, of course."

I took out my chequebook and paid them in full.

There were smiles all around as I left the store to return home. Orenstein and his boys were coming from the opposite direction. The lads went into the apartment, while Orenstein stood on the sidewalk waiting for me. Very quietly, he asked, "Have you been receiving anonymous phone calls?"

I nodded. "For the last couple of weeks. Not every day, but every so often."

"You have a theory?" he asked, looking up at me.

"Yes. I suspect we have the same theory. One question I have asked myself with no answer has to do with the fact that Joel is an only child. Unusual around here, is it not?"

"I believe his mother has health issues."

"You believe or you know?"

Orenstein, as usual when faced with such a question from me, did not answer. I had to infer that he knew. I did a lot of inferring.

He walked up the stairs and into his house. I, of course, was left standing outside with several unanswered questions.

I went upstairs to prepare for the delivery of my new purchase. I moved the two broken overstuffed chairs toward the front door to clean around where they had been. I made more coffee and went to check out the Internet. Mostly, I devoted myself to reading about the opening of the hockey season and, more specifically, the upcoming confrontation with the Leafs.

The rookies who had made the team had had outstanding amateur careers. One of the three was expected to be a star. He was the fellow I had noticed in the preseason game. I should have applied to be a scout.

The doorbell rang. Jack, the sofa fellow, came up the stairs, shaking his head. "Is there a back door?"

"There is a fence. Do you think you can get it over?"

Jack and a helper carried both of my mother's chairs outside and left them on the curb. Jack drove the truck up the alley. He had a ladder in the back, which he put against the fence.

I borrowed a ladder from Shmully and put it on my side of the fence. The garlic bed was going to take a beating. The two men were able to lift the couch, which was carefully wrapped, onto the top of the truck. Jack climbed the ladder to put a thick tarp on top of the fence. I climbed the ladder on my side. Jack and his friend moved the sofa to the top of the fence. Jack and I balanced it there. The other fellow came around to the garden and climbed the ladder behind me. He and I were holding the thing on an angle and slowly moving it down. Jack had joined us, and the three of us were able to set it down safely.

Next we had to get it up to the second floor. Since the staircase was outdoors and metal, we could slide it up using a rope and manpower. By the time we had got it up to the back gallery, we were all perspiring. After a pause, we wedged it into the house. With a few minor adjustments, the sofa fit just as I had envisioned it. It changed the entire character of the room. Looking around, I decided to rearrange the entire space. But not this minute.

I went back downstairs with the two gentlemen to watch them load the two chairs into the back of their truck. We wished each other well. Jack looked particularly pleased. I thanked him profusely. Jack reversed to drive down the alley to pick up his ladder.

I turned to go back into my house. Mrs. Orenstein was standing on the landing. I could never read her face, never predict what she might say.

She nodded in my general direction. "Are you going to fix up your garlic bed? I was looking forward to next summer when you harvest."

"As a matter of fact, I was just going to do that now. And I may plant some more bulbs. We really haven't had much of a frost."

She nodded and went back into the house. I decided that the landing was her pulpit, her Hyde Park Corner. The other thing, a minor mystery, was the obvious difference in age between Orenstein and his wife. Theory: She was the younger sister of the first wife. This was the only explanation, and it would follow custom. Of course, I could not ask. And Orenstein would not volunteer the information.

The garlic bed was not entirely ruined. I smoothed out the area and rearranged the mulch.

Once back inside, I remembered I hadn't really eaten. While munching on a bagel, I put together a cheese omelette and made more coffee. Sitting at my table, I ate while admiring my new bed.

My cell rang. "Martha here. The news is not all bad."

"That is good to hear."

"She has some heart issues which need to be attended to."

"And her mood?"

"Much improved since we know what it is we are dealing with. We have a diagnosis."

"You are not dealing with the unknown any longer."

"You know, some days you really outdo yourself."

"Thank you for the sort-of kind word."

"You have your interview this afternoon? You are planning to behave?"

"Scout's honour."

"Try not to belittle the interviewer, even though this person is likely to be a third of your age."

"You forgot to add something."

"Go on."

"Someone you likely taught or supervised."

"So your job is to tell me how I did."

And she rang off.

I scanned the morning news on the Internet. There was nothing truly outrageous: corruption probes, another demented suicide bombing in the Middle East, government bungling, the murder rate in Chicago was very high and measures to reduce it had failed. Maybe Molly and I would avoid going there. In the tumult of the last few days, I had all but forgotten about her.

I wondered how she was doing. I also wondered if anyone had broached the subject with her of her going to live with an old friend. Somehow, I doubted it. She had moved from a hamlet in the North to a psychiatric unit in a big city hospital to a group home in the same big city, all in a matter of a few weeks. That was a lot of change for a young person; for anyone.

On second thought, I supposed her experience mirrored mine. So we would be two transients discovering life in the big city together. I would be experiencing life in a way I never would have predicted: not through religious rite but on the ground, hands on. Transcendence in a different form.

There was activity in the alley. Tanzer had brought back Orenstein's truck. It looked cleaner than it had the day it came from the dealer. I went out to check.

Tanzer greeted me warmly. "Ready for your new car?"

I walked around the shiny vehicle. He proudly pointed out the new alarm system and gave me a quick tutorial on how to use it properly. The new glass had been tinted to match the rest.

Inside, all the shards from the broken window had been removed and the rugs had been shampooed. Orenstein came out to inspect as well. Tanzer told him about the new alarm and assured him that I knew all about it. I insisted that he go over the basics for Orenstein's benefit.

If Shmully could appear pleased, I guessed he was. The two men walked together down the alley talking in Yiddish. They presented a startling contrast. Tanzer towered over Orenstein and outweighed him by a hundred pounds at least. And when the car dealer put his arm around him, Shmully disappeared.

I needed to move Ferguson's car. Reading parking signs in our *quartier* required long and serious study. Understanding them was a hopeless task.

By the time I got to where I parked it the night before, the ticket person was starting his route up the street. I figured I made it by no more than five minutes. Now the task was to find an alternative parking spot. I drove around for about twenty minutes with no success.

Passing our alley, I decided I could pull in behind Orenstein and not offend the meter readers, I hoped.

Reading the newspaper online, I noticed an ad for the car sharing service. I read the blurb and checked out the local parking stations. There were several in our area. This could be a rational solution to an issue that might present itself if Molly went to a special school at a distance from here. I knew I could use Orenstein's SUV. I saw that option as an emergency one only. So I followed the instructions to join the car-sharing outfit. This took about forty-five minutes.

No sooner did I finish than Ferguson called. Without preamble, he started in. "I have been accepted at the Manoir. I am moving in a month. I beseech you to come by to check out my library."

"I am fine, thank you, and how are you?"

"You coming by later today?"

"My schedule is rather full."

"We both know you can be annoying. Stow it. See you later."

I could just sit around and have my schedule filled by others. I did not have to do a thing. By the time I got off the phone with Ferguson, I had confirmation that I was accepted by the car sharing outfit. This was further proof that I was joining urban, secular life.

I stared at my new couch, still not used to it being part of my space. I realized that I had not sat on it. I also realized that I had to buy some decent throw pillows. I had no idea where to do that. Surely some knitting store around here would have some. I knew I had passed one recently but I could not remember where it was.

Looking online for the store and at the same time for pillows produced more results than I would have thought. Of course, I did not find the knitting place I was thinking of.

I wanted to get some air and was feeling a little peckish. I started walking down the Main. The partly cloudy fall day required a jacket and, of course, my trusty Canadiens cap. Past Mont-Royal Avenue, there was a restaurant that had a menu in the window advertising many varieties of macaroni and cheese. How *nouvelle cuisine*. And there were people in the place.

At the corner of Rachel was a coffee bar where I purchased the darkest coffee they had. It was good and strong. I decided to walk east down Rachel. I passed the paint shop where I had bought the paint for my renovation. Those guys were in there working away with several customers at once. Farther down the way was an instrument shop where musicians were walking in and out with violin cases and at least one cello.

A block from Saint-Denis Street was a large church where banners were hanging, advertising upcoming musical offerings. Up the side street, the car wash was open and had a lineup waiting to get in.

Before returning Ferguson's car, I planned to get it washed and filled with gas.

I crossed Saint-Denis, knowing that I could probably find a store that sold pillows. Perhaps on the way back I would look. I did not want to stop; I had a good pace going. On the corner of Saint-Hubert was a knitting store that was not open on Monday. I looked in the window. There were pillows on display; none of them appealed to me. They were too old-fashioned and stodgy- looking. I kept going and passed some interesting restaurants whose menus were posted in the window or outside. I would read them some other time.

A Japanese car dealership was next. Very tempting. Holding my breath, I kept going.

A block or so east, an Italian takeout restaurant had some tables inside where people were eating. The counter in the rear had an array of choices. I was hungry. I chose some lasagna and mixed vegetables cooked in olive oil and garlic. A roll and a glass of water became a delicious lunch. I sat beside a couple from New York whose son was at university in Montreal. When they visited, they arranged to come here to eat. The food was good and relatively inexpensive.

They asked me what I did. I told them I was a private detective. They both thought that was interesting and changed the subject to talk about their son's girlfriend, whom they did not like. She had a tattoo. They reminded me to pick up some pasta sauce while I was here to take home for later.

Excusing myself, I went to the counter to pay and get some sauce. I chose a rosé. On my way out, I thanked them for their advice. I left quickly. I did not want to get into a discussion about their son's choice of companion. I would have defended her to the hilt.

It was time to go back home and get organized for the rest of the day. Saint-Denis Street from Rachel to Mont-Royal had a fascinating array of boutiques. One had the sort of throw pillows I was looking for. I noted the name and website. Tomorrow was soon enough.

Walking up Mont-Royal to the Main, I passed more boutiques, which seemed to cater to a different crowd. Places sold leather clothing, vinyl records, and boots. These boots looked serious, like maybe you were going to stomp something. There was the occasional restaurant and a few bars where some patrons were standing outside smoking.

By the time I walked back to the duplex, I needed to hurry to get ready for the appointment. I took a quick shower. For the outfit, I decided on subdued socks, blue button-down shirt, dark slacks, and the new blazer. The black walking shoes would do for footwear. One more brush of the hair, and I was ready to go.

Mrs. Orenstein was in her pulpit as I went outside. "You have a date?"

"Mrs. Orenstein, I have a very important meeting and I do not want to be late." She nodded and went back into her flat. The door was not slammed.

Progress.

I drove back to the car wash on Nicolet Street. Luckily, there was only one cab in front of me in line. The car wash door opened, and the attendant let both of us in. I left the keys in the car and walked back to the rear of the place where the cash register was. The owner came over to ask whether I wanted my car done inside and out. The price was more, but worth it.

He started talking to the cabbie in Arabic. They were old friends. The attendant could not get the cab to start. Everybody pitched in to push it out of the garage into the back alley, where the driver and owner worked at getting the motor going again.

Ferguson's car was finished. I quickly drove away, looking for a gas station. In downtown Montreal, there were very few gas stations. I dropped that idea for now. I needed to find parking, pay the meter, and run to my rendezvous. It was four twenty-five.

I put the car in a lot next to the computer store and ran through the two blocks to get to the building off Dorchester. I entered exactly at four thirty, the clock above the front desk informed me. There was a person sitting behind a teller's window. I gave my name and said I had an appointment with Susan Epstein. I had to sign in, and this time I was given a badge that said, impressively, "Guest/Invite(é)."

A few minutes later, a young man who also was wearing a badge came down the stairs to introduce himself. "I am Claude Drouin. Ms. Epstein is not available this afternoon." I followed him to a meeting room off the main entrance. There was a small, round table with three chairs. I was to sit in any one of them.

Mr. Drouin put his laptop on the table, opened it, and was looking over the screen at me.

"This interview should take about an hour. I hope you have arranged your parking accordingly."

He was not as young as I would have predicted, perhaps in his forties.

"I am parked in a lot around the corner. So I am all set."

"I am going to review your application, and if I have any questions, I will ask them."

"Fine."

He started reading, "How long were you in the priesthood?"

"Thirty-six years."

"And you left because?"

"I felt it was time to. I had accomplished all that I needed to."

He moved the computer slightly to the side so he could maintain eye contact more easily.

"You were always in the north?"

"Yes."

"You were never moved around?"

"No. I was a fixture in the small communities around James Bay."

"I read your recommendation from the bishop. I tried reaching him by phone. I spoke to his secretary, who confirmed that you were very good at your job. I could not speak to the bishop himself. Do you know why not?"

"I cannot answer that question."

"What was your relationship with the bishop?"

"This bishop—none, really. Over the years, I served under several bishops. I had decent relationships with most of them. And one or two I got along with very well. We hit it off personally."

S. John Diamond

"I have to ask you about abuse. The fact that you were not moved around may indicate that you were not involved in any abuse."

"It could also indicate that the supervision in my part of the world was lax."

He looked directly at me. "Do you sense that I have a bias in this area?"

"I sense that because I was a priest, I am suspect."

"I have worked on some of those files. I did interviews with men who had been abused in schools in the fifties. It was not a pleasant experience." He looked up as if to gauge my reaction.

I returned his gaze with no apparent reaction. I hoped.

"Did you get involved in the schools?"

"I was involved everywhere: the school, the hospital, the jail."

"That is how you met Molly?"

"Yes. At school."

"Tell me about her."

"She would come by for a chat before she went home. She had an interest in the outside world."

"And then what happened?"

"I do not know exactly. I was called to a meeting at the school after Christmas a year or so ago. Molly was not the same child. She was withdrawn and extremely uncommunicative."

"And you suspected something?"

"Yes."

"Did you have any contact with her prior to this meeting, over the holidays?"

"No, I was too busy with my duties. When school began, she did not come around."

"You did not suspect anything?"

"After the first week, yes. And then the case conference was convened."

"What do you think happened to her?"

"She was attacked."

"Do you suspect she was raped?"

"Yes."

He nodded. "The evidence supports that. Why, at your age, in your retirement, do you want to foster her?"

"Because I think I can make a difference."

He looked at me. "You do not lack confidence."

I shrugged.

"We need to go over your financial situation. I assume you are not in this for the money?"

Since these figures were fresh in my mind, we accomplished this rather quickly.

"I or Susan will get back to you regarding your monthly stipend."

"Do you know how long this process is going to take?"

"You know the answer to that. You know how bureaucracies work."

"Or don't work."

He was about to get up. "Is that why you left the Church?"

"Largely."

"Could you expand on that?"

"Well, I just felt that we were not responding to the needs of the people. We were more concerned about other issues. We had lost the reason for our existence. I felt the hierarchy was just that, a hierarchy— out of touch."

He nodded. I started to get up from the table. I looked over at him. "Where you taught by brothers?"

He looked down as if remembering an experience, "Oh, yes. I went to a *Collège Classique* in Quebec City. Classes were all day, including Saturday morning."

"And were you abused?"

"Not physically. The abuse, which is not the right word, was more subtle. The mere weight of the curriculum did not leave much time for anything else."

"Were you ever taught to have fun?"

"More by accident. One or two of the Brothers were fantastically funny. They were also the most effective teachers. They did not need to pick on any of the students, to scapegoat anyone."

"And, of course, that would extend into the dormitory."

He smiled.

"You have managed to turn this interview around. You have exposed some memories in my life as I tried to do with you. Your interview technique was more effective than mine."

"What is the next step?"

"We will meet later this week to review all the candidates. You will receive a letter shortly after that."

We both stood and shook hands. He escorted me to the door, making sure I gave back the guest pass.

Once outside, I checked my cell; there was one call from "anonymous." As I walked across the grassy median on Dorchester, I had two thoughts. The first was that blame really was a useless human trait. But my, oh, my, was it powerful.

The other was the very real fear that my application to be a foster parent was going to be rejected.

CHAPTER FORTY

The lot was nearly empty when I got back to Ferguson's car. I had to focus on where I might find a gas station. I drove east on Sainte-Catherine. On the corner of Lambert-Clossé was a service station that provided gas the old-fashioned way: someone came out to pump the gas.

I asked the fellow to check the oil. We both decided that it should be changed. I took his card and told him I would call to make an appointment.

I made my way over to Ferguson's. Luckily, the garage door was open, so I drove in to park the car in its spot. I took the elevator to Ferguson's floor. I knocked on his door.

"Come in."

"I could be a deranged neighbour."

He was sitting at the table fussing with his medications.

"You want to borrow sugar from a diabetic?"

"Do I sense a certain malaise?"

"You do."

"You could hire Doris to help you pack the apartment."

"I already called her."

"And she agreed?"

"I guess so; she could not stop laughing."

I started to look through his library. The books were divided by era; Old Testament, New Testament. They were also alphabetical according to author.

On first brush, nothing stood out. Some of these books looked too valuable to give away.

Some others may have had sentimental value. I chose one book from the Old Testament and one from the New. Both on the history of textual transmission.

I showed them to Ferguson, who agreed they were good choices and okay to take.

"Have you eaten?" He was looking up from the couch.

"No. As a matter of fact, I am hungry."

"Doris made a pasta sauce. It is in the freezer. And I think we have enough pasta around for two. We may be a little weak in the salad department."

"Is that grocery store open down the street?"

"Yes, it is."

"Fancy a walk?"

"As a matter of fact, yes."

I took the frozen sauce out and put the container in a pot of water to start to thaw.

Off we went to the new store. Neither one of us met anyone on Greene Avenue we knew. A first.

Once inside the new grocery store, it took me a minute to get used to the brightness and the layout.

I had never been in a place like this. Everything was perfectly in order. Everything was exhibited in such an artistic way. In fact, I felt like I was in a museum. I could look, but I should not touch. I needed to control myself, since I was hungry.

Ferguson and I agreed on a bread. We had a choice of fresh pasta or the packaged variety. We chose both. Reg insisted on iceberg lettuce. I chose the celery and green pepper.

We shared the bill.

Sarah Lazarus appeared before us. She was not alone. She introduced us to a young man who appeared to be several years her junior. I introduced her to Ferguson.

She appeared to be happy. "Great new store, eh? I cannot stay away."

As she passed me, she looked up to say, "I really do need to speak to you. Call me."

Ferguson and I continued up the street, Ferguson was quietly chortling to himself.

"What is so funny?"

"You."

"Oh, come on. I walk up the street and I meet someone I know. What is so funny about that?"

"Need I remind you that up to a year ago, you were not fair game to the opposite sex. Now you are. That may be the biggest challenge you face in your retirement."

"You are not attractive to the opposite sex even now?"

"You know something I do not know?"

"Not specifically. I was reading more stuff about the shenanigans that go on in seniors' residences. Naughty bunch of folks. You may have that to look forward to, Padre."

We were standing outside his building.

"There was this guy whose ministry was around Saint-Sauveur in the Laurentians. One afternoon, he was administering to one of his flock when the husband came home early, suffering from the flu . . ."

Back in the apartment, I was still giggling. Whether it was true or not, it was a great story. Ferguson went into his den and came out with two crystal glasses and a decanter of sherry.

"Fancy some?"

"Great idea."

I stood sipping the sherry. "Ferguson, this Molly thing is all wrong."

He stood looking at me and said nothing.

"She does not belong in the city. Molly belongs on that farm that Doris was talking about—a self-contained safe space. It may have been wrong for Doris's kids, but it is perfect for Molly: fewer distractions, quiet, more attention, more intimate. This city plan is nonsense."

"And your part in this?"

"At the moment, the best thing I can do is see that Molly is taken care of in the best possible way. Living with me here, now, is just not right. It does not fit."

"You feel better with that?"

"I do, and I am in the best position to advocate for it. That is the one thing I am sure about."

"You had better speak to Martha. And for the record, I agree with you."

There was a pause, and then I said, "I sense that my involvement with Molly will not end here. Molly will re-enter my life at some later time."

"What a declaration. You are sure about that?"

After a long look at me, he nodded and sat down on the couch.

"I have never heard you so positive about anything. As for your assumption, obviously time will tell, but you know, later on you will be more settled here, and so will she."

"My feelings were getting in the way of being dog-shit practical."

"Speaking of practicality, I need to eat."

I started on supper. Thawing the sauce was more of a challenge. The sauce dislodged into a saucepan, and I added a little water to bring it almost up to a boil.

I started up the water for the pasta and quickly put the salad together. Doris had left a jar of her low-fat dressing. I cut the bread very thinly. I did not want to put butter on the table. I organized the table settings. Ferguson was ready.

"I am having water; same for you?"

"Same."

Reg said grace. We started on the salad and bread.

The rest was ready. The sauce was superb. Credit to Ferguson, he ate slowly and kept his portion small.

"As usual around here, we will not leave the table hungry."

Ferguson nodded and then continued, "Your friend Orenstein is going to take himself to a mikvah tomorrow."

"Really. Of course, a ritual cleansing before Yom Kippur."

"You know that in the next week or so they finish reading the Five Books of Moses, which they immediately start again. Moses is denied permission to enter the Holy Land. After all he has done, the great leader is denied the prize he has striven for."

"Familiar paradigm, isn't it?"

His phone rang. "I will be there, and I feel fine. I am the picture of health."

"You have to go to the clinic tomorrow?"

"Yes."

My phone rang. "Well at least you behaved yourself. Nice technique to turn the interview around."

"I am fine, thank you, and how are you?"

"Listen, you dork. You know how things work around here. I get blamed for you."

"You have broad shoulders, and I guess we could get you a flak jacket."

"What are you doing later?"

"I am involved in a theological or metaphysical discussion with Rev. Ferguson, which has been interrupted twice. We haven't reached the fork in the road that will determine which way it will go."

"Pardon me. I have a case conference to prepare for. Maybe I will call you when I am finished."

"That would be fine."

Ferguson looked over at me. "We are popular this evening."

"I had an interview this afternoon with the foster care people."

"Did you behave?"

"Why does everybody ask that? The fellow who interviewed me has a bias against priests, both personally and professionally."

"You no doubt acquitted yourself well."

"Neither one of us drew any blood."

"I assume that was Martha who called you?"

"How could you guess?"

"I could tell by your tone and your body language."

"Is there more to tell about your relationship with her?"

"When my wife died, Martha was very supportive. She checked up on me. Even though I knew my wife was terminally ill, I was devastated when she passed. We had been together forever. Others said that they would be in touch. Martha followed through."

"What are you suggesting?"

"It is obvious that she is interested in you as more than a friend."

"I am not used to that. I have witnessed it, of course. But aside from a couple of teenage crushes centuries ago, I have had no experience with that sort of thing. From what you have said, neither has she, really."

"True. And perhaps I am becoming too paternal where both of you are concerned."

"You know, it is a little bit like starting on a trek without a map or a compass."

"Isn't that life, really?"

"That is partly why I left the Church. I no longer trusted the map or the compass."

"Why were you never promoted?"

"You want the vernacular answer or the ecclesiastical one?"

Ferguson started to laugh. "I think right there you have answered my question."

My cell rang. I did not recognize the number. "In case you are wondering, that young man I was with on Greene Aveneue was my nephew, Elyse and Martin's son."

"Why do you folks start conversations from the second paragraph, Sarah? And yes, I did think you had lucked out."

"A group of us break the holiday fast together. We're a very eclectic crowd, and I wondered if you wanted to join me as my guest."

"Is it okay to attend if one has not fasted?"

"There is no means test."

"Thank you very much, but I may have other plans."

"Martha."

"Yes, I may be spending the day with her."

Sarah hung up.

Ferguson looked over at me and said nothing.

I called Sarah back; she did not take the call.

I looked over at Ferguson. "You know, I think I stepped into the middle of a long-simmering feud and stoked the coals."

"Are you surprised that this sort of thing happens?"

"I would like to think that those two would have the resources to move on. Anyway, I quite innocently stepped into this kerfuffle."

The cell rang again, this time the caller was known. "I am just parking downstairs. I will be up in a minute."

"The door is open."

"Martha?"

"Martha."

I buzzed her into the building. She entered the apartment dressed in a red blazer, beige slacks, and red flat shoes. She had a touch of makeup on.

"Nice getup."

"Fucking PR. I've spent so much time on bullshit that I needed to work until now finishing the important stuff."

"Would you like a drink?"

"Not on an empty stomach, thank you."

"I could make you something."

"Not necessary. I hear the grocery store is open down the street."

"Let me heat up some pasta for you. We have enough left over to feed you in fine style."

"Sold."

I went into the kitchen to organize her dinner. Ferguson's stove did not have a timer. I wound up the cute little chicken timer that Doris bought. When I came back to the salon, Martha and Ferguson were sitting on the couch, engaged in conversation.

"Salad? Bread?"

"No bread. A little salad would be nice."

"Iceberg lettuce or green leaf?"

"Iceberg would be fine, thank you."

I went back into the kitchen to fix her a salad. There were several minutes left on the timer.

"Do you want your salad now or with your meal?"

"This is a first-rate restaurant. With my meal, if you don't mind."

She got up from the couch to come into the kitchen to get some water. I had opened the oven to check on her dish. She filled her glass from the canister in the fridge. I closed the oven; she stretched up to give me a kiss. It was not perfunctory.

"What was that for?"

"When I first met you, I did not understand what you were about. I still don't, but I appreciate you."

"Ditto."

"Typical. Mother was right."

We went back into the parlour. Ferguson was dozing in his corner of the sofa. When I attempted to remove his glasses, he woke up.

"Do you want to lie down?"

"What? And miss all the fun?"

I joined Martha at the table as she ate. "This is really good."

"What did you expect? We have a reputation here."

"That fellow who interviewed you is not someone I know."

"Where did he come from?"

"He had done some work in Quebec City for Social Affairs. My sense is that he is being groomed for management. Susan Epstein, I know. In a way, I am glad she was unable to see you."

Ferguson, from the couch, asked about Molly.

"She is doing well. She is very adept at using modern technology to communicate."

Ferguson looked over at me. "And you—are you adept yet?"

"I went into the computer store on Sainte-Catherine Street, and I was told to go to the Apple store. The Apple store was a madhouse; I could barely hear, let alone understand what the very young woman was going on about. All I know is I need to spend some time on it, which I have not done yet."

Martha's phone buzzed. She went into the den to take the call. When she came back, her face was ashen. "Spoke too soon. Molly went AWOL."

Ferguson broke the silence. "I bet that there is a very logical explanation."

Martha, clearly agitated, responded. "I cannot go in there and yell and scream. The Group Home coordinator would ream my ass for interfering. In the hierarchy, we are on the same level."

"So can I assume we are not going to spend the night driving the streets?"

"Not necessarily. And especially if you find her," she said, looking directly at me.

Ferguson, who was now lying on the sofa with his legs out, said in his laconic way, "Count me out of this one."

Martha went over to Reg, bent down, and gave him a big kiss on each cheek.

She walked by me at the table. "Coming?"

"What about the dishes?"

"Go, Glasheen. Duty calls!" Ferguson bellowed.

CHAPTER FORTY-ONE

I drove Martha's car to Notre-Dame de Grace, which was about fifteen minutes west of Ferguson's apartment. She had me go down Monkland, which is a main thoroughfare in the area. The street was lined with boutiques, so there was traffic.

"You know, we are going at this the wrong way."

"How so?"

"We need to think like Molly. What would have been so important that she would have missed supper? The last time she did this, she was tending a sick cat."

"Funny, we have several years of education and life experience between us, and we are reverting to mind reading."

"Did any of the staff canvass the immediate neighbourhood, like by knocking on doors? Maybe she helped an old lady with her groceries."

"How fucking practical can you be?"

She pulled the car over to use her cell. She had a text message from the coordinator to the effect that Molly had yet to be found and all communication was to go through her.

She phoned the woman, whose name was Therese. "Martha Lang calling concerning Molly. I would like an update on her situation. You can call me at . . . [etc.]"

Martha then looked at me. "You know, this place is becoming as bureaucratic as the Church."

"Hardly."

"I know the house parents very well. They have been with us forever. And I am not allowed to speak to them."

Her cell rang. "I was wondering if you had the resources to canvass the neighbourhood. And if not, my friend and I would volunteer to do so."

There was a pause, Martha listened, and then said, "How long is this going to take?"

She listened some more and finally said, "Please keep me informed, and thank you."

"We are to stay out of it. She is organizing the search."

"Bullshit. We both have too much invested in this to sit on the sidelines. Agreed?"

S. John Diamond

She turned to look at me. She was smiling. "Screw them."

"Exactly."

We started driving up and down streets in the neighbourhood. Nothing.

"Therese has alerted the police. And she was organizing a flying squad of staff from other homes to begin a search. That could take hours."

"Let's go ring some doorbells."

We parked near the group home, but not too near. There was a half moon; otherwise, our way was lit by streetlights.

Many of the residences were fourplexes: one entrance in front, another one on the side.

We chose to go together. Martha put on her hospital dog tags. She also carried business cards, just in case.

We went together. We rang eight doorbells and spoke to five people. No luck.

The group home was the only single dwelling on the block; it was a fine, well-maintained older residence. We canvassed on the other side of it. Again nothing.

Across the street, we did the same thing. No results.

Two cars pulled up in front of the group home. Two people emerged from each car. Three women and one man, the flying squad.

Martha and I started walking up the street. The four workers emerged from the house. Both cars were then parked properly. And then, the four split in two to repeat what we had just done.

Martha said to me, "Let's go to Monkland to get coffee and wait."

Martha was able to find parking. There was a choice of two coffee shops, one on the west corner and the other on the east corner. Both were busy, and since I had no preference, we went into the western one. Martha entered first, and I followed a few paces behind. The aroma of coffee was thick and welcoming.

At the counter, Martha ordered tea. I wanted plain old black coffee and a sweet. Martha chose a cookie. She insisted on paying.

We spied a table for two in the corner. The crowd was a mixture of young couples, students, and folks like us. As I carried the tray, Martha was greeted by a couple of people as we edged our way through the crowd. No one acknowledged me.

Once seated, Martha placed her phone on the table. There was no activity.

The coffee was excellent. I devoured the less-than-fresh sweet roll. Martha nibbled at the cookie. Conversation was next to impossible above the din. Martha broke off half the cookie to give it to me. It was much better than what I had chosen.

Her phone buzzed: a call from her mother, which she did not pick up.

There seemed to be no reason to stay, so we left. Outside, she returned Mrs. Lang's call. The hospital called: they wanted to see her on Wednesday, Yom Kippur. Martha agreed it was important and that she would take her there.

We started walking down the street. "There goes our road trip. Mommy duty."

"Another time. I have put it on my agenda. Do you cross-country ski?"

"Not for years. I think the last time was at university. A bunch of us used to go regularly."

"I will do some research. I am sure there are some really good trails around here in winter."

"Rushing the season, aren't you?"

"Just thinking ahead."

She put her hand through my elbow. "What are you doing Wednesday night?"

"I have no plans. Sarah Lazarus called to invite me to a dinner party. When I said I was busy, she slammed off. She guessed I was busy with you."

"Damn her."

"You guys going to bury the hatchet one of these days?"

"One of these days."

"Why the jealousy?"

She took her arm away and turned me around to face her. "Because she is a two-faced bitch."

A couple, who had been following us, gave us a wide berth on the street corner and tried not to stare too intently.

"I am leaving this whole subject alone. And I regret bringing it up."

"Stop patronizing me."

We walked in silence. After another block, Martha said, "Did Sarah mention who was hosting?"

"No. But she did say it was going to be an eclectic crowd."

"Their name is Stone, Barbara and Phil. Both professors: one at Concordia and the other at McGill. And the crowd would be very interesting. Trust me. Phil teaches physics. Those guys are really from another planet."

"So, what did you have in mind for Wednesday?"

"Watching hockey together."

"Serious?"

"Since I know you are a fan, I have sort of followed the fact that the season starts Wednesday night."

"I accept. I will cook for you."

"I will bring beer and peanuts."

"Will Molly's disappearing act, her third, create a problem for our plans?"

"It might. Someone could decide that she is at risk in an unlocked environment."

"Except for her run from the hospital, these two from the group home can be easily explained."

"Do you want to leave this to me? There will be a discussion in about a week or so. I think the evidence to place her in a monitored unit is weak, as well."

Martha's phone rang. She listened for a moment. "Oh, isn't that good news. So she was not very far away, then. Thank you so much for calling. You have a good night, too."

"So our young friend gets more interesting with each passing day. You were right; she was visiting down the street. Something about a young girl confined to a wheelchair. Molly stayed for supper."

"Good girl. Nice to be able to intuit behaviour at least some of the time."

"Mind reading was part of your training?"

"Not overtly. More or less a by-product."

"I need to run you home, don't I?"

"You have another idea?"

"I do, but I don't have the energy to follow through at the moment."

I shifted mental gears. "You know, Molly does not belong here in this situation. She belongs on a farm or someplace rural and quiet with few distractions and lots of attention."

We were stopped at a red light. Martha turned to look at me. "I hate when you are right, which you seem to be most of the time."

The car behind honked.

"It's the only thing that makes sense at the moment. Her life should not be an experiment. Surely you have the resources to place her in an environment where she can experience some stability, some success. Her staying with me now is wrong all the way around. Her going back to her village is impossible. Leaving her in a similar situation in the city is too risky. She will wander off again."

"I will phone Claire. And what about your application to be a foster parent?"

"Let it stand for now. I am curious to know how they deal with me."

We drove in silence over the Mountain back to the Plateau. I nodded to Mother. I really should go visit. At the moment, I felt a sense of completion around the Molly situation. For the first time in a few weeks, a weight was lifted. The cemetery could wait.

Martha double-parked in front of my door. She leaned over to give me a kiss. It was a long one. She patted me on the knee. "You had better go in; this episode tonight really tired me out."

"Yes, I think we both need some rest. We will speak soon."

I got out of the car and watched her slowly drive down the block and make a right turn out of sight.

CHAPTER FORTY-TWO

I checked the mail on the way into the apartment. There was an envelope from the Social Service Centre, which I started opening on the staircase. Standing on the top stair, before I opened the inner door, I read that my application to be a foster parent was being reviewed and I would be contacted shortly.

Well, at least I was not disqualified. Perhaps I could find out more from Martha.

I looked around the apartment. If I was going to entertain, I would definitely need to seriously vacuum and dust the place. It was too late now. I looked online for recipes that one might consider for a pre-hockey dinner. What went with beer and peanuts? Ordering a pizza was too predictable. Hot dogs and frites was a possibility. Chili was a more interesting choice. I would try that out on Martha to see if that was acceptable.

I wrote to her asking about the letter and the menu. There was no immediate response.

The sports site was loaded with hockey talk. The American sports site was full of US college football, baseball, and professional football. Hockey was down the list.

I wrote on my calendar where I thought the Habs would finish in April. I then skipped to the middle of June to record my Stanley Cup prediction and ultimate winner. Not the Habs. But I could always dream. I then deleted all that stuff. I remembered I was no longer a lonely priest living in a small community in the North with time on my hands. I had graduated to the big city and so-called retirement. Something about the law of unintended consequences, which I thought was so much psychobabble; maybe it was true, or at least in my case, it seemed so.

I went back to read emails from organizations whose blogs and blasts I should unsubscribe from. I started the dreary process, then stretched out on the new couch and picked up where I had left off when I awoke refreshed at five.

There was a note from Sarah, with sort of an apology for her behaviour earlier. In essence, she was writing that we should just be friends. I chose not to write back. I thought that was what we were—just friends.

I sat back to listen to some jazz radio on the Internet. I turned the sound up while I undressed to take a shower. Martha had written back to say chili was fine, but could it be vegetarian?

And she would chase after the foster care folks. And by the way, the Juvenile Court had sent a subpoena in the Joel abuse case. I wondered how all that was going down in the community, especially with Rabbi Shinder and his daughter and son-in-law. As for Orenstein, he would no doubt give me marching orders if necessary. There was nothing I could do at the moment. The justice system was doing its job; what good it could do was a question for another time.

More questions for little Joel, answers to which he would mumble through. I still worried about how he was feeling. The beating was bad enough; now came the inquisition. Which was worse?

A shower was relaxing. My mind wandered and managed to fix on nothing in particular. I sat in a robe in front of the computer, looking up vegetarian chili recipes. To my surprise, there were many. I printed off a few and was determined to create the best non-meat chili in the Plateau. My friends in the north would be amused at this. Chili was best with game meat.

Next, I looked up mikvahs in Montreal—more specifically, where one might be located around here. Sure enough, there was one within walking distance. Water was universal to religions.

After a snack of melba toast, I decided on a walk. I was going to put off dusting the apartment until later. I did remember to take one of the recipes with me to make sure I had enough of the basic ingredients. A vegetable store on Parc had tofu, chickpeas, and red kidney beans, in addition to the mandatory greens. I would pick up a bread later. I returned to the apartment with my purchases.

Mrs. Orenstein was standing guard on the landing. "Those people called to ask about you."

No secrets around here. "Yes. They seem very thorough."

"Well, what is Shmully going to say? That you are a cannibal? What nonsense."

I started to laugh. "Mrs. Orenstein, it would be so much simpler for them if that is what he said." She snorted, turned, and walked back into her house. Another triumphant performance.

Shmully came out in shirtsleeves to tell me that a subpoena had been issued. I told him that I already knew.

S. John Diamond

"Martha?"

I nodded.

"The family wants a deferral until after the holidays. I will see what I can do."

"Will they permit that? After all, it is a serious case."

"I can only ask. But they have granted such delays before."

"I rather think few do not accede to your wishes."

"Were that always true."

With that, he turned and went into his flat. Was he more abrupt than usual, or was it just me?

The post had not arrived yet. After sorting out my purchases, I went back out to start another walk—I knew not where. Down Saint-Laurent, and as if by a magnet, I was drawn to the movie theatre now owned by Sheila Green and her family. The place looked the same. The double feature attracted the same crowd as last week, judging by the traffic.

Mike Green would be in dialysis this afternoon if he had gone on Saturday.

Time for some atonement on my part. I made my way down to Pine Avenue and then west to the Royal Victoria Hospital. I eventually found the dialysis unit in the maze that characterized the place. I had brought my cross, which I pinned on the lapel of my jacket. But no Mike Greene.

There was an exit through a parking lot back onto Pine.

Up to the General I went. This time, I went in through the lower entrance and went to the sixth floor. The unit was located on the second floor of the west wing. I waited an eternity for the elevator and was about to take the stairs when the car came. Down I went, putting on my calling card.

Opposite the elevator was a sort of waiting area. To the right was a corridor with examining rooms on the right. At the far end was a room that opened up into the dialysis unit. There was a young woman seated at a desk behind a banquette. "Can I help you?"

"I would like to visit Green, Mike Green."

"Just a minute, sir."

To my left were dialysis chairs filled with people receiving treatment. They were four chairs to a space, two on one side and two on

281

One Last Confession

the other. From what I could see, the area was filled with occupied chairs.

A tall woman loomed in front of me. "And you are?"

"My name is Terry Glasheen. I would like to visit briefly with Mike Green."

She looked at my lapel. "Yes, Father, I will take you to him."

We passed several groupings of four chairs, the patients attached to machines that were enormous in comparison to the small kidneys they were replacing. Amazing, really.

In the back, in the right corner by the window, was Green. He was sleeping under a hospital blanket with his chair reclined and earphones on. The earphones were plugged into a small TV, which was playing a talk show.

Ruth, the head nurse, or so her dog tag said, nudged Green's arm. He woke up, looked at me and said, "Are you here to administer last rites?"

Ruth laughed uproariously. "I will leave you two alone."

He took off his earphones, a concession I appreciated.

He did continue to look at the TV.

He then looked at me. "Why are you here?"

"To apologize."

He did not respond. He looked at me cold-faced. After a minute or so, he said, "You prick."

I did not respond; I continued looking down at him. One of the assistants came to offer me a chair.

Green looked up at him. "Albert, that won't be necessary. This gentleman is leaving."

He put on his earphones, changed the channel on the TV, and looked away.

Two seconds later, he tore off his headset and yelled, "Nurse!"

Two people came running, a nurse turned off the dialysis unit, and Albert the assistant started massaging Green's legs.

"Left leg, left leg. What are you trying to do, kill me?"

Green was able to stand close to his chair. In a few seconds, the pain abated and he sat back down.

"Now, Mr. Green, I can adjust everything down. You will have to stay longer. Is that okay?" the nurse said.

"What choice do I have? And Albert, tell this gentleman to leave."

The assistant looked at me, as if to ask, what gives?

"Come on, Mike, what are you telling me? Stop joking."

"I am not joking. Get this guy out of here. I do not want him here, ever."

I was on my way out when Albert caught up to me. "What was that all about?"

I turned to look directly at him, "I think he blames me for his being on dialysis and maybe a bunch of other things."

"I guess you'd better go, then."

"I guess so. Nice making your acquaintance."

The assistant stood in the entrance of the unit and watched me walk down the corridor to the elevators.

At least I had atoned. And the more I thought about it, so had Green.

CHAPTER FORTY-THREE

I took the elevator back up to the sixth floor. There was no sale today. I walked east toward the main entrance. Halfway down the corridor was the chapel. I decided to go in for a minute. I sat alone in the room. The space was quiet. To the right was a very elaborate wood sculpture whose symbolism escaped me. There was no little plaque with a title to give me a clue. After a few minutes, I was able to calm down and focus on the rest of the day.

That was the second time in my adult life I had been excused. I started to laugh to myself. Welcome to the real world.

I was going to call Ferguson to find out what he was up to. Perhaps I would call Martha to find out if she had any information on Molly's status and her role in the court date with Joel's family.

The more I simply sat, the less I wanted to leave. A grey-haired woman entered the room behind me. I turned, she nodded to me. She had a cross on her lapel. I did not want conversation, so I got up to leave. I did not acknowledge her on my way out.

The general hubbub at the main entrance was jolting. I quickly went outside to get away from the din. On the walkway to the left and right of the door, staff and patients were smoking. There was a staircase opposite that led up to street level. I turned left to walk down to Côte des Neiges.

Martha called. "You have created a stir."

"Seems to be the theme of the day."

"Let's call it a split decision. Some want Molly close by. Others agree with you that she should live outside the city. Claire will ultimately make the decision."

"I would think she would be in my court."

"Cannot tell with her. And I really cannot intervene with her on your behalf."

"So be it. And the subpoena. What is your role in that?"

"I will appear along with the executive director and our lawyer. I am getting used to these things, unfortunately."

"Goes with the territory, I guess. Be prepared for a delay in the hearing. Orenstein will request that it take place after the Holidays."

"I thought as much. I am spending tonight with Mother. I assume you do not want to do the same. We will speak tomorrow. Have a good evening. Any plans?"

"I thought I might chat up Ferguson."

She rang off. I had reached Côte-des-Neiges. I decided to cross and continued walking west. At some point, I would walk down to Sherbrooke Street to head to Reg's apartment.

The sun was directly in my eyes. Through the trees, I could see the college that was being remodelled as a condominium. This may have been heresy, but I thought it a nice looking building. As for buying a unit, I did not think that was realistic.

At the first corner, I took a left turn, mostly to get out of the sun's rays. I crossed to the west side of the street. The homes were large and well cared for. Many seemed to have tradesmen's vans parked outside: contractors, electricians, and the like. There was a sign saying I was entering Westmount. At Montrose and Mount Pleasant, there was a school for girls. Cars were parked outside, waiting to take the students home. Many of the parents were standing outside talking.

At Mountain, I turned left and made my way down the hill to Sherbrooke Street. I was at the back of Ferguson's building. I phoned him. There was no answer. I walked over to the little park facing the Temple. There was activity around the building in anticipation of the evening's service.

There were two security people standing outside the front doors talking.

Ferguson was not in the park. I walked back to Greene Avenue. He was not in the diner, nor was he in the coffee shop across the street. I went into the grocery store, which was crowded with afternoon shoppers. There was another exit that led out into a patio by the side street. There was Ferguson talking to his friend, the retired professor. They were off to the side in the shade.

I sat with them. "Hope I am not interrupting anything important."

Ferguson looked positively robust today. He looked over his glasses at me. "I sensed you were in the area. The Prof and I just finished a rather lengthy walk. And no, we have not solved all the issues of the day." They both chuckled as if at some private joke.

Ted looked over at me. "You busy next week? Wednesday, to be exact? I have talked Ferguson here into reviewing a book at the library on Atwater. The work is a secret. The fact that Reg has agreed I consider a coup."

"*Winnie the Pooh, Macbeth, the Hardy Boys, Elmore Leonard . . .* oh, please tell us."

Ferguson looked over his glasses again at me. "You really are a snot, you know?" and then burst out laughing.

"I guess I will have to show up to find out what the great sage of Westmount has to offer. Anyone want something? I fancy a coffee and a sweet."

They both said they were fine. I went back into the store to get black coffee and a sweet roll with lemon topping. As I was waiting to pay, I felt a hand on my elbow and someone reaching up to kiss me on the cheek. I turned; it was Sarah. "Nice work. I just heard about what you did for Sheila Green."

Given our last communication, I was taken aback, "I, ah, well, she is a nice lady and she deserved to come out a winner." We walked out the side door together. "Listen, I am sitting with some friends—please join us."

"Gotta run. I just came from school. I need to get myself organized for tonight's festivities. See you again."

"'Have an easy fast,' I believe one says."

"Correct, and thank you."

She hurried across the intersection and up the street.

Ferguson was eyeing her. "A woman in every port, eh?"

"I had this notion that it is not too late for you and Claire."

Ferguson looked down. I had struck a nerve.

Ted began to recount their afternoon activities. "We walked from here to the Apple store on Sainte-Catherine. I was trying to urge old pokey here to at least consider entering the twenty-first century by buying a small notebook."

Ferguson came back from wherever he went. "At least I enjoyed the walk and the conversation. As for the rest, what a waste of time. I cannot type. I could hardly see the keyboard. My fingers were too big for the keys. And then, old boy, we walked back and here we are."

"I got it. You are going to review the *King James Bible.*"

Ted got up from the table. "Gotta run. Flossy needs to be walked and fed."

I looked up at him. "I hope you are talking about your dog."

He smiled and rolled his eyes. "See you next week at the surprise party."

I looked over at Reg. "I hit a nerve, did I?"

"Not your fault. It was a long time ago. I really do not want to talk about it. She is coming to supper tonight. Please join us."

"Thank you for the invitation. But under the circumstances I do not think it is a good idea. She has the task of deciding Molly's fate."

"Oh."

"Oh."

"I like your odds, as one of my parishioners used to say. He was a horseman, and he used to attend service in the morning and go to the track in the afternoon. He claimed I had an effect on his wagering."

I brought the uneaten sweet, which had been bagged for me, as we walked up the street.

At Sherbrooke, my bus was waiting at the light. We said our goodbyes, and I hopped on.

I had to stand until the Main. The Saint-Laurent Boulevard bus was coming up the hill as I crossed Sherbrooke Street. There was a line of people at the bus stop on the northeast corner. I also stood going up to my stop. One young student did offer me a seat, which I declined with thanks.

Our street was not busy. Many of my neighbours were having an early dinner before sundown.

I had no mail. The late afternoon light came in the kitchen window. I had left the two books I had borrowed from Ferguson on the counter. I picked up one of them, and a paper fell out onto the floor.

It was not a bookmark. There was writing on the inverse. It was a letter from Claire to Reg dated fifteen years ago. The book had kept the script legible. I started reading. After the first paragraph, I stopped and put it back in the book. It was a love letter. There were two sheets of heavy stationery folded carefully. I wondered for a moment if the conversation this afternoon and this letter were linked, but I knew the answer, and the subject was now closed—forever.

I thought of taking myself out for supper. The more I thought about it, the more it was a good idea. All of my new-found friends were busy.

I read some stuff online. I found out that the holiday would be over tomorrow night around eight in the evening—seven fifty-three to be exact.

I had bought a small blender somewhere along the way, which I took down from the top shelf in the cupboard. It required cleaning to get rid of the dust it had collected. While it was drying in the drainer, I organized all the ingredients on one side of the sink and the spices on the other. I had not asked Martha what level of hotness she could tolerate. I decided to tone the recipe down, just to be safe. She could always add hot sauce or one of the extra jalapenos (they came packaged as four) I had picked up at the grocer's.

There was an old pot under the sink that was perfect for simmering chili. I was sure the thing was fifty years old.

I started with the sauce first. Then, as that was slowly cooking, I used the blender to dice the vegetables, which I then sautéed in olive oil. I poured them into the pot. I drained and added both the chickpeas and the red kidney beans. I left the tofu out of the recipe. Not everyone liked tofu, and I was a little put off by the texture.

While that was cooking, I ran to the computer to look up a General Tao's tofu recipe. I had seen the dish on the menu at the Chinese restaurant Martha and I had gone to a few nights ago. Miraculously, I had all the fixings except rice, which surely I could pick up at the *dépanneur* down the street. I turned off the stove and put my jacket on to run the errand.

Orenstein was coming out of his flat at the same time as I was coming out of mine. He was alone. He nodded in my direction. He was not wearing leather shoes; rather he had on old high-top running shoes.

"Have an easy fast," I said to his back as he was running down the stairs. He turned at the bottom.

I went to my favourite *dep*. One of the plate-glass windows had been smashed and covered by a combination of green plastic bags and opened-up cardboard boxes. Inside, the storekeeper was his usual jovial self.

"This nonsense happens all the time," he told me with a shrug.

"Are you going to put bars on the windows?" I asked.

"I have to now. Insurance, you know."

I found rice. Then I decided to see if he sold specialty beer, the locally brewed stuff. He did, and I chose three bottles with the most decorative labelling. I had no idea if they were any good. He nodded as I placed them on the counter. "They sell well." The packaging alone was worth it.

I returned home with my purchases. The street was eerily quiet. Someone should mount a neighbourhood watch, I thought.

I had received an email from the foster care people, which I carefully read twice. There were two parts to it. The decision on my application to be a foster parent has been deferred to a later date.

There was a name and a phone number for me to call, at my convenience, to discuss an "alternative option" in the meantime. There was a CC to Claire Thomas. The letter was signed by the fellow who interviewed me. The original was being mailed to me. Somebody had created a compromise. I wondered if it was Claire. And I also wondered if this was her last hurrah. She no longer had the same influence she once had.

Martha called. "I just found out what they have offered you."

"Do you always start your conversations in the middle?"

She started to laugh, to giggle, actually.

"Just with you. I am fine, thank you. And what do you think of their offer?"

"What offer? They have deferred their decision. I scared them off."

"They want you to volunteer weekends at one of the group homes."

"Oh, lovely. Saturday night? Sunday morning? That sort of thing."

"Yes, something like that."

"Oh, balls. There goes my social life."

"Look, you are not the usual candidate who applies to be a foster parent."

"I am not the usual type who does a lot of things."

"Pat on the back to you."

"To change the subject, I bought some very interesting local beer for our hot date tomorrow night."

"I hope you mean that."

"Mean what?"

"Nothing. What is the main course?"

"A very creative veggie chili, just for you."

"I will bring a very interesting bread to accompany your fine dish. Could I bring a lettuce for some salad?"

"Fine."

"What time am I expected.? And do not say 'whenever.'"

"Six thirty sharp. Puck drops at seven thirty. Or so."

"You should call to speak to that group-home person to find out exactly what they have in mind for you." She rang off.

I wanted to call those people to tell them to put their ideas in a dark place and to withdraw my candidacy. I put the phone down on the counter with a little more force than I intended.

Good thing they were idiot-proof.

I looked outside into the back alley. A couple of figures were eyeing Orenstein's SUV.

I grabbed my phone and ran down the stairs yelling and screaming at the top of my lungs. On my way out the door, I had grabbed a broom, which I had neglected to put away. The two youngsters took off up the alley.

They could have been armed. They could have stood their ground. That thought only occurred afterward. As I was turning to go back into the house, a police car drove slowly down the *ruelle*. The driver stopped to look at Shmully's car. The car stopped, and a tall, blonde police woman got out, putting on her hat. She came over to the fence. She asked in French what had happened. When she heard my answer—more precisely, when she heard my accent—she switched to English.

"Yes, I saw two men dressed in dark clothes. They were young, boys really. They did no damage to the car. The SUV belongs to my neighbour. If I see them around here again, I will call the police."

As I was climbing the stairs to my flat, I wondered why the fancy alarm did not go off. I concluded that Orenstein had disabled it.

I phoned the Social Service Centre to speak to the person about their alternative proposal. Emily wanted me to leave her a message on her voicemail or alternatively send her a text or email message. Her return phone call interrupted my dusting the apartment. I recognized the number.

"Am I speaking to Mr. Glasheen?"

I could not place the accent or the age of the caller.

"Yes. You can call me Terry."

"I am Emily Leclerc with the group home department. I believe you received a letter from us concerning volunteering weekends."

"I did."

"I am a little bit familiar with your file; we should meet to discuss this further. Do you have a car?"

"I have access to a vehicle. Does my volunteering depend on having a car?"

I realized my tone was one of impatience, bordering on exasperation. I had a choice. I took a deep breath.

"Ms. Leclerc, I am available to meet with you. When would be convenient?"

"Wednesday, tomorrow, at eleven. Are you free this weekend?"

Belying my growing hostility to these folks, I had managed to lighten my tone, even though I was sure that I might give myself a hernia.

"I am available at eleven, and I am free this weekend."

"Tomorrow, then. I look forward to meeting you."

When I rang off, I let out a big breath of air. I had not realized how much I had invested in this whole process, and there was roadblock after roadblock. In the meantime, Molly, I supposed, was safe for now. She could wander off again, and then what?

I phoned Martha. "Who is Emily Leclerc?"

"I am fine, thank you, and how are you? I sense your growing hostility to the process. And by the way, it is Emilie—she is Haitian. She was found on the streets of Port-au-Prince when she was fourteen. She has come a long way."

"You are telling me she is a success story. I can only hope Molly becomes the same."

"Mother wishes you well and wonders when you will visit next? And no argument from me. Though you do understand where they are coming from? You are an unknown entity."

"I will rent space on a billboard."

"I like when you get a certain kind of pissed off."

"Tell Mother that when my schedule permits—and, after all, I am retired—I will come calling to take her out dancing."

Martha relayed the message and then returned to the line. "She accepts."

"Later, then." I rang off. Then I turned the damn thing off.

Returning to my chef fantasy was not what I wanted to do. It was probably the safest thing I could do. I needed to calm down, pure and simple. I needed to forgive. And that was a real fight right now.

I focused on making General Tao's tofu with rice. I had to scale down the rice recipe for two. I used the entire box of tofu with the idea that I would freeze what was left over for another time. The salt content on the box was alarmingly high; nevertheless, I soldiered on.

Once I started eating, I felt better. I turned on the TV to watch a baseball game. The two teams were playing out of the string. Neither one was going to be in the playoffs. I switched that off and turned on the computer to listen to the jazz radio station. That was the perfect choice.

I finished eating and judged the dish a success. After cleaning up, I lay on my new couch. I moved a lamp around so I could read. After about five minutes of looking at last Saturday's newspaper, I dozed off.

I woke up with a start. Both my hands were balled into fists. I had been in the middle of a dream which involved holding off a gang. My sense was the gang was made up of familiar faces, none of whose names I could remember now. I went to the fridge to get a small bottle of cold water, which I drank in one gulp.

I was still in fight mode. I put on my jacket and Habs baseball cap and went out to walk it off. The clock on the cell registered twelve seventeen a.m.

At the end of my block, I turned left. At the next block, my eye looked north. Under a street light, I could see the outline of someone swaying back and forth. I could not make out anything else. I walked toward the light, which was set back from the curb at the corner of the alley that continued from our street. When I got closer, I realized who it was.

Rabbi Shinder was deep in prayer. I stood in front of him for a while. I was going to move on, leaving him to his devotions.

He opened his eyes, which took a moment to focus on me. He did not say anything, nor did he acknowledge my presence. I started walking up the street past him. There was no one else around.

"Excuse me, Mr. Glasheen."

I turned to face him once more. "Do you still take confession?"

CHAPTER FORTY-FOUR

I looked up at him. His face was haggard. His body was slightly stooped. I remembered his carriage being tall and erect.

"You want me to take confession from you?"

He nodded. "I know this may be highly irregular."

There was something about the whole presentation which compelled me to nod my head.

I followed him to his lower office. My mind raced through the scenario: Yom Kippur, confession, my dream. My upset. And last but not least, something Ferguson told me the other day, which, right then, I could not remember.

There was a large candle on the Rabbi's desk. There was no other light.

I sat in the same chair as before. He sat behind his immaculate desk. In the corner on a clothes stand was a white cloak-cassock. Purification.

I did not move. I did not speak. He sat before me with his hands folded on his desk in front of him.

He had removed none of his outdoor clothes.

I waited. He said nothing. He stared at his hands.

His hands were large and smooth; I tore my eyes away from them.

I remembered. "Moses asks for forgiveness for the sin of the golden calf."

He looks up at me. "What are they going to do with me?"

"I do not know."

Again silence.

"Moses is denied entrance to the Promised Land."

"After all he has done for His People."

I repeated, "After all he has done for his people."

He looked up again. "What are you going to do now?"

"Nothing. I am going home. I have heard your confession. You will know your penance."

He was looking down at his hands. "I have all day today to work that out. Don't I?"

I said nothing. I slowly got up and left his office, probably for the last time.

CHAPTER FORTY-FIVE

The air outside was good. I walked up the path toward my street. Halfway, I turned my head to the side to retch.

I stumbled home. Orenstein's house had a night light in the front parlour. I had left my light on in the staircase inside.

I went up, washed my mouth and face, and sat on the new couch shaking. I wanted a shot of Jameson's; actually, I wanted the whole bottle.

I went to my computer and wrote Claire Thomas that I was withdrawing my application to be a foster parent.

I wanted to write Martha. I could not. I feared I might say all the wrong things and all the right things. So, in the end, it was safer to say nothing.

I just sat. Maybe I slept. First light came. I did not look at the time.

We knew so much, and yet we knew so little.

CHAPTER FORTY-SIX

I went out and started to walk. I was on autopilot. I just kept going. I went up the mountain, past the cross, whose lights went out as I went by. A little farther on was the cut in the rock where the road narrowed; luckily there was little traffic. There was an open gate into the cemetery on the right. The city was displayed before me, and in the distance was the outline of the Laurentian Mountains.

Mother's grave. I stood over it and stared. "She was very helpful to us, very supportive." Rabbi Shinder's words came back to me. I needed her to be both supportive and helpful one more time. I could see her in my mind, not as she looked at the end, but from an earlier, more vibrant time. I remembered the tributes that extolled her passion for teaching. And how she was able to move even the most difficult student, including those in the prison. Everyone got caught up in her spirit of joy. She deserved her rest. It was well-earned. "Forgive her her sins."

I started to leave, looking for the gate that would lead me back down the mountain.

I remembered something I had read about Yom Kippur: the notion of the closing of the gate, ending one cycle and beginning a new one. How apt.

On my street, men were slowly walking to prayers. I wondered how Rabbi Shinder was going to experience this day. I also wondered about Orenstein. There was no doubt in my mind that this evening he and I were going to meet.

I spent the rest of the morning inside trying to sort out things. The more I ruminated, the more edgy I got. The Internet provided some respite from my conflicted feelings.

My cell rang. It was Martha. "Mother's test this morning was very demanding. She can't be left alone. Tonight is off. Rain check?"

"Sure. Sure."

Maybe she picked something up in my voice. "You okay?"

"Honestly?"

"I know you sent me some messages. I have not read them. Yes, honestly."

"Like shit."

"Something happen?"

"Yes. But look, you are busy with Mother. It will wait."

"You sound remote, like you are in the middle of something."

"Later. Send Mother my best."

Life's experiences led one to this moment. Really?

I knew the answer to that and was having trouble accepting it.

On the Internet, I happened onto Martin Luther King's "I Have a Dream" speech, which I watched from beginning to end. I was seven at the time and remembered watching it with Mother.

When it was over, she was in tears. I now understood why.

At ten p.m., Orenstein appeared at the back door. I invited him in.

We looked at one another. He looked as haggard as I felt.

"Rabbi Shinder addressed his congregation today and announced his resignation. You know something about that?"

"Did he say anything else?"

"Yes."

"Now what?"

"The authorities will be informed."

"Is there more?"

"The community is in shock. You and I are . . . what's the word . . . pariahs."

"Blamed?"

"You more than me."

"For being truthful. Did he really do it?"

"We will never know. At least not now. Only two people know: Joel and the person who did it."

"It bothers me. It does not bother you?"

"Perhaps. The law will be happy; they have a guilty party. The community will blame us for nosing around. They will blame you more, because you are an interloper. And we will be left with several unanswered questions."

"And Joel? What about the victim? Who sees to him? Who speaks for him? Will they make him testify?"

"Not this way. And I hope his needs are being met as well. Are you okay with me? After all, I dragged you into this."

"I believe I agreed to be dragged in."

He nodded. "You know that sometimes life is not voluntary."

We both smiled at one another and shook hands, with his back turned, he said, "By the way, there is a new situation. Tomorrow. Ten thirty?"

"Tomorrow, ten thirty."

I turned to look out at the grey street. Life really was not voluntary.

SPECIAL ACKNOWLEDGEMENT:

The final draft could not have been completed without the generous help of Katherine Townsend and Alexis Diamond. Their editing skills pulled the manuscript together, keeping the dialogue flowing as I intended.

To you both, a hearty Bravo

ACKNOWLEDGMENTS

I had a lot of help and encouragement in writing One Last Confession. Jack Kugelmass sent me an article from the New York Times which gave me the idea for the story. Judie Diamond, Adriana Palanca, and old friend Richard Monaghan encouraged, helped, and supported the work. Alan Surkis challenged me to write a novel and demanded that I get it published. Friends Margaret Lefebvre and Phyllis Frankel read early drafts and were very enthusiastic in their praise. John Stevens edited the manuscript early on and was convinced the story should see the light of day.

Special mention to Katherine L. Turnbull and Alexis Diamond for proofreading the final draft. They also suggested improvements that added to the narrative.

My sincere thanks to all and sundry.

www.ingramcontent.com/pod-product-compliance
Lightning Source LLC
Chambersburg PA
CBHW061138120626
46546CB00005B/1836